DEADLY
LUST

DEADLY LUST

McCAY VERNON
and
MARIE VERNON

PINNACLE BOOKS
Kensington Publishing Corp.
http://www.kensingtonbooks.com

Foreword

Historic St. Augustine, Florida, with its colorful past, has been home to pirates and villains, marauders and despots. In the late 1980s a serial killer chose to make this, the nation's oldest city, the venue for his multiple slayings. William Darrell Lindsey, born and raised in this quaint seaside town, murdered at least six women in St. Augustine and one in North Carolina. He is suspected of numerous other murders following the same pattern as those to which he has confessed. The true story of his crimes exposes the lurid underbelly of drugs, prostitution, and crime that taints even this most seemingly placid of communities.

For star-crossed William Lindsey, life was never easy. As a three-month-old infant, he lost both his parents in a tragic automobile accident. Today he sits in a six-by-nine prison cell waiting for the cancer he has to end his life. His odyssey has been a compelling story of a man whose macabre compulsions drove him into drug addiction, sexual aberrations, suicide attempts, and, ultimately, murder.

Of the plots that play out in the lives of human beings, most have at least some positive aspects. But there are no winners in this saga of serial lust murder—the killer, his victims, their families, and society itself are all losers. Lindsey, dominated by his bizarre, seemingly uncontrollable need to control, torture, rape, and kill women, derived only fleeting pleasure from the fulfillment of his fantasies. Ultimately he lived the life of a hunted animal. But the killer's personal tragedies are dwarfed by comparison to the pain, suffering, and brutal deaths he inflicted upon the defenseless women he chose as his victims—young women who were leading the desperate lives of street prostitutes as they fought the ravages of crack cocaine addiction.

The depths of sorrow the parents and families of these young women have endured is far greater than anyone who has not lived through the same experience can fathom. It was prolonged torture for them to watch their daughters, some of them already mothers themselves, fall prey to the curse of drugs. They were forced to stand by helplessly as the women's addictions forced them into prostitution, enslaved them to predatory drug dealers, pimps, and johns, and exposed them to life-threatening diseases. To see them abused by these men, then cast aside when they were no longer useful, multiplied the anguish. Then came the final tragedy—the women's brutal and senseless deaths at the hands of a serial killer.

There is a universal fascination with serial killers— those who murder not just once, not simply in the heat of passion, but cold-bloodedly, deliberately, again and again. This bizarre and most difficult to understand of all crimes compels us to search deep within ourselves, within our dreams and hidden fantasies, in an effort to understand such a killer's motivation.

William Darrell Lindsey represents the essence of the enigma posed by serial lust killers. To gain insight into the overwhelming compulsion that led a man to kill brutally and seemingly at random involves exploring his life, the lives of his victims, and the environment in which he chose to live. Nor can such research ignore society's views on criminal activities within a community.

It can only be speculated how many more women would have fallen prey to St. Augustine's serial killer had not a rare phenomenon contributed to his capture—complete cooperation between two law enforcement agencies in communities six hundred miles apart. Buncombe County Sheriff's Department in Asheville, North Carolina, and St. Johns County Sheriff's Office in St. Augustine, Florida, displayed the finest of cooperative police work in bringing William Lindsey to justice.

Serendipity played a part in Lindsey's capture as well. When one considers the ease with which a nomadic killer is able to conceal himself within a culture that includes drug dealers, prostitutes, pimps, and johns, it is understandable that Lindsey's heinous crimes remained unsolved for so long. As this story explores the shadowy subculture within which Lindsey operated, it provides revealing insights into the pervasive ease with which crack cocaine can contaminate an entire segment of an otherwise model community.

In their search for the killer during the years he remained at large, police investigators were forced to sift through a myriad of suspects and informants, many with long criminal records. A number of these men and women offered false information about the murders. Some even claimed credit for the crimes, a not-unusual event in high-profile homicides. Each time investigators were forced to use their resources pursuing these false leads, the killer gained the advantages of both time and having suspicion diverted elsewhere.

The victims William Lindsey chose to kill present an equally intriguing but far more tragic human story. Without exception, they were young women locked into the unyielding grip of crack cocaine addiction. In order to feed this insatiable habit, they lost control of their lives, and ultimately of life itself. Even before death, their existence was one of crack-driven humiliation, desperation, and frequent physical abuse. They were stigmatized as "worthless crackhead whores," especially by those who capitalized on their addiction. Those insensitive to the women's life circumstances viewed their deaths at the hands of a killer as predictable and even justifiable.

Interviews with the victims' families and others who knew them yielded a far more compassionate view of these women. Lindsey's victims could have been anyone's daughter, anyone's sister, anyone's neighbor. They were little girls who danced in school performances, who drew hopscotch squares on the sidewalk, who played with dolls and giggled with their girlfriends. While some of their family situations portended less than optimal outcomes, in most cases they were part of warm and loving families, not "throwaway children" as some would assume.

So what went wrong? What compels a woman to sell her body five or ten times a night, to risk contracting AIDS, to face the possibility of being physically and emotionally abused, to jeopardize her very life? This book documents how the quest for crack cocaine can consume and destroy once-normal, rational human beings. It also explores the subculture that revolves around crack cocaine and its use—the drug dealers, the pimps, the johns, the prostitutes, and the serial killer in their midst.

The issue of race also plays a role in understanding the background against which Lindsey's murders occurred. What forces at work within St. Augustine's African American community may have facilitated the murders and made their solution doubly difficult? How does the white community's past record of discrimination contribute to the social problems involved? Is there a workable solution to the economic factors that make dealing crack cocaine appeal to many young Black males as their only viable option for survival and success?

Without question, the acts William Lindsey committed, the manner in which he took life not once but multiple times, are repugnant to contemplate. However, like other serial killers, he was a man driven by a lust he was unable to control, one that yielded sadistic sexual gratification only when he could inflict pain and death upon his victims. As is true with all lust-driven serial killers, his acts of killing brought only temporary surcease from his compulsion; with each successful murder and the macabre thrill it provided, the need to repeat the act in fantasy and reality was reinforced. Capture and imprisonment—or death—were the only fates that could come from the wretched dilemma he faced.

Despite repeated attempts to interview William Darrell Lindsey, "the Crack Head Corner Killer," he declined to meet or correspond with us. His refusal necessitated an exhaustive investigation and extensive interviews to gather the facts required to understand the man and his crimes. In writing this story, we have relied upon the records of law enforcement agencies, interviews with the detectives involved in the various investigations, discussions with persons whom Lindsey grew up with, employers, personal contacts with other serial killers, and a thorough study of the literature on serial murder.

Without the full cooperation of Sheriff Neil Perry, of St. Johns County, Florida, and that of Sheriff Bobby Medford, of Buncombe County Sheriff's Department, North Carolina, this book would have been impossible. From the former agency we obtained complete transcripts or summary reports of interviews conducted on the suspects questioned by St. Johns County detectives. Equally valuable information was made available from Buncombe County. In addition, we interviewed in depth the lead investigators and detectives in the Lindsey case from each of these jurisdictions. Through their assistance and cooperation we are able to present a much more rounded and authentic version of events than would otherwise have been possible.

While numerous personnel of these law enforcement agencies lent their assistance, special thanks are due to Detective Frank Welborn, who conducted much of the investigation into Lindsey's St. Augustine killings. Sergeant Jackie Patronska, of the St. Johns County Sheriff's Records Department, was especially helpful in guiding us through the voluminous material on file in her department. Advice from Kevin Kelshaw, spokesperson for the St. Johns County Sheriff's Office, saved us hours of going through blind alleys in search of the information and contacts we required. Former detective Jennifer Ponce offered critical insights into the investigation process, as did Special Agent Allen Strickrott, of the Florida Department of Law Enforcement. In Asheville, North Carolina, Detective John Harrison, the man who arrested Lindsey, was gracious enough to give us his insights based on three decades of experience in law enforcement. We are grateful for the time he spent going over the case with us, showing us the crime site, and pointing out Asheville's red-light district. For information about police diving squads, we are grateful to Officer Tim Willingham, formerly of St. Augustine Police Department, now a member of the Jacksonville Sheriff's Office.

Interviews with William Lindsey's family and people he grew up with were valuable in providing understanding of his arcane personality, especially his early years. In order to gather data on Lindsey's boyhood, we interviewed his schoolmates from first grade through high school, especially those who grew up in his neighborhood. Jackie Johnson, Donald Heyman, Joe Pomar, Charles Brantley, Dickie Brantley, and Herbie Wiles were especially helpful.

Billie Sue Lockley, best friend and confidante of Lindsey's late adoptive sister, Sue Alice Lindsey, gave us good descriptions of the home where Lindsey grew up and the family dynamics. Jean Bain, who worked with Lindsey's father, also offered valuable insights as well as information that put us in touch with other people who knew the Lindseys. Likewise, Alice Roberts, Margaret Brantley Hall, and Kathleen Rockwell provided help in rounding out this phase of Lindsey's early years.

For information about Lindsey's marriages, interviews with Joan Forsyth and Shirley Hammond, sisters of Lindsey's first wife, Willa Jean Willis Lindsey, supplemented information available from detectives' interviews.

Agnes Marjenhoff, sister of Lindsey's second wife, graciously shared with us specific factual information, documentation of the marriage, and photographs. Marjenhoff's daughter, Rose, and her son, Fred, also assisted us with valuable information and family photos of Lindsey.

Lillian Vaill and Joyce Bradley were helpful in locating relevant people in the Palatka area to interview. Kay Guthrie shared her familiarity with many of the suspects in the case and the places they frequented as well as helping with the photographs in the book.

Debbie Thompson provided background on Lindsey's work history and behavior during the two years he was her employee and neighbor. Additional facts regarding Lindsey's employment history were contained in interviews detectives conducted with his employers and coworkers.

Assistant State's Attorney Maureen Christine, the prosecutor in the Lindsey case, made full records from her office open to us. These contained data that included pictures, interviews, and court information. Victims' advocate Mary Alice Colson guided us in understanding the impact such crimes have on victims' families. Debbie Christopher, office manager in the state's attorney office, was helpful in dealing with data from her department.

Fred Thomas provided an interesting description of how he came upon one of Lindsey's crime scenes, as did Jack Shelton, of Asheville, North Carolina.

Most of the information regarding the killer's victims was obtained through direct interviews with their families. A major reward from researching this story has been in meeting and coming to know these parents, brothers, and sisters who, while still mourning the loss of their loved one, generously shared with us their recollections, insights, and photographs. In particular, Melvin and Mildred McQuaig, Nancy and Jackie Bennett, Stacey Snead, and Malvera Lucas took time from their active lives to provide reminiscences of the victims' lives and discuss the influences that resulted in these tragic deaths.

Coverage by the *St. Augustine Record* and *Florida Times-Union* provided information about the legal processes involved in Lindsey's ultimate confession and sentencing. The photographic expertise of Gili Lochner added considerably to the book. We are particularly indebted to her for her assistance with the cover design.

It should be noted that while real names are used for Lindsey, his victims, and their family members, some suspects and others who were interviewed by the authors and by law enforcement have been given pseudonyms. Many of the dialogues included in this story have been taken directly from police records and other interviews. A few have been carefully reconstructed from the known facts. The majority of the quotes from William Lindsey were taken from his confessions to investigators.

We, the authors, were motivated to tell William Darrell Lindsey's story for a number of reasons: first of all, we are residents of the area in which his crimes occurred. Although McCay Vernon never met William Lindsey, he grew up in the same neighborhood, delivered newspapers to Lindsey's boyhood home, attended the same schools Lindsey attended, and was employed for a time at the same restaurant where Lindsey later worked. St. Augustine being a small, close-knit town at that time, they had a number of acquaintances in common. Further motivation for writing Lindsey's story was the fact that Dr. Vernon, a psychologist, has been involved in many homicide cases as a court expert and has written widely on forensic issues. The opportunity to examine the life of one such killer close-up added excellent material to the research he is currently doing on serial lust murder. As coauthor, Marie Vernon brought to the story her extensive experience as a journalist and freelance writer for newspapers such as the *Baltimore Sun* and *Cleveland Plain Dealer.* She has authored two historical books, *The Garrison Church* and *Speaking of Our Past.* Her skills as an interviewer resulted in an accurate portrayal of the victims and their families. Her abilities as a novelist were used to bind together the mountain of facts collected into a coherent whole.

By exploring William Darrell Lindsey's life, his crimes, his confession, and his sentencing, we hope to contribute to the knowledge of what forces form and motivate a serial killer. While it cannot be stated positively whether or not it is possible to identify and root out the fierce internal rage that leads such individuals to kill, the more clues to such behavior we can discover, the closer we come to addressing and preventing the deadly phenomenon of serial lust killing.

Prologue

1996: Season's Greetings

In December 1996 the historic town of St. Augustine, Florida, was celebrating the Christmas season with the "Nights of Lights," an annual display of twinkling bulbs strung from every tree, lamppost, and downtown building. Even the boats in the harbor sported colorful Christmas decorations. The usual influx of tourists thronged the town square, explored the quaint shops on St. George Street, toured the ancient fort, and enjoyed horse-drawn carriage rides through the narrow cobblestone streets.

Nothing in the festive holiday atmosphere suggested that a serial murderer, who had eluded capture for nearly a decade, was about to be exposed. Nor did St. Augustine's residents suspect that one of their own—a man who had grown up in this quaint seaside town—would be revealed as the killer.

The unraveling of the trail of brutal murders began innocuously enough with a Christmas card, one of many Sheriff Neil J. Perry, of St. Johns County, Florida, received that year. By its postmark—*Marshall, North Carolina*—Perry recognized the card as having been sent by one of his former part-time deputies, Fred Thompson. This was no surprise as the two had periodically stayed in touch since Thompson retired from his St. Augustine insurance business to return to his hometown, near Asheville, North Carolina.

But the holiday season was always a busy time in law enforcement—lots of traffic accidents, domestic fights, DUIs by those who had celebrated too heartily—so the card, along with other mail, lay unopened until after New Year's.

On the January day that Sheriff Perry finally slit open the envelope, he had no idea that it would contain the key to the savage killings that had plagued local law enforcement for nearly a decade. Nor was he aware that the contents of the envelope would initiate an investigation that would ultimately stretch the resources of his department to the limit. In the process a sordid side of charming, historic St. Augustine would be revealed, an underbelly of drugs, crime, and prostitution scarcely discernible to the millions of tourists, who flocked there each year, nor to most local residents.

Ultimately the card and its contents would play a decisive role in bringing a brutal serial killer to justice and allowing the grieving families of his victims to feel that some measure of justice had been achieved.

But for now, the envelope lay unopened as St. Augustine celebrated the coming of a new year.

Chapter 1

November 1988:
St. Augustine, Florida

The man drove slowly, carefully down West King Street. He would take his time. No hurry. The pickings were always good around here.

A cold, windy night, though. But that was better. Fewer people out on the street. Less chance anyone would notice. . . .

At 7:00 P.M. on Tuesday, November 29, 1988, twenty-seven-year-old Anita McQuaig Stevens stood shivering at the intersection of King Street and Riberia in West Augustine. The sweatpants she was wearing under the shorts she'd pulled on before rushing out of the house offered little protection against the brisk east wind that was causing the temperatures to drop rapidly toward the forties—unexpectedly cold for November in St. Augustine. Hugging her arms against her sides, she turned her back to the breeze for a moment. Her long blond hair whipped across her face. She shoved it back impatiently. It had been hours since she'd had a hit—she needed a fix and she needed it bad.

Pacing impatiently, she continued to scan passing cars. In this area of town known as "Crack Head Corner," it was rarely difficult to find a john willing to pay cash or a few rocks for a "date." Finally Anita spotted a blue sedan cruising slowly up King Street, its driver peering inquisitively through the windshield. The middle-aged man behind the wheel slowed, then honked his horn. By waving to him, Anita responded to the signal used by the johns who prowled this area looking for prostitutes. The car pulled to the side of the road. The man leaned across to roll down the passenger-side window and asked if she was looking for a date.

He appeared to be in his late forties or early fifties. Old. That was safer, actually. Nothing special about his looks. Anita considered for only a moment. "Forty bucks for a straight up," she said. He nodded and motioned for her to get in.

Anita jumped into the passenger seat, slammed the car door closed, and directed him to head toward the bridge on State Road 312, some five miles distant. As they pulled away from the curb, she took a closer look at the man. He looked vaguely familiar . . . maybe someone she'd dated before. Hard to remember. Bill. That was the name he had given her that time. But who knew if that was true—most of the johns never gave their real names.

They drove east on King Street, turned south on US 1, then left onto the Route 312 Bridge over the Matanzas River. As they drove, the man removed one hand from the wheel and started to grope between her thighs. Anita pushed him away. Payment first, then sex. She had learned that the hard way. Just a few weeks before, a john had stiffed her, then dumped her out miles from home. Another guy had stolen her money and jewelry. This john didn't seem like that type, but you never knew.

They cleared the Route 312 Bridge and Anita

pointed to an unpaved dirt road off to the left. The area of Fish Island was relatively safe. Police stopped by sometimes to rout out the vagrants who set up temporary shelters under the bridge, but most of the area was deserted. Anita motioned to the driver to stop the car near a cattail-fringed pond surrounded by dense undergrowth of palmettos, wax myrtles, and sawgrass. Several piles of construction debris had been dumped next to the dirt track. Here it was dark and silent, with nobody one in sight.

Only the two people in the car that night can say exactly what happened to turn sexual lust into murderous fury. Whatever the motivation, an altercation began, then quickly escalated into physical violence. Anita immediately sensed she was dealing with someone far more powerful and dangerous than she had anticipated. Even so, she was totally unprepared when, without warning, the man struck out, smashing his fist into her face. Before she could recover, he landed several more crushing blows, then seized the triple herringbone necklace she was wearing and twisted it savagely about her neck. Terrified, she pulled loose from his grasp, leaped from the car, and fled into a palmetto-covered area near the pond. She heard his footsteps close behind, crashing through the thick fronds in furious pursuit.

Her heart pounding in terror, Anita raced on, until she found herself hemmed in by the dense undergrowth. Bloodied by the stiff, razor-sharp palmetto fronds and uncertain which way to turn, she hesitated. In that fatal moment he caught up with her. During the pursuit he had picked up a one-by-six board from the debris lying nearby. She saw him raise the timber to strike her and held up her arms to ward off the blows. Her feeble defense was to no avail. A fierce blow knocked her to the ground. She rolled, trying to shield herself, but he continued to rain brutal blows and kicks to her face and body.

No matter how loudly Anita screamed or how desperately she struggled to escape, she was no match for the man's strength and maniacal fury. Even as she rolled into a fetal position he continued beating her mercilessly. Sometime during her final tortured moments, the left side of Anita's face and her eye socket were crushed. Savage blows splintered her upper and lower jawbones as well as her nose. Soon the palmetto fronds in the area were slick with Anita's blood.

When she was finally beaten into unconsciousness, the man dragged Anita's body through the palmettos back toward the pond. His rage still unabated, once clear of the thicket, he grasped the waistband of the pink corduroy shorts she was wearing over her sweatpants and tried to rip them off her. When the deadweight of her body made that attempt unsuccessful, he used his pocketknife to slit both pant legs up the front. He stripped her sweatpants down to her ankles, then pulled up her sweatshirt and bra, exposing her breasts. He then burned her with cigarettes and bit her neck and inner thigh. Finally he violated her body in the most degrading fashion possible, shoving broken tree branches into her vagina and anus. That done, he dragged Anita's lifeless form, the tree limbs still protruding, some fifteen feet to the pond and heaved it into the chill, dark swamp water.

Panting and drenched with sweat from his exertions, he watched as Anita's remains drifted slightly away from the cattails and reeds toward the center of the pond. After a few moments, he stooped and dipped his hands into the water to wash away the blood smeared on them. Then he straightened, listened for a moment, and returned to the car.

She'd asked for it, had it coming. Just like all the others she'd tried to put him down. But he couldn't go home like this. Blood on his shirt, his pants.

Mother's house.

That would be safe.

On November 30, 1988, at approximately 11:00 A.M., Eugene Wells, an employee of the Anastasia Mosquito Control District, was collecting water samples from the borrow ponds on Fish Island and identifying potential mosquito-breeding areas. As he was turning around by one of the ponds, he noticed something floating in the water, stopped his truck, and got out to check further. His first thought was that it was a department store mannequin that had been discarded. Returning to his truck, he put on a pair of water boots and stepped into the edge of the pond to get a better look. It was then that he realized that what he had taken to be a mannequin was actually a woman's body.

As Wells was a lieutenant fireman for the Bakersville Volunteer Fire Department, his first thought was to call St. Johns Fire and Rescue Dispatch using his hand walkie-talkie. The dispatcher there told him to secure the area until law enforcement officers arrived, which he did.

Sergeant Elliott A. Gribble, of the St. Johns County Sheriff's Office, was in the vicinity of State Road 312 when he overheard on the fire/rescue channel that a body had been found in a borrow pit off Fish Island Road, approximately northwest of the radio tower. He responded and upon arrival saw the brown pickup truck belonging to the Mosquito District and its driver, Eugene Wells. Gribble reported the following:

Mr. Wells was securing the road, protecting tracks he observed in the roadway. He then led us to a water filled borrow pit and pointed out the body. We observed

*a seminude body of a white female. She was near the
southwest bank wearing a light-colored shirt and tan-
looking shoes. The shirt appeared to have been lifted
over the chest, exposing her breasts. I observed several
foot tracks in the area as well as a red cigarette lighter
and two blue strings. This evidence was not molested
and secured for further evidence collection.*

At that point Sergeant Gribble notified his captain
that the crime scene appeared to be a homicide and
the entire area was secured for the homicide unit. Investigators and crime scene analysts arrived and it was
immediately obvious from the condition of the body
that this was a murder. They began collecting evidence,
but because the area was in frequent use as a dumping
place for debris, there was difficulty in determining
what articles might have been connected to the crime.
Deputy Christopher Bonnevier photographed the tire
tracks, but because there were many in the area, none
could be identified as belonging to the killer's vehicle.

Investigators noted that the body was that of a white
female, between twenty-five and thirty-five years of
age. She was partially clothed, wearing a white sweatshirt with a design of boxing gloves and the letters
TKO, boxing shorthand for "technical knockout" on
the front. The sweatshirt and her underwire bra had
been pulled up. Her pink corduroy sweatpants, which
appeared to have semen stains on them, were found
hanging from a bush about fifteen feet from where
the body was found. (Lab tests later failed to demonstrate that the pink sweatpants had semen stains,
although they tested positive for the presence of
blood.) Gray sweatpants had been pulled down
around her tennis shoes. She was still wearing jewelry,
including a gold herringbone necklace, which had
apparently been tightened around her neck, as there

were ligature marks present. On her wrist she had a blue yarn bracelet.

The body was removed to the morgue for an autopsy by St. Johns County medical examiner Robert J. McConaghie. This revealed that all of her injuries, except for a bruise to the side of her head, appeared to be postmortem. The medical examiner noted multiple injuries, including hemorrhages of the larynx and hyoid on the right side, a blow to the left side of the head and eye, forceful blows to the mouth and nose with fractures of the anterior face, a blow to the back of the right thorax, perforation of the rectum with a sharp-pointed wooden object, vaginal tears—possibly caused by a foreign object—a possible cigarette burn under the left chin, and possible bite marks on the neck and right thigh. There were multiple scratches on her face, back, buttocks, and left side.

After examining the undigested food in the victim's stomach, and noting the body's full rigor when found, he estimated the time of death at most likely between 6:00 and 7:00 P.M. on November 29. A blood alcohol screen proved negative. The condition of her abdomen and cervix revealed that she had been pregnant at some time in the past. A rather puzzling discovery was that there were old bird-shot pellets embedded on the right and back side of her head. As her third molars had not yet erupted, he estimated her age as being in the early twenties.

A police sketch artist did a rendering of the victim's face, which was published in the December 1 edition of the *St. Augustine Record*. Anyone with information regarding the crime was asked to call Sheriff Neil Perry's office. Jonathon Tremble who had known and dated Anita, called the sheriff's office to say that the woman in the picture appeared to be Anita Stevens. He was questioned as to his relationship with her. "I liked her a lot," he said, "but I wasn't in love with her or anything like that. It was kind of a friendship. 'Say, hey. How are you doing?' This and that."

He added, "It's a very sad thing that has happened. I just feel sorry for her mom and dad. I mean, it's sad when someone is killed and it's an accidental death or a car wreck. That's one thing, but when you see a beating, that makes you really sick. I hope you get whoever did this."

At the time of Anita Stevens's murder, local law enforcement had no reason to believe it was anything other than an isolated killing. On January 30, 1989, Detective Mary LeVeck entered Anita's case into the FBI's Violent Criminal Apprehension Program (VICAP) system. LeVeck's report listed Anita's vital statistics, her identifying features, the details of the crime and where it was committed, evidence collected at the scene, and cause of death. The FBI Academy in Quantico, Virginia, was contacted. Agent Alan E. Burgess responded that the case would remain in the system indefinitely and would be compared to all other cases submitted to VICAP. In the event that a linkage was made, his letter stated, Detective LeVeck would be notified immediately.

It would be many years and many murders later before either law enforcement or Anita's parents learned who the perpetrator was. Only at that time would they learn the complete details of the killer's actions that night. Meanwhile, his sadistic killing spree was not finished. In his deadly lust for sex and violence, he would strike again . . . and again . . . and again. . . .

Chapter 2

The Two Sides of St. Augustine

Explore our Treasures . . . Nation's Oldest City gives endless enjoyment
> —Headline in 2002–2003 edition of brochure, *Explore St. Johns County*

He drove back through the center of town, down past the Fountain of Youth, Ripley's Believe it or Not, the Castillo de San Marco. Midmorning now, the streets and sidewalks full of people. What would they think, those camera-toting tourists if they knew what had happened last night under the bridge. . . .

St. Augustine, Florida, on the surface, would seem a most unlikely locale for a serial killer to carry out his heinous crimes. Since the April day in 1565 when the army of Don Pedro Menéndez de Avilés routed the French Huguenots and claimed the area for Spain, the city has attracted sun seekers and fishermen, tourists and artists, motorcyclists and schoolchildren, honeymooners and sailors, foreign travelers and retirees, bird-watchers and archaeologists. Its chamber of commerce boasts: "It's scenic, it's tourist-driven, and it's a great place to live."

In short, nothing in the appearance of this haven on Florida's northeast coast, blessed by sun and sea, suggested that it might attract and harbor a sadistic killer. To comprehend fully how, in this historic enclave, a man managed to butcher six women without coming under suspicion, it is essential to understand a bit of the town's character. More important, it is necessary to be aware of the contrast between the St. Augustine most visitors see and the darker side, which is hidden from view.

Each year over 3 million tourists visit St. Augustine, the oldest continuously occupied European settlement within the continental United States. They come to tour the Castillo, the ancient Spanish fort where the Native American warrior Geronimo was once held prisoner. They climb to the top of its 1874 lighthouse, where a Fresnel lens casts its beam some thirty-five miles into the Atlantic. They admire the alligators, crocodiles, exotic birds, and other animals at the century-old Alligator Farm and wonder at the many oddities displayed at Ripley's Believe It Or Not Museum. Some are even brave enough to sip the sulfurous waters of the famed Fountain of Youth, supposedly discovered by the Spanish explorer Ponce de León.

Five different flags have flown over the city as various nations claimed it as their own. From Menéndez's arrival in 1565 until 1763, St. Augustine was under Spanish rule. It fell to Great Britain in 1763 and was reclaimed by the Spanish in 1784. In 1821 Florida was claimed as a territory by the newly founded United States of America, and in 1845 it became the twenty-seventh state in the Union. In 1861, with the outbreak of the Civil War, Florida joined the Confederacy and remained under that flag until the Union regained control in 1862.

While each governmental entity that claimed St. Augustine as its own left its mark on the city, it is the Spanish influence that has prevailed most strongly over the years. Street names, architecture, Minorcan cuisine, and old-world pageantry are part of daily life in what has been called the "most European of American cities."

If one were to hop aboard one of St. Augustine's omnipresent tour trolleys, many of the major attractions would be found along King Street, a thoroughfare that bisects the very heart of this historic town. A tour highlight would be the much-photographed Bridge of Lions, where flags flutter from the bridge's stanchions and a flotilla of sailboats and motor yachts bob at anchor in the harbor. From here, one obtains an impressive view of the Castillo de San Marcos, the Spanish-built fort whose battlements overlook the harbor, its cannons aimed seaward.

At the east end of King Street, trolley drivers point out such sights as the beautifully landscaped park known as the Plaza de la Constitución, which surrounds the old slave market, the impressive Cathedral-Basilica, which flanks the square, and the balconies and crenellated towers of Flagler College's Spanish-style buildings, designed and built by the late railroad baron Henry Flagler. Students at Flagler take their meals in a magnificent dining room whose windows were created by the famed glassmaker Louis Comfort Tiffany. At the intersection of King and Cordova, the train passes the Casa Monica Hotel, a building that once served as the St. Johns County Courthouse, but which now stands in newly restored splendor. A favorite tour stop is the Lightner Museum, once an exclusive hotel catering to wealthy winter visitors, now a repository for an eclectic

mix of memorabilia, with a charming café tucked into
what was once the hotel's indoor swimming pool.

Farther along, just before East King Street ends, the
trolley pulls into the San Sebastian Winery. This is the
end of the line, as far west as most tourists will travel.
A few blocks farther, past US 1, past the San Sebastian
River and the plush offices of the Florida East Coast
Railroad, East King Street becomes West King Street.
Here begins the other side of St. Augustine, the one
where tour trains don't go.

Today the area known as West Augustine has taken
a number of steps to revitalize itself. But to truly comprehend the culture that prevailed there at the time
Anita Stevens was murdered, it is necessary to see that
neighborhood as it was back then. West of US 1, the
first building one encountered was a cut-rate liquor
store, an undistinguished concrete building with bars
on its doors and windows, its parking lot littered with
trash and discarded beer containers. Down the street
a bit farther, amid ill-kept storefront businesses, the
Big Bear Pawn Shop's sign proclaimed, CASH IN A FLASH.
Near the pawnshop unemployed men seeking day
work waited outside Labor Finders employment
agency. Interspersed among the surviving shops were
vacant buildings, many of them decaying and win-
dowless. On nearby Masters Drive bail bondsmen
provided "get out of jail" money to those requiring
the service.

The parking lot of Pic 'n Save Supermarket, at the
corner of King and Palmer Streets, was a favorite
hangout for prostitutes looking for dates, as was a fast-
food restaurant a block or so away. The Pic 'n Save was
also a favorite target for petty thievery by the prostitutes. The names and locations of the grocery store
and the nearby restaurant would surface in police re-

ports time and again as detectives delved into the backgrounds of the murdered women.

The farther west one traveled on King Street, the more dilapidated the homes and businesses became. Sidewalks disappeared, ditches and yards flooded with water after each downpour, weeds sprouted along the roadsides, and abandoned buildings and trailers were left to molder. In front yards battered cars rusted slowly as they sagged on flat tires. On the side streets off this thoroughfare, sewage service was spotty and outhouses still remained in some areas.

While the majority of West King Street's residents, largely African Americans, struggled to lead upstanding and productive lives, the prevalence of crime and the area's atmosphere of neglect made daily living difficult and sometimes dangerous.

In the early 1980s, some three miles from downtown St. Augustine at the intersection of West King Street and Volusia, was the area known to police, local pimps, prostitutes, and drug dealers as "Crack Head Corner." At this intersection on the north side of King Street, just past the tracks of the Florida East Coast Railroad, a convenience store with barred doors and windows shared a large gritty parking lot with a garish purple building that was once a car wash. This area functioned as a local gathering place. Diagonally across on the south side of the street, another vacant lot served the same purpose. The yards of adjoining houses, cluttered with a variety of plastic lawn chairs, car seats, oil drums converted to barbecues, also offered informal outdoor-meeting areas.

During daytime hours the social scene at Crack Head Corner consisted of clusters of idle men— mostly African Americans—gathered in the parking lot or clustered around the oil-drum barbecues in the yards of some of the nearby houses, a few with brown paper bags containing open bottles of liquor. Local residents stopped by the convenience store to buy cigarettes, bread, milk, and lottery tickets.

In late afternoon and at night, the scene at Crack Head Corner changed dramatically. Provocatively clad prostitutes paraded up and down the street or perched on the hoods of cars lined up in the parking lot, the better to see and be seen. Drug dealers brazenly hawked their merchandise. Johns and druggies cruised up and down looking for women and/or drugs, both of which were readily available. Both the pushers and the prostitutes often aggressively approached the cars and pickup trucks that slowly passed or stopped to solicit a date or buy some rock.

While Crack Head Corner was at the heart of the drug and prostitution trades in St. Augustine, these enterprises also operated in the predominantly African American area of St. Augustine known as Lincolnville. Lincolnville, founded in 1866 by freed Civil War slaves, is located on the east side of US 1 and south of King Street. This enclave has been occupied by or visited by such prominent persons as baseball notable Jackie Robinson, civil rights leader the Reverend Martin Luther King, and musician Ray Charles. Charles, who was blind, received most of his education at the Florida School for the Deaf and the Blind, located within the historic area of St. Augustine.

While prostitutes and drug dealers made their "connections" at Crack Head Corner and in nearby Lincolnville, they often proceeded to more remote, nearby rural areas for their sexual liaisons and the exchange of money for drugs and/or sex. Ironically, the seclusion these hideaways offered presented a very real danger to the prostitutes. A john bent on demanding rough sex, attacking his date, or dumping her out of the car and driving off without paying could do so with little fear of interruption.

These rural areas where prostitutes and johns held their rendezvous were pockmarked with numerous borrow pits, which are water-filled ponds of varying depth. In this area of Florida, the water table is extremely close to the surface with much of the land being swampy or else only a few feet above sea level. Consequently, in order for new construction to take place, building sites require fill dirt. The soil for this is obtained by excavating holes—"borrow pits"—that immediately fill with water. (The "lakes" that grace many of the more expensive housing developments in the area are, in fact, gentrified borrow pits.) In Anita Stevens's case, as in the later St. Augustine murders, the borrow pits offered the killer an immediate solution to the problem of disposing of his victims' bodies.

The dichotomy that existed between historic downtown St. Augustine and West Augustine explains in part why crimes committed in West Augustine caused scarcely a ripple in the fabric of the wider community. Although it was an open secret that West Augustine and Lincolnville were the centers of the town's drug and prostitution trade, it was all too easy for citizens of St. Augustine and surrounding St. Johns County to ignore events that took place in that section of town where few whites ventured, except those in search of a fix or sexual gratification. That is not to say that such activities did not affect those living elsewhere—addicts coming down from a high were often desperate to get enough cash for a fix and resorted to burglary, housebreaking, and car theft. Quite often they targeted the more affluent neighborhoods, as well as West Augustine for their criminal activities.

It should be noted, too, that throughout West Augustine there were many modest residences occupied by hardworking, law-abiding people. Those residents

were as likely to be victimized by the criminal element
as were those living in more upscale areas. Religious
life was also strong in the community—St. Paul's
African Methodist Episcopal Church on King Street
enjoyed the historic distinction of having offered its
pulpit to the Reverend Martin Luther King during
the civil rights conflict. The Woolworth's five-and-
dime store in downtown St. Augustine had been the
site of an historic civil rights protest, as had the Mon-
son Hotel on the bayfront. By the late 1980s overt
racism was frowned upon, but such mementos served
as a reminder of the humiliation and abuses some elements of St. Augustine's white community had
heaped upon Dr. King and his followers.

At one time Florida Memorial College, an all-black
institution, had occupied a large tract in this area. By
the end of the 1980s, all that remained was a crum-
bling arched entrance overgrown with weeds and
kudzu vines.

At the time of Anita Stevens's murder, there existed
in West Augustine and Lincolnville a close-knit subculture consisting of prostitutes, drug dealers, petty
thieves, pimps, johns, and some cabdrivers. These individuals tended to lead precarious lives, pursued on one
hand by the police and, on the other hand, preyed
upon by each other. The johns frequently abused the
prostitutes, who were, in a physical sense, essentially
helpless to defend themselves. The drug dealers and
pimps also subjected these women to brutality and ex-
ploitation. Yet the women, too, were predators in that
they often ripped off johns and dealers. Many of these
individuals, when arrested, readily informed on one another, either to curry favor with the police, to avoid
arrest, or to obtain reduced sentences.

For the killer, this was the ideal setting within which

to carry out his crimes. His victims were not only available and vulnerable, most of the people with whom they associated on a daily basis had criminal records and were readily fingered as suspects.

For the police investigating Anita's murder, Crack Head Corner's subculture offered a tangled web of accusations, false confessions, and convoluted relationships, all of which made identifying a clever killer a nearly impossible task.

Anita Stevens's addiction to crack cocaine had driven her to prostitution, as was true of other women whom the killer would later choose as his victims. For these women, tethered to $100-to-$200-a-day drug habits, with little education, children to support, and no legal trade or profession, life offered few options. To support their expensive habit on the minimum-wage jobs they were able to obtain was clearly impossible.

The women's desperate quest for the next fix inevitably led them to risk being beaten, robbed, raped, arrested, or, in the worst case scenario, murdered. To cope with these dangers, the prostitutes employed a loose network through which they kept each other informed of which johns were given to brutality, what the men's sexual preferences were, whether or not they tipped, and which ones had access to a good supply of crack. But because the women were forced to compete with each other for johns, such information was not always shared.

Further back in time—in the '40s and '50s—St. Augustine supported several houses of ill repute. These establishments offered some degree of protection to their employees and their customers. As a young man, the coauthor of this book waited tables in a St. Augustine restaurant where the owner of one of the brothels regularly brought his "ladies" to dine at noon on Sundays when his business was slack. However, that era had long since passed, leaving the women no choice but to pick up their dates on the streets and service them in dangerous areas such as backcountry roads and isolated trailers.

The police also posed a constant threat for the prostitutes. Of the women who became the killer's victims, all had been arrested, and most had served jail time for prostitution, drug offenses, and/or theft.

During the course of the investigation, dozens of prostitutes were interviewed. Most seemed to lead aimless existences, moving frequently from one place to another, from one man to another. Kelly, who was interviewed by Detective Mary LeVeck, reported living in numerous locations over the course of a year or so. "That was when I lost the house and I was kind of on the street and I lived over on Anastasia Beach. Really on the beach. I owned a car, but the motor was blown up and it had been sitting for like a year 'cause I didn't have the money to fix it. Then I moved in with Phil. We went and stayed at his sister's house, the dirty trailer that sits right there on King Street. Then after we moved from his sister's house, we stayed at his mother's. Then we got an apartment over on the island. A couple of months I lived over there. Then I split up with Phil and went to live with some friends in the trailer park. I stayed there for about three weeks. Then I lived on Bridge Street. I was with Raymond then. I just moved from there."

Her account of an endless chain of residences and equally endless alliances with one man after another was a story detectives would hear repeated time and again by prostitutes as they pursued Crack Head Corner's elusive killer.

* * *

The men who came to Crack Head Corner seeking the services of the prostitutes were a varied group. They ranged from well-to-do businessmen with homes in the more upscale areas of town to out-of-town visitors looking for action, to down-at-the-heel drifters, to fellow addicts. Between these extremes were the construction workers, lawn-care maintenance men, and others who labored in unskilled or semiskilled jobs, some relying on day-to-day employment. The vehicles they drove ranged from Mercedes and Cadillacs to beat-up pickup trucks and rusted-out compacts. Racially they were just as diverse, although most were either Caucasian or African American.

The one single characteristic that defined most of the johns was their view of prostitutes as available merchandise, to be used, sometimes abused, and almost always depreciated.

A number of the johns who frequented Crack Head Corner were what locals referred to as rednecks or racists. The antipathy of these men toward African Americans was often enflamed by white prostitutes who dated African American males. One such individual who became a suspect in the murders was a thirty-three-year-old white male restaurant worker named Hale Banks who had a violent past, with arrests for burglary, aggravated battery, damage to property, and other such crimes. When speaking of Anita Stevens, he told detectives, "She was a pretty good old gal. Then she went down there and started liking them niggers. It wasn't no secret."

Banks then lied, claiming, "Me, I just go down to Crack Head Corner for recreational purposes."

Another man who reflected the racist element among those who frequented Crack Head Corner was Wesley Trout, a self-employed masonry contractor.

Speaking of white prostitutes who dated African American men, he expressed his feelings thus: "I don't care what happens to none of them. They can all kill each other as far as I care. It don't really matter to me whose body they found in the borrow pit."

Trout's ex-wife described her former husband as a white supremacist. "His name is very strong in KKK," she said. "He hates blacks. Often he throws bottles at them from his truck. He's got several shotguns and rifles. He also keeps a pistol and an ax handle under the seat. When he sees a white woman with a black male, he'll say, 'Sorry goddamn bitch! Somebody needs to blow her brains out. Somebody needs to kill that bitch. She ain't nothing but trash.' He used to brag all the time that he ran over some guy, a black guy. He thought it was funny. He kept the guy's shirt under his truck seat as a souvenir."

The racists made life miserable for both white and African American prostitutes—that the women were willing to expose themselves repeatedly to this sort of danger and abuse once again illustrates the overpowering seduction of their addiction to rock cocaine.

The pimps were another component of Crack Head Corner society. Many of them were also drug dealers. In addition to selling drugs and pimping, some of these men ran houses where, for a fee, a prostitute could use a room in which to have sex with a john and/or get high.

The pimps and dealers were known by colorful aliases such as "Dump," "Rat," "Fat Boy," "Poochie," "Gator," "Sheephead," "Bo Bra," "Snakeman," "Cookie Monster," and "Thumbtack." The prostitutes were among their major customers both in terms of the drugs they themselves used and what they persuaded their johns to buy in order to party. In St. Augustine, African Americans controlled the crack cocaine trade. It is one reason the white prostitutes were so heavily involved with these individuals.

One witness interviewed after Anita Stevens's murder reported that he had picked up a prostitute in West Augustine and drove her to a particular bar. When he stopped the car, approximately ten black males ran up wanting to sell drugs. The woman gave a young man of about 16 $20 for two rocks of crack cocaine. Later they returned to the same bar and the woman got out of the car this time, saying she could get a better deal from "the main man."

During the course of the murder investigation, a paramedic, who was questioned regarding one of the suspects whom he had treated, reported that it wasn't uncommon when driving along King Street to be approached by men wanting to sell drugs or sex. The paramedic stated, "This one man says to me, 'I got young women, I got old women, they're making me bunches of money. I got a condo out on the beach, real nice condo, and I got a nice car. If you need anything (meaning sex or drugs), you just come to me and I'll get it for you.'"

But the prostitutes' dealings with pimps and dealers amounted to far more than a simple commercial transaction. As former detective Jennifer Ponce, who was involved in the search for the St. Augustine killer, reported, "The dealers wine and dine the prostitutes to get them hooked. Once hooked, the women are totally under the dealer's control." She described the dealers as subjecting the women to sexual activities with multiple partners, intercourse with animals, being photographed in lewd poses, as well as subjected to torture and bondage. "They use them for sexual 'dog and pony' shows," Ponce said.

A lot of the brutality that prostitutes faced occurred

when they were desperate for a fix and were forced to buy their rock on credit. Because the dealers could not seek police help to collect their debts, they relied on such strong-arm methods as brutally beating the women. They worked to develop such a reputation for brutality that their customers would be afraid to renege on payment. Thus, they, too, became suspects during the murder investigations.

The last, although peripheral, members of the Crack Head subculture were the cabdrivers. Because most of the street prostitutes either lacked the money to buy a car, could not get credit, or, in most cases, had had their driver's licenses suspended (as was also true of many of their clients), they depended on taxicabs for transportation. Prostitutes when released from jail often called a cab for transportation back to the streets. Thus, the cabdrivers got to know these women, sometimes even driving them around while they conducted sexual acts with their johns in the cab. In St. Augustine, as in other small towns, many cabdrivers also had criminal records. (As recently as 2002, of the 112 hack licenses issued in St. Augustine, seventy-three [65 percent] were awarded to drivers with a history of criminal and/or traffic offenses. Six were on probation at the time their licenses were issued.) Thus, some of these drivers were also into drug sales, buying hot merchandise, and pimping. With this background, it is easy to understand that cabbies were often a source of customers for the prostitutes, pimps, and drug dealers. Conversely, when a prostitute was murdered, cabdrivers were often one of the primary providers of clues to solving the crime.

In investigating Anita Stevens's murder, a detective questioned a man who drove for American Cab. He described what was, for him, a typical evening. At 7:00 or

8:00 P.M. he picked up a white male who advised him he was looking for female companionship. He described the man as follows: "Dark hair, medium longish length, sort of lumpy features, had a mustache and sort of a scraggly beard. Not real well-groomed. Semiportly, not a fat person, but neither was he like athletic or anything. I got the idea he was probably a construction worker type. I think he was sitting around out at Arnold's (a local bar) and reached the decision that he would rather go out and pay for some [sex] than to spend all his money buying drinks for female bar flies and go home frustrated."

The cabbie drove him to Lincolnville to look for a prostitute named Alicia. When unable to find her, they encountered Ecstacia on Riberia Street, south of King Street, and she got into the cab. According to the cabdriver, Ecstacia directed the cabdriver to take them to another address where they bought drugs. He drove around the block while this transaction was going on, then picked them up again and took them to the male's residence, a mobile home on St. Augustine Beach.

When interviewed, the man confirmed that he had paid Ecstacia $20 for oral sex and that they had freebased coke together. After about two hours, he said, they left his mobile home, called a cab, and went to Lincolnville to purchase more crack. They returned to the mobile home for more sex, more drinking, and more smoking. When finished, they walked to the nearby convenience store and called the cab again. At this point the cabdriver told them he disapproved of their activities and asked them to get out of his vehicle. At about 3:00 A.M. the man left Ecstacia at a bus stop while he got back into the cab and went home. "I think he had spent something like a hundred and twenty dollars on her that evening," the driver stated. When asked if he felt that the man had been angry about the way Ecstacia treated him, the driver replied, "No, more like stupid and confused."

In one of the later murders, Detective Mary LeVeck reported having called in the cabdriver who was known to have transported one victim shortly before her disappearance. The cabbie admitted to having the victim as a fare only when detectives began to focus on him as a suspect. Even after giving his affidavit, he refused to make known his phone number or address, saying he did not wish to become involved. He did, however, agree to a polygraph as to the veracity of the account he had given.

For a killer in search of victims, Crack Head Corner and its environs offered an ideal hunting ground amid a mélange of people living on the fringes of the law. The prostitutes were available and hungry for cash or crack. The area's racial structure and society's bias threw suspicion on its African American habitués. Johns, drug dealers, and cabdrivers with criminal records became suspects, deflecting suspicion from those not in these categories.

Within this seething subculture, a careful killer was able to achieve relative anonymity. Here he was free to seek out his vulnerable victims, lure them into his vehicle, beat them into submission, and, ultimately, in a frenzy of anger and lust, kill them.

Chapter 3

Anita Stevens: A Victim of Crime/A Victim of Crack

Long before their deaths, the women who fell victim to the St. Augustine killer were, in many respects, destroyed by an equally deadly enemy—addiction to crack cocaine. Trapped in the drug's relentless tentacles, they abandoned careers, children, families, and—most telling of all—self-respect. Even in death they were stigmatized as "prostitutes," "crackheads," "street whores." Such castigation of their lifestyles made it easy to overlook the horrendous dilemma these women faced and the struggles they endured trying to survive. It also ignored the heartbreak and desperation of the families who had to stand by helplessly as their loved ones sank deeper and deeper into the irreversible traps of addiction and its companion, prostitution.

A tragic and chilling case in point was Anita McQuaig Stevens. This young woman—Anita was only twenty-seven when she was killed—grew up surrounded by a devoted family, in a community that, until her downfall, accepted and supported her in every way possible. As Sheriff's Deputy Jennifer Ponce, who was involved in the investigation of Anita's murder, put it, "Everybody

around town knew and respected Anita's family."
Anita's story vividly illustrated the power of crack cocaine to take total control of a person's life. In her case,
as in that of the other victims, this addiction contributed directly to her death.

At the time of the book's preparation, Anita's parents, Mildred and Melvin McQuaig, still lived in the
house on Newcomb Street in St. Augustine that
Melvin had built when he came home from World
War II. "With a little help from my friends," Melvin
said. Tucked away slightly west of South Dixie Highway, Newcomb Street is located in a neighborhood of
modest single-family homes. The McQuaigs' residence was one of the better tended, its yard neat with
typical north Florida vegetation that included orange
trees and semitropical plants.

Inside, the house was very obviously family-
oriented. The living-room furnishings were worn
and comfortable. Photographs of the McQuaigs' six
children, fifteen grandchildren, and fifteen great-
grandchildren smiled at visitors from the every available surface. A dining table, capable of seating a
large family group, occupied the area between living room and kitchen. A framed display of Melvin
McQuaig's souvenirs of his military service hung on
the wall nearby.

This was the home where Anita grew up, the
youngest of the six McQuaig children. As a child, she
had every reason to believe that her life would follow
the path of her successful older siblings.

Anita's mother, Mildred, was a personable, attractive lady, with white hair and a ready smile for visitors.
Anita's father, born and raised in St. Augustine, was
somewhat more taciturn, but his reserve masked a
warm, friendly manner and a quiet sense of humor.
Melvin's military career had begun with a stint in the
pre–World War II Civilian Conservation Corp (CCC),

an organization established during the Depression to provide work for young men. From there he enlisted in the Florida National Guard and later the U.S. Army, where he served until honorably discharged in 1945. He continued part-time in the army reserves, earning many commendations, finally retiring in 1981. He was a printer by trade and worked in this occupation at the *St. Augustine Record*'s printing plant. He also served as a supply sergeant at nearby Camp Blanding.

Mildred McQuaig worked from time to time at various jobs outside the home. As a former employee of the now-defunct Kresge dime store, located on St. Augustine's historic St. George Street, she is one of the group that still meets annually, dubbing themselves "the Kresge Girls." But her major focus over the years was on her home and family. "I don't suppose young girls today would be happy wearing homemade clothing," she observed, "but I sewed the dresses for all three of my girls."

All of the McQuaig children except Anita had done well in their careers and marriages. Most had settled fairly close to home. Son Melvin Jr. heads a very successful food supply business in St. Johns County. The others hold responsible positions and are highly regarded in their community, as are their parents. The McQuaigs remain to this day a close-knit, supportive clan—a recent gathering at Melvin Jr.'s home included sixty-four members of the immediate family.

Religion had always played a strong role in the McQuaigs' family life. Their children, including Anita, regularly attended Sunday school and services at nearby Pentecostal Holiness and Calvary Baptist Churches. At every stage of the trauma Anita was to bring into their lives, her family was helped to survive through hope, prayer, and deep religious conviction.

Anita was born on April 31, 1961, at nearby Flagler

Hospital. Her infancy was marked by considerable illness, as she was born with only one kidney. This problem was compounded by a kidney infection, pylitis, which had to be treated with strong medications. "She became so terribly thin that her little wrist was hardly as big around as two of my fingers," her mother recalled. Mildred sometimes speculated that the strong medications Anita received as a result of this illness may have predisposed her to drug abuse when she was older.

However, once the renal disease was under control, Anita thrived. She quickly grew into a pretty, pink-cheeked little girl with wavy blond hair and a ready smile. At age six she began attending nearby Evelyn Hamblen Elementary School, where she proved to be an average student. Her blond, blue-eyed looks made her a natural to be chosen as the "little Dutch girl" in her school's annual parade.

By age thirteen, the first signs of the recklessness and willingness to experiment that would mark Anita's later years appeared. At this time a neighbor called Mildred McQuaig at work to report that she had spotted Anita and a girlfriend leaving the McQuaig home in the middle of a school day carrying a suitcase. Anita's mother rushed home and searched the area, but the pair had disappeared. In spite of a frantic survey of the neighborhood and panicked phone calls to friends, relatives, and police, Anita could not be located. For five days not a single clue to the two girls' disappearance surfaced. Meanwhile, family, police, and volunteers scoured the surrounding area for them, their desperation mounting with each passing hour.

Finally a phone call from police in Pennsylvania ended the McQuaigs' nightmare. The girls had been taken into custody and were being held in a juvenile facility seven hundred miles distant from St. Augustine. The McQuaigs immediately boarded a plane—Mildred McQuaig's first flight—to retrieve their daughter. It turned out that the girls had gone from the McQuaig home to busily traveled US 1 and hitchhiked north, taking rides with a variety of truck drivers. The motive the girls offered for their escapade was that Anita's friend, unhappy living with her father and stepmother in St. Augustine, wished to return to her mother's home in Connecticut. That two thirteen-year-old girls escaped unscathed from this dangerous venture was little short of miraculous.

By the time Anita entered seventh grade at Ketterlinus Junior High School, her long blond hair and developing body were attracting the boys' attention. Apparently, she was conscious of the effect she was having on the opposite sex; photographs taken at the time showed her posed seductively in a bikini. Anita, however, also gave evidence of a domestic side. She stood out in her ninth-grade home economics class to the extent that she was the only student her teacher relied upon to go to a nearby supermarket and purchase supplies for the class. In recognition for her outstanding record as a student at Ketterlinus Junior High School, she received a national award, "Who's Who Among Vocational and Technical Students in America."

At home she enjoyed experimenting with foods, collecting recipes, and cooking a variety of dishes. "Even today we in the family use some of the recipes that Anita found," her mother recalled. Anita also enjoyed decorating. Later, no matter how limited her living quarters, she always kept them tidy and clean.

But by then it was the mid-1970s, a time when young people all over the country were experimenting with drugs. The St. Augustine area with its open harbors and proximity to Interstate 95—a major drug route between Miami and New York—was no exception. Even at the junior-high level, drugs—both marijuana and cocaine—were all too readily available. It was also a time when the old restrictions on sexual behavior no longer seemed to apply. For pretty, popular, headstrong Anita, the combination was to prove disastrous.

Her social life soon began to revolve around drug use and association with those who reinforced her habit. Her mother, Mildred McQuaig, felt that it was about the time of the ninth-grade prom that Anita first experimented with drugs. Experimentation with marijuana soon progressed to crack cocaine. "She was bright, but her problems soon overwhelmed her," a former acquaintance said.

At age sixteen, while still in ninth grade, Anita became pregnant. She dropped out of school, and on September 16, 1977, a hastily arranged marriage took place between her and nineteen-year-old Frank Dubose, a boatyard worker, who was the father of her child.

The marriage was to be a relationship marked by drugs, alcohol, and physical abuse. Even before the birth of her child, Anita was forced to move back home with her parents. The marital situation had deteriorated to such a point. After young Dustan was born, Frank Dubose, not wishing to assume responsibility, left the state, failing to provide financial support for his son.

Anita and her infant son lived for a time with her parents, then, later, in a house next door. As a ninth-grade dropout with no vocational skills, she could obtain only menial jobs, mostly waitressing in restaurants in the St. Augustine area. A man who was later interviewed by police as a possible suspect in her murder recalled, "I dated her around 1980 when she worked at Granny's Kitchen (a restaurant). Sometimes I slipped over to her house when her parents were gone. She seemed like a pretty good old girl."

Although devoted to young Dustan, Anita could not break away from her addiction to cocaine. Crack became her drug of choice, trapping her ever more deeply within the drug culture that flourished in St. Augustine. Later, she began to frequent the African American area of West King Street, especially those areas where the only white women were usually prostitutes.

There Anita became enmeshed in a segment of society for which drug use had progressed far beyond simple experimentation or recreational use—it was an all-encompassing way of life. Soon every waking moment became a quest for the next hit, the next high. Not only was her craving for crack cocaine relentless, it was also expensive. The quickest way to obtain the crack cocaine she craved—and actually the only way available to her—was to prostitute herself. As most of the drug dealers were African American males, Anita quickly became dependent upon them. An acquaintance reported, "I seen her on the streets. She was a white girl, but she was mostly with black guys. A different guy most every time."

The McQuaigs, desperate to help their daughter, entered her into a drug rehab program, one of several such programs they would eventually try in their efforts to halt the course of her addiction. At times her rehab sessions were court ordered. A prostitute who was interviewed after Anita's death stated that she had been talking to Anita on the street and that Anita "had some kind of trick lined up where she could go to this drug program to keep from going to jail.

"She never gave me any specifics," the woman said. "It was just like, 'I gotta turn myself in in the morning or I'm gonna be in trouble.'"

Feeling that a change of scene would remove her from undesirable associates, her parents agreed to

take care of young Dustan while Anita moved to Cape
Canaveral.

As the booming center of the aerospace industry,
the Cape offered plenty of opportunities for employment. Anita immediately found work as a waitress at
Fat Boys Restaurant and Bar. There she met Parke
Stevens, a six-year U.S. Navy enlistee. They began dating, and once again Anita became pregnant. On
January 2, 1985, three weeks before the birth of her
second child, she and Stevens were married in a
church ceremony in St. Augustine. Parke, an alcoholic, had promised he would stop drinking. The
couple moved to military quarters at Patrick Air Force
Base, near Cocoa Beach, Florida. Anita took part-time
work as a telephone solicitor.

Before Anita's expected due date, she was rushed
to the hospital, where it was discovered that the baby
was in distress and would have to be delivered immediately. Unable to locate her husband, Anita made a
frantic phone call to her parents, who made a hasty
drive down Interstate 95 to be present at the birth. On
January 28, 1985, Anita gave birth by cesarean section
to a son, Parke Stevens Jr.

Signs had already developed that this marriage was
in serious trouble; again drugs and alcohol were the
main problem. "It (the marriage) was a disaster,"
Stevens later reported. Anita's older son, Dustan, then
eight years of age, lived with them for a time, but his
stepfather was abusive. Dustan soon returned to live
with his grandparents and, at times, with Anita's older
sister.

In October 1985 Parke, an alcoholic with a record
of arrests for driving while intoxicated and domestic
violence, was assigned by the navy to attend an alcohol rehabilitation program in Orlando. The day the
program ended, Parke told Anita he was filing for a
divorce. Anita was given thirty days to remove herself

and the two children from base housing. Shortly after the divorce was final in April 1986, Parke Stevens left on the USS *Forrestal* for a six-months tour of sea duty.

The demise of her second marriage made it all too easy for Anita to succumb once again to the lure of crack cocaine. In June 1986 she moved back to St. Augustine with her children. She got a job in another restaurant, but her reputation as a drug user made her an easy target for the dealers. Her first day on the job she told her mother that an ex-boyfriend and drug pusher, Burt Long, "shoved cocaine right across the bar to me."

For the parents, this was a time of tension and anxiety. For instance, Anita went on a date with Jack at around 8:00 one evening and her parents retired at 11:30. At 12:30 A.M. the phone rang. It was Jack saying that Anita had left him to go to the rest room and didn't come back. He'd waited almost two hours before leaving the restaurant. Anita arrived home at 3:45 A.M., claiming that she hadn't left Jack at all, that they had just had breakfast at Denny's.

At times Anita was caring for her children, taking them to the beach or shopping, and playing games with them. But when she was coming down off drugs, she became irritable and abusive toward her parents and her children. Often she left without saying where she was going or when she would be back. Sometimes she dropped off one or the other of the children with friends, then failed to pick them up when she'd promised. At other times she came home only long enough to beg some money from her parents or siblings or to sleep off the effects of another binge. Holidays were particularly trying, as Anita would promise to be on hand for family gatherings but generally failed to show up.

From that point Anita's life was on a rapid and tragic one-way downward spiral. In order to support her drug habit—at its peak costing as much as $200 a day—she sank deeper and more desperately into prostitution. A man who had previously dated Anita told of her lack of discrimination: "Anita would do anybody, anytime for a buck. She was the type that if a damn car would stop to pick her up, she was gone. It could be Joe Yuan from Taiwan. I mean, somebody would have to be desperate [to take the chances she did]."

Another man, when questioned by the police, recalled, "She'd gone downhill. Started liking them niggers down there. I saw her with a little girl named Connie Terrell, who's down there on West King Street all the time. This is just what everybody knows."

When police interviewed Connie Terrell after the discovery of Anita's body, she confirmed that they had been friends. (Connie, who would later become another murder victim, was, like Anita, heavily involved in drugs and prostitution.) By this time both women had suffered the consequences of the dangers to which they exposed themselves in picking up strange men. Connie recounted an episode when the two of them had been together in a motel room and a man tried to kill Anita, eventually leaving her unconscious in a bathtub.

In August 1986 Anita was kidnapped and raped by several African American men. According to the report she filed with the St. Johns Sheriff's Office, she was leaving the parking lot of the St. Augustine post office with her son eighteen-month-old Parkie, strapped into his infant car seat beside her. A black male, whom she later claimed to have known "years ago when she did cocaine," asked her for a ride to the local Hardee's fast-food restaurant. She allowed the man, whom she knew by the names "Rail" or "Railroad," into her car. As they were driving along, the man, seized Parkie and demanded money. She gave him the $42 in her purse, but he said that was not enough and threatened to kill the child. Frightened, she drove to her house and took $100 of her mother's money, which Rail grabbed from her along with her jewelry, including her wedding ring. He then had Anita drive to a dark area near a cemetery, where they met a black man driving a white car, whom Rail referred to as "the Boss." Rail handed the money and jewelry to the Boss, leading Anita to conclude that Rail owed the Boss money for drugs.

After this transaction, Rail forced Anita from the car and raped her. Three more black males joined them. She heard Rail offering her to the other men in return for cocaine. According to Anita's account, the four men then took turns raping her throughout the night. From time to time other men—some black, some white—stopped to observe what was going on. Some of them even sat in her car and smoked crack while the rapes were going on. These were people she recognized only by their street names—"Bullet," "Bushwacker," etc. She heard one of them rationalize the rape by saying, "She was hot in school and has it coming."

Anita reported that at first she resisted the rapes, but stopped when the men threatened to harm her child. At daybreak they let her go without harming, Parkie, but threatened to burn her parents' house and kill her children if she turned them in.

Anita returned home and her mother accompanied her to the emergency room of Flagler Hospital, where she filed a report of the incident. As there was suspected sexual assault, vaginal samples were taken and sent to the state crime lab. Later she signed an affidavit notarized by Detective Gribble of the St. Johns County Sheriff's Office.

Eighteen-month-old Parkie was also examined at the hospital. On arrival he had a temperature of 100.9

but was alert and playful. He was given a prescription for amoxicillin, and his mother was instructed to see that he drank plenty of liquids.

At about this time a custody hearing instigated by Anita's former husband Parke Stevens caused the boys, Dustan and Parke Jr., to be taken from Anita and given to her parents to raise. (Oddly enough, after Anita's death, Parke Stevens once described her as "a great mother.") In spite of her fierce devotion to both her children, and her determination to raise them herself, Anita's uncontrollable drug habit made this hope unrealistic. At times after the breakup of her second marriage she did manage to live on her own, although mostly she stayed with a series of different men. Occasionally she moved back to the family home. For a while she was living in a travel trailer, which she apparently used as a base for prostitution. Men known only by their street names—"Dark Mike," "Don Juan," "T-Man," "Dump," and "Lucky Early"—came and went. Neighbors complained how "she had a different man in there every night." The bartender at a local hangout Anita frequented resented her because "she picked up a different man each time she came in the bar."

Anita's reputation as a "rip-off whore" brought her in conflict with some of the people with whom she associated, and that placed her life in danger. An acquaintance reported seeing her with a black eye. "'Red Bird,' an habitue of Crack Head Corner hit her with his fist because she would not do what he wanted," she said. Others reported that "Anita was scared of the dealers she owed money to," which was undoubtedly true. Another woman related a time when she was with Anita and they "smoked up $1,998.98 worth of rock in about forty hours." (A three- or four-day crack binge can consume up to fifty rocks a day, at $5 to $10 per rock.)

Diana Richardson, a prostitute who later became another of the killer's victims, was interviewed following Anita's murder. She spoke of a man who committed suicide after living with Anita. "He was an older man. He used to pick up 'rock stars' (the street term for crack-addicted prostitutes). Anita took him to the cleaners really bad. She was smart about it. She came and stayed a bit before, you know, to get him interested. It was a plan. Anita wanted the money. If the money was there, she was going to be, too. She spent every dime he had until he didn't even have a place to live."

The man's son was bitter regarding Anita's relationship with his father. "He was in love with Anita. She stole a lot of Dad's stuff and got him started on crack. I know for a fact that he had this gorgeous fish tank, like a hundred-gallon fish tank, and he ended up selling it. He got ten rocks of crack for it. Dad had a business, but he ran up huge debts from buying crack for 'the girls.' Then he lost his business. He was totally broke. He asked my mother for two hundred fifty bucks and went out and bought drugs with it. He was living in a shack with no hot water, no plumbing, or anything. After that, he put a hose from the exhaust into the car, rolled up the windows, turned on the motor, and died of carbon monoxide poisoning."

"A lot of people were upset about what Anita did," a woman acquaintance and fellow addict, confirmed. "She used quite a lot of people. Because of the drugs. It was because of her habit."

Malcolm Wilson, one of the many suspects interviewed in the search for Anita's murderer, testified that Anita would bring her tricks to the gas station where he worked and try to persuade him to cash their checks so they could buy drugs. Wilson's assessment of the uses to which the money would be put is revealing: "When an asshole comes in at two o'clock at night and tries to get me to cash a ten- or twenty-dollar check, I know he ain't going out for ice cream."

In spite of his awareness of the sort of men Anita was dating, Wilson was genuinely attracted to her, as were a number of other men. "We went out a couple of times until one day when I went over to get her, I found there was some characters there, the kind that even I don't deal with. It's like a bad penny, you know. I chucked it once and I didn't want it back in my pocket."

He said that after Anita moved to Palm Coast, she sometimes stopped by the gas station where he was working. "She ran in and gave me a big hug and I got kind of embarrassed because she reeked with this funky-assed perfume. I didn't know what she wanted, what she was going to ask for now. But she told me she was doing really good. I said, 'That's great, Anita. At least you got out of the bullshit here.' It's sad. There again she conned."

Wilson said he frequently tried to warn Anita of the hazards she faced if she continued her drug use. "I told her, 'How the hell do you know what's cooked in that stuff (crack cocaine)? Somebody could put rat poison in and see how you spin.' She'd say, 'They're my friends.' I'd tell her, 'They're *not* your friends. They're gonna grab your ass one way or another.'"

Wilson also presented an insightful analysis of Anita's relationship with her parents: "She could con her mom into believing the moon was shit, you know? Her dad, he knew better. Her mom and dad are sweethearts. They was conned. That family has done more than their share for that girl."

Wilson, himself a recovering addict, was all too aware of how difficult it was for those emotionally closest to the user to deal with the problem: "As long as you feed the habit, you get crap. Me and her dad used to have lengthy talks on how you do not help an alcoholic or drug addict by feeding the source. You got to cut the ties. When you stop baby-sitting, then they grow or they fold. [I told her parents] you got to Baker Act her (commit her involuntarily to a mental-health facility). If she don't pertain to the system (obey the rules), she goes to the work farm. She needs to get into a program where it's well structured and you either work for what you get or you do without. [That's] when playtime is over."

In spite of Wilson's realistic view of Anita's proclivity for deception, she frequently conned him. "Lots of times I loaned her money, ten, twenty bucks. She'd say she needed diapers and stuff for her little boy, Parkie, and I'd feel sorry for the kid. 'I'll pay you back,' she'd say. All this shit. I knew where she was going. Out West (West Augustine). Where the crack dealers and the johns were."

He also admitted he found her attractive, although by this time her looks were beginning to fade due to the rough life she was living. "Okay, we liked each other. I even went so far as me and her was gonna share a house together. I was only there maybe a day. The first night she left me alone with her two boys. The next morning I woke and there was no one there except me and her boys. I called her mother and had her come get the kids. That ended any hopes of a real relationship, even though we remained friends and I tried to help her."

While Anita's mother continued to help and support Anita, her father advocated more of a "tough love" approach. When, in February of 1988, she was jailed for taking his car without permission and driving while her license was revoked, he was ready to allow her to pay the penalty for her actions. His wife pleaded with him not to do so and he relented. Instead of receiving a jail sentence, the charges were dropped and Anita was released on her own recognizance the following day. At this time she had five previous convictions and two revocations on her driver's license.

Toward the end of her short life, Anita was living at Flagler Beach in a travel trailer belonging to her parents. She would occasionally return to her family's home until her addiction and subsequent lifestyle created too many problems. At still other times she was in various drug-rehabilitation programs. While in one drug rehab program, Anita was asked to draw a series of pictures to illustrate her life as she saw it. The result was a touching revelation of a young woman aware of the forces that are destroying her, but unable to break free from them.

Although she insisted she was desperate for help, even when admitted to rehab centers she failed to show up, or else managed to get booted out before completing the program. This is not uncommon behavior for crack addicts. Those few who do get to the stage of recovery have usually failed in rehabilitation an average of six times. Jean Borden, a chef at the tech center where Anita had been a student, offered to mentor Anita, as did Lois Turner, the McQuaigs' pastor, but their efforts were equally in vain.

Through all of this, Anita's parents—her mother in particular—clung desperately to the hope that a cure could be found for Anita's now-overwhelming addiction. Like any parent going through the excruciatingly painful ordeal of seeing her child's life destroyed, Mrs. McQuaig clung desperately to any thin thread of hope and refused to give up on Anita. "She was never mean or talked bad to us, and she loved her children above all else," Mildred McQuaig recalled. "That was what made it so hard to see her going down that path."

By the late 1980s Anita's addiction had seized total control of her life. On several occasions she overdosed and nearly died. Often her parents were out at three and four o'clock in the morning searching the streets for her. Numerous times she arrived home with injuries received in fights. Trips to the Flagler Hospital emergency room became almost routine.

When Malcolm Wilson was interviewed after her murder, he felt the perpetrator would be found in West Augustine, where the drug dealers operated. "I'd say somebody out West (West King Street) murdered her. Maybe they ran out of uses for her. Maybe she ran her mouth. What these assholes do out West is to use them crack prostitutes until they're done, and when they're done, let them flop. It's sickening."

Despite the depths to which she had sunk, Anita never stopped caring for her children, even at times when she had lost custody. In her final year of life, she wrote a letter to a friend in which she stated:

> I'm working again, six days a week from 2 pm til 8 pm at La Bella's (restaurant) on A1A south. I have Mondays off but as soon as Michelle (her sister, who was caring for the children) can, I would like Parke and Dustan for a weekend. I have arranged to work from 5 to 9 on the weekend. She permits them to come and my naibor [sic] Francie will babysit them hours I'm away. Her husband Donnie will take Dustan fishing on the pier and I can see them out the window of the restaurant, plus they will eat dinner where I work. I really miss my babies. We can work it to where no one will know (that the children were with her as she was not supposed to be permitted to see them alone).

Her parents and sister mostly cared for the children, but as Anita became hopelessly in bondage to her drug habit, her former husband sued for custody of his son Parke Jr. Richard Watson, the hearing judge, appointed a guardian *ad Litem* to insure that the child's interests were being protected. An evaluation was conducted to see if Anita was a fit mother. In November 1988 the guardian *ad Litem* visited the McQuaig home to discuss the matter of the child's custody with Anita and the McQuaigs. "I will do anything it takes to keep my boys," Anita pleaded. The guardian, aware of Anita's inability to function responsibly as a mother, replied that she felt it would be best if the father were allowed to have custody.

Furious, Anita stalked off. She pulled on her gray knit jogging pants, pink corduroy shorts, and a sweatshirt with a pink collar stenciled in front with the letters TKO and two boxing gloves. At four o'clock she left home, saying she was going to Connie Terrell's house to retrieve a purse she had loaned to Connie.

That was the last time Mildred McQuaig saw her daughter alive.

After a sleepless night waiting for Anita to return, Mrs. McQuaig begged her husband to go search for Anita, but he refused to participate in what had become a familiar scenario. In an effort to get his wife's mind off the turmoil at home, Melvin McQuaig suggested the two of them spend the night at their cabin on the river. While he was getting ready, Mildred went searching for Anita, but to no avail.

The following day, Anita's parents, Melvin and Mildred McQuaig, went to their cabin on the St. Johns River. They returned home on December 1 to find the copy of the *St. Augustine Record* that had been delivered to their driveway. When she opened the paper to the front page, Mildred immediately recognized the drawing and description as Anita. Frantically she tried to contact the sheriff's office, but when unable to get through, she phoned the St.

Augustine police. It was there that she learned that the murder victim had already been identified and was, indeed, Anita.

Mildred McQuaig would not be the only mother in St. Augustine to face that dreadful moment. Anita's killer was still at large . . . and still hunting for his next victim.

Chapter 4

June 1989: Constance Marie Terrell

It was safe to go back.

At first the story had been on the front pages, then inside. But even the newspapers had forgotten by now. Nothing about her for a long time.

He'd be careful, though. Mama was wrong. He wasn't headed for trouble.

By summer, law enforcement officers had questioned an extensive list of potential witnesses, anyone who could be considered a possible suspect or informant in Anita's case—mostly other prostitutes, pimps, and drug dealers, as well as Anita's family and friends. Despite these intensive efforts and the cooperation of the FBI, no significant clues were uncovered. Anita's slayer remained a mystery.

June 1989. Summer had arrived full-blown in St. Augustine. The snowbirds had long since headed North, and a lazy sort of peace had settled over the community. Meanwhile, the initial shock waves stemming from Anita Stevens's murder had subsided. The women of Crack Head Corner were once again risking their lives jumping into the cars or pickup trucks of most any john who agreed to their offer of a date. If the need for a fix was desperate, the women took their chances even with men who demanded rough sex or were known to be dangerous in other ways.

On June 11 of that year, the local newspaper carried numerous ads for gifts suitable for Father's Day—neckties, shirts, and golf equipment. Temperatures along the First Coast were hovering in the nineties, and a tornado had been reported in the Florida Panhandle. That Sunday morning Robert Sikes and his wife decided to go fishing at the borrow pits off Holmes Boulevard, near Thompson Bailey Road, little realizing they were about to uncover the next link in a chain of vicious sexual murders that would plague the community for most of the following decade.

At approximately 7:50 on Sunday morning, Sikes and his wife unloaded their boat from their truck, launched it, and pushed away from shore. They had been in the water approximately three minutes when an object—something bright red or purple—caught their attention. Moving closer, they realized that what they were seeing was a female body, lying on the bank, half in, half out, of the murky water. The petite, slender woman had been positioned on her back and was naked except for the red T-shirt that had been pulled up above her breasts.

At approximately 8:40 on the morning of June 11, 1989, Deputy Folin L. Christmas, of the St. Johns Sheriff's Office, was parked in the Li'l Champ's lot on State Road 16 at Collins Avenue when he was approached by a white male. The man introduced himself as Robert Sikes and said that he wanted to speak with Christmas about something very important. He told the deputy that while fishing at the pit off Four Mile Road, he had spotted a body lying on the bank next to the water. He offered to show Christmas where the body was, but first he wished to take his wife home.

Deputy Christmas followed the couple to their home. Sikes parked his vehicle and rode with the deputy back to the area where the body had been spotted. Christmas got out of his vehicle and approached, walking on the left side of the road in the grass to preserve any tire marks that might be present. He saw a female body lying on the bank with one foot in the water. The body appeared to be nude except for a pinkish purple shirt bearing the logo BUCKWHEAT, pulled up above her breast. A small yellow nylon rope was tied around the victim's neck. Although stripped of her clothing, she still had on several rings and a small pair of earrings.

Christmas notified the sheriff's office and secured the scene until Lieutenant Robert Taylor and Sergeant Larry Mahn arrived. Sheriff's Deputies, Randy Capo, and Terry Isaacs were also summoned to secure the scene, setting up their vehicles to prohibit access to the area. Deputy Christmas then took a written statement from Robert Sikes and gave it to Deputy Meade. Detective Mary LeVeck arrived on the scene and assisted deputies with photographing the crime scene and searching for evidence.

A police sketch of the area where the body was discovered along with indications as to where various pieces of evidence were located in relation to the body was entered into the files. The diagram showed two large bodies of water separated by a roadway. Several tire impressions were taken and several beer cans and two white socks were collected as evidence.

At approximately noon that day, technician A. Miller, from the Florida Department of Law Enforcement (FDLE), arrived and began processing the body. A possible fingerprint was located on the back area.

A half hour later, Investigator Kenneth Moore, of

the medical examiner's office, arrived and assisted in removal of the body. Doctor Robert J. McConaghie, the medical examiner who conducted the autopsy, noted in his report that the woman had died of a gunshot wound to the head. This was confirmed when he recovered a flattened lead bullet from her brain. She had also suffered a hemorrhage of the larynx, suggesting that she had been strangled as well. He also noted that she had pelvic inflammatory disease, abrasions on her right arm, and traces of recent cocaine use and possible alcoholic intoxication. He estimated the time of death as occurring twelve to sixteen hours prior to discovery of the body.

The body Sikes had discovered was that of Constance Marie Terrell, a friend and frequent companion of Anita Stevens's. Connie was one of the women who had been interviewed after Anita's death. She was a logical informant—like Anita, the petite twenty-eight-year-old with still-girlish features was known to frequent West King Street, prostituting herself to satisfy her constant driving need for crack.

Like Anita, Connie Terrell was part of a large, close-knit family with deep roots in the St. Augustine community. Connie grew up in the same home in which her mother had been raised and in which her parents still live today. During the lifetime of Connie's grandmother Claire King, the Bennetts and their family shared the home with her, enlarging and adapting the old house to the needs of their growing family. In a recent interview, Connie's mother, Nancy Bennett, pointed to one of the home's interior doorways—"I was born in that very bedroom," she said.

Connie's father, Jackie Bennett, grew up on nearby Masters Drive in St. Augustine. Like most natives, he has a deep and abiding appreciation of the easygoing, close-to-nature lifestyle the St. Augustine community offers. He told how, as a boy, he and friends would cast their mullet nets into the Tolomato River, load their catch into a tin washtub, place the tub onto a wheelbarrow, and peddle the fish throughout the neighborhood.

The Bennetts' home, located at the end of a long driveway and bordering on a tidal marsh, reflected the laid-back lifestyle typical of longtime Florida residents. Surrounding it were the homes of several of the Bennetts' seven children. Inside, the old house provided much evidence of Jackie Bennett's remodeling skills and Nancy Bennett's homemaking ability.

The Bennetts' home was warm and comfortable, and there was obvious closeness among the siblings. They have a strong religious faith, and musical and artistic ability abound in the family. In addition to his work as a surveyor, Jackie Bennett played in a country music band on weekends, entertaining in such local spots as the High Chaparral and the Lantern Lounge. (It appeared the genes for musical ability were passed on to Bennett's son Todd, who has perfect pitch, a talent that brought him success in his work as an organ installer and tuner.) In short, everything about the family would lead one to expect that Connie's life would be a happy, normal one.

Connie, a middle child of seven, was born on August 9, 1962. At the time the Bennetts were living in Ocala, where Mr. Bennett's work as a surveyor for the Florida Department of Transportation had taken them. Connie started first grade there at Blessed Trinity parochial school. The following year the Bennetts returned to St. Augustine. Although the move to St. Augustine put the Bennetts closer to their extended families, Mr. Bennett's work still involved a commute on his Kawasaki motorcycle each day to Deltona, some ninety miles distant.

While much of Nancy Bennett's career had been as

a mother and homemaker, she always made use of her love of fabrics and her talents as a seamstress. For a time she operated a fabric shop, the Silver Needle, on nearby Masters Drive. She later sold that business but returned to carry on a drapery and slipcover business, Cover-Ups. Her children still benefit from her skill as a seamstress—on a recent morning daughter Deanna stopped by with several pairs of her husband's pants to be hemmed.

Through their membership in a motorcycle club, the Bennetts have traveled extensively. As a result of their motorcycle trips to Colorado, Utah, Wyoming, Arizona, and New Mexico, the remodeled living room of their home was decorated in a Southwest theme.

Upon their return to St. Augustine from Ocala, the Bennetts attempted to enroll their children in the local parochial school, but were unable to do so because of overcrowding. Connie entered a public school, Crookshank Elementary. At seven she made her First Communion at the Cathedral-Basilica, wearing the same veil that had been worn by her grandmother, her mother, and her sisters before her.

Connie, although not a particularly good student academically, excelled in art. At home she was the family clown, joking back and forth with her sisters and brothers and performing clever takeoffs on classmates and school friends. She was also a "neat freak," insistent on picking up and organizing any possessions left scattered throughout the house. In short, Connie, surrounded by her four sisters and two brothers, was brought up in a devoted family with deep religious faith. By all indications she seemed well on her way to a happy, productive life.

Then, at about age twelve, Connie developed scoliosis, a condition involving an abnormal S-shaped curvature of the spine. The small-framed child was forced to wear a cumbersome brace for several years, a disfiguring device that made it impossible for her to sit comfortably or bend to retrieve objects.

Unfortunately, this highly visible physical disability occurred during Connie's early teens, a time when to be different from the in crowd is to suffer social ridicule and rejection. Insecure adolescents can be unbelievably cruel to one they perceive as different, weak, or handicapped. Not only was Connie forced to endure the discomfort, disfiguration, and limited range of motion imposed by the device, but at school she was teased by insensitive classmates. For example, when she dropped a pencil or a book, some of the boys would kick it out of her reach. On one occasion a girl deliberately burned a cigarette hole in Connie's school dress while she was in the lavatory.

Connie's lack of academic ability, combined with the social ostracism caused by her scoliosis, continued to plague her in high school. By the time she was no longer required to wear her brace, the damage to her self-esteem was ingrained. As an outsider she found it all too easy to seek acceptance from other rejected teens, who turned to drugs for temporary feelings of confidence and self-worth.

Connie's parents were unaware of the magnitude of the drug problem in St. Augustine, even though it was endemic in the community at that time. In retrospect they realize that it was in high school that their daughter began experimenting with marijuana and perhaps cocaine as well.

While still a high-school student, Connie became romantically involved with Billy Terrell. In 1980, when Connie was in eleventh grade, she became pregnant, dropped out of school, and married Billy. Connie's parents reluctantly supported what they felt from the beginning to be a precarious union. Terrell, who worked in the building trade as a framer, was reputed to be excellent at his job, but it was also rumored that he was a heavy drug user. Still, they and the rest of the family rallied around and helped the young couple set up housekeeping. Connie and Billy's first home was a tiny travel trailer, so small that when guests were present for dinner, Billy had to sit with his feet in the bathtub.

On February 9, 1981, Connie's daughter, Kimberly, was born. Two years later, on March 18, 1983, she gave birth to a son, whom she named Jackie for her father. The Terrells moved to a larger apartment on the beach and seemed on their way to settling into the same pattern as Connie's older siblings, building a life for themselves centered around work, home, and extended family. Construction in the St. Augustine area was booming and Billy had plenty of steady work. Connie was employed sporadically, sometimes baby-sitting for her older sister, sometimes cleaning houses or working at a nearby day care center.

But it soon became evident that drug and alcohol abuse was beginning to seriously impact the young couple's lives. In an interview with a woman who later knew Connie, Detective Mary LeVeck learned that it was Connie's husband who got her started on the drugs that led to her addiction.

"I know her husband got her started on drugs," the informant said. "They started doing crack and Connie used to go out West (West King Street) in her car and cop drugs for him."

When Connie and her husband were arrested for possession of marijuana, it became even more obvious that the marriage was in serious trouble, with drugs contributing to its turmoil and physical violence.

By the time Kimberly was six years old and young Jackie was four, Connie and Billy had divorced. After that, Connie's addiction had become the compelling force in her life. While devoted to her children, she was able to care for them only periodically. At times they lived with Billy, at other times with their grand-parents.

Much like her friend Anita Stevens, Connie's ad-diction to crack cocaine inevitably led her into prostitution, the only way she could possibly pay for an ever more demanding drug habit. She obtained her supply of drugs and money from many of the same dealers and johns with whom Anita dealt. Both women became members of the same subculture comprised primarily of pimps, prostitutes, and drug dealers.

As time passed, Connie's craving led her to aban-don caution and common sense when dealing with the men who desired her services. When questioned by police after Anita's murder, Connie admitted that she had been beaten up by a white male who took her to the woods, forced her onto the hood of his car, and raped her anally. "He was a real jerk," she said. "He threw all my clothes into the palmettos. I had to walk out there and get them. He said he was going to pay me, but he didn't." At that stage of her addiction, she was more perturbed by the loss of the money—and the drugs it would buy—than by the indignity and physical pain of the rape.

As far as identifying Anita's killer was concerned Connie was unable to help. When asked if she thought Anita had been killed by one of the black drug dealers, Connie replied, "They do stupid shit like that . . . giving money or crack to whores for sex, then beating them up and taking it back."

Connie was less forthcoming about her own activi-ties. One of the prostitutes interviewed by Detective Mary LeVeck after Connie's murder said that "Connie was real, real quiet about the business she did. I mean, if you live on the street and you associate with these people who, you know, deal drugs, you don't say nothing. You keep your mouth shut or you wake up dead. That's the rules of that game."

The same informant described Connie as "just a little cutie pie. She was always in a pretty little skirt, she wore decent clothes. Some of the other girls are with the shorts that are wicked, you know, their cheeks all hanging out. And I mean this is in the winter. But Connie wasn't like that."

In her never-ending need for rock cocaine, Connie continued to take the same risks that cost Anita her life. Living on the streets, she wound up staying with one man after another . . . anyone who would give her a place to hang out and enough rock to get high on.

A woman who knew her at that period said, "After Connie divorced her husband, she stayed with Morgan. He cared a lot about her. Like he'd have her kids over there and stuff. He would wash her clothes for her and let her stay (in his house). He's pretty nice to all the girls. He's an older man and he's got a temper, but he wouldn't hurt anybody. While Connie lived with Morgan, she kept messing up, stealing and whoring, until he wouldn't have anything to do with her."

Most of Connie's dates, like those of the other women of Crack Head Corner, were brief, twenty- to forty-five-minute affairs involving a short drive down one of the county roads to a secluded spot where they could engage in either oral sex or regular intercourse without interruption. At other times the sex took place in the houses or trailers occupied by one of the parties. The police investigations later revealed that a black man, Boris, with whom Connie was involved at one time, maintained a room in his house where the prostitutes could pay to bring their johns for sex or to get high. There were several of these houses in St. Augustine. Most of their owners also dealt in drugs along with operating a "hot sheet" room or two, which they rented to those needing a place to have sex.

Connie, like many of the other prostitutes, period-ically developed temporary live-in relationships with the johns, drug dealers, and pimps with whom she as-sociated. Some lasted only a few days or weeks, others a year or more. One of these men, Wiley Simms, was interviewed by Detectives Frank Welborn and Mary LeVeck on June 12, 1989. He said that he had met Connie the previous October. "I met her on the street. She was a prostitute," he said. Two weeks later she moved in with him. "But she still would often spend the night at Boris's."

"So she was living with you and him sort of at the same time?" Detective Welborn asked.

"Three or four nights a week, she was living with me. That started breaking apart about April. That's when I asked her to leave. I packed up all her clothes and took her over to Boris's house. She wouldn't get out of the car. I just told her, 'Get your ass out of the car. That's it.' She appeared at my door a couple of times after that. One time she entered the house. The second time I did not allow her to come in. And she was trying to coax me out of the house to sell me drugs."

In this, Connie was following a pattern common among the more physically attractive prostitutes. With her slim figure and almost childlike features, she, like Anita, attracted men who became infatuated with her. She would move in with such a man and remain with him so long as there was a steady supply of drugs and/or money. In other cases she continued to work the streets in order to support the man. However, these liaisons generally terminated when the men be-came too controlling or the drugs ran out and the fighting began.

Even when Connie's appearance had clearly begun to show the effects of chronic drug abuse, too many beatings, and much hard living, she was still able to at-tract admirers. Her long dark hair and petite figure—she was five feet two inches tall and weighed one hundred pounds—made her extremely appealing to men.

When questioned by Detective Mary LeVeck about Connie, Shanelle, a fellow prostitute, admitted that she had "hated Connie because she was so pretty."

Shanelle revealed something of her own and Connie's lifestyle in the report she gave the detective:

> Like I said, we just couldn't stand each other. It was like a code, I didn't like her and she didn't like me. Then after I came back from prison, she came up to me and said, "Hi, how are you doing?" And I said, "Hey, girl, how you doing? When did you cut your hair and everything?" It was like we'd never had any problems. So I got so I liked her and we'd hang out. She'd tell me about certain things that happened in the street. And I talked to her. But after she started hanging out with Oswan (a pimp and drug dealer) even though she knew how I felt about him. They got real close and I got jealous and was saying nasty things to her . . . messing with her. It just pissed me off.

Detective LeVeck asked Shanelle how Connie obtained her dates. "Did she walk the street and have guys pick her up, or did she set things up ahead of time?"

"I think she did a little of both," Shanelle said. "Like she'll stand out there and a guy she knows will come along and they'd get in the truck and go somewhere. [Other times] she'd set dates where she'd say, 'I've got to meet somebody at eight o'clock.'"

When asked if she had ever heard anyone call Connie names, Shanelle replied, "People would call her whore or tramp, somebody did junkie. Just people in passing. But they do shit like that. Of course, Connie was born and raised here, so she knew almost everybody in town." (This kind of abuse occurred periodically to all the prostitutes, but it was especially vitriolic when directed at local women who prostituted themselves or a white prostitute such as Connie seen with an African American man.)

Given Connie's lifestyle, it was inevitable that sooner or later she would come into conflict with the law. Shoplifting and prostitution in support of her drug habit cost her a term in the county jail, as did driving with a suspended license and failure to pay traffic tickets. On a number of occasions, her name showed up on the police blotter when she was caught riding with men in cars in which police located drugs and paraphernalia.

Still, Connie had no difficulty finding men who would support her habit—for a time, at least. "All of them are in love with Connie," one such man stated. "There's other men out there that love that woman. One guy bailed her out [from jail]. I gave her canteen money when she was locked up."

Don Harkins was one such person. He held a well-paying job local factory. After meeting Connie on the street, they arranged a "date." A second liaison came a few days later. Soon Harkins found himself falling in love with the attractive, likable young woman.

Harkins, a user himself, although not an addict, was fully aware of Connie's problem. "When I first met her, I knew within minutes she was hooked on drugs."

In spite of that—or perhaps because of it—he persisted in the relationship. By Christmas, Connie had agreed to move in with him. According to Harkins, their relationship grew very close, even though he realized that she was living with another man at the same time and was still turning tricks to support her drug habit. "I fitted her profile perfectly," he conceded ruefully. "I made good money and could supply her with drugs at least one or two days a week."

Harkins later claimed that in his efforts to "help"

Connie, he even tried to have her incarcerated to keep her away from the drugs. "Connie was killing herself," he said. "She needed medical help bad. And she was taking me down financially—I was still into drugs at that time, but she used every day. We would burn one hundred dollars, maybe two hundred dollars of my money on weekends. I said to her, 'If you want to quit, we'll do it together and I'll help you go through it. We'll go see doctors. . . . We'll go to rehab.'"

But Connie was clearly not interested in quitting. "It was too easy for her to get drugs," Harkins said. "And I fell into the same trap. I was just helping her die . . . killing her myself by giving her more drugs. I just fell right down with her."

While Harkins offered a somewhat sanitized version of their relationship, claiming that his motive was to help, others who were interviewed following Connie's murder reported that she had often suffered physical abuse at his hands. Harkins once hit Connie in the head with a flashlight, knocking her unconscious. Another time he struck her in the kidney with his fist. This is not surprising since cocaine abuse and violence often go hand in hand.

However, it was not Harkins's violence that ended his relationship with Connie—it was when he saw her giving oral sex to an African American male. "I knew from the start she was a prostitute," he said. "But if you don't see her do it, you can live with it. But when I saw her do oral sex with that black man, it came home to me."

Apparently, Harkins still continued to have feelings for Connie as he bemoaned the fact that when he got into a fight and was badly hurt, Connie never came to see him. "She knew I couldn't work and had no money. But seeing her with that black man, that kind of helped me get over my feelings for her. My love eventually turned to pity."

In his statements to the detectives after Connie's murder, Harkins claimed, "Connie tried to come back to me after that and sell me stuff she had stolen. I told her no, to get out. The last time I saw her was about May sixth. She knocked on my door and got in. I gave her a coat she had left at my house and made her leave. I later saw her at Boris's place, because that's where I bought my drugs. He was a big dealer. I may have had sex with her there. He had a room for that."

Eventually the drugs and prostitution took a visible toll on Connie's appearance. A friend who had attended school with her said, "Connie had been chubby and real cute as a girl. When I saw her some years later, I didn't recognize her because she was so thin. But Connie never looked like a whore. She dressed nice, not like Delicious, one of the black female prostitutes who dresses real provocative."

During this period Connie stayed off and on with Boris. He, too, was abusive to her, once admitting to having punched her in the eye with his fist. In spite of his frequent abuse of Connie, Boris testified, "I don't know anybody that hates her. She's got friends. People like her and care about her. She was a nice person."

Boris undoubtedly spoke from his perspective as a black drug dealer and someone who had used—and had been used by—Connie. He was aware of the rejection and contempt she faced from some of the local people with whom she had grown up in St. Augustine. "Some people would pass Connie on the street and call her 'whore,' or 'nigger lover.' Sometimes they even threw things at her."

It was from Boris's house that Connie departed on Saturday, June 10, 1989. She had been drinking heavily all afternoon, but that failed to satisfy her craving for a few rocks. She informed Missy, one of the house's habitués, that she was going to "meet a guy.

"Wait for me—we'll party when I get back," Connie told her.

The evening was still warm and steamy as Connie headed for Crack Head Corner, where she could be virtually certain to pick up a date. Still feeling the alcohol buzz, at about eight or nine o'clock that evening, she was walking west along King Street when a dark blue Ford LTD pulled to the side of the road. The driver honked, then rolled down the window. Connie stepped toward the vehicle.

"Looking for a date?" she asked.

"How much?" the driver said.

She tilted her head to one side. "Depends. What kind you want?"

"How about just for straight up?"

She looked him over, trying to estimate the best price she could get from him. He looked to be about forty or so, his clothes nothing special, the car not too new. Definitely not a big-money guy. "Thirty dollars," she said.

He nodded and shoved open the car door. Connie jumped in and instructed him to drive out to Holmes Boulevard. "I know a spot out there where we won't be bothered," she told him.

When they arrived, Connie showed him where to pull the car into a small clearing out of sight of the road. After the motor was turned off, the two of them climbed into the backseat. Connie stripped off her pants and underclothes, but she merely pulled her T-shirt around her neck, allowing most of it to hang behind her neck. The man loosened his belt and unzipped his pants.

He groped Connie's exposed breasts while she massaged his limp penis. But even after a lot of groping and fondling, the man could not get an erection.

Connie, perhaps remembering the many humiliations she had suffered at the hands of various johns, began laughing at his dilemma.

Her laughter quickly turned to shock and terror when the man exploded in rage and began pounding her with his fists. Connie fought back desperately, but at a mere one hundred pounds, she was no match for him. He wrestled her onto her back. Then, before her alcohol-fogged brain could register what was happening, he grabbed a piece of rope shaped into a noose from under the front seat. With one swift motion he jerked it around her neck.

Realizing her life was at stake, Connie struggled harder. Choking and gasping for breath, she pleaded with him to stop. Ignoring her pleas, he kicked open the car door and climbed out, yanking her along with him. Once free of the car, he threw her to the ground and began to beat her unmercifully, raining blows on her face and body with his free arm, all the while pulling the rope tighter and tighter. As the noose cinched about her neck, Connie, fighting for every breath, clawed with both hands at the rope. So desperate was she for air that she hardly felt the blows that landed on her ribs and abdomen.

Connie's terror reached new heights when she saw the man reach back into his vehicle and pull out a rifle. In despair she raised herself on all fours and begged, "Please! Please! Don't hurt me anymore!"

Holding the rope in one hand, he pointed the rifle toward her head. Looking straight into her eyes, he snarled, "Bitch! Whore!"

To escape the fury that distorted his face and burned in his eyes, she turned her face away from him. As she did so, a bullet from the rifle ripped through her brain.

In the aftermath of Connie Terrell's murder, local law enforcement was faced once more with the onerous task of piecing together the events leading up to the death of a local woman. The interview Detective Mary LeVeck, of the St. Johns County Sheriff's Office, conducted with Boris, the drug dealer and pimp from whose house Connie had departed just before her death, offered insight into the lifestyle and convoluted relationships between the pimps, drug dealers, and prostitutes. It also revealed the endless details detectives must check out in the course of their investigation. Understandably, many times such interviewees offered the most self-serving statements possible and made transparent attempts to cover their own illicit activities. Investigators were well aware of this, and hoped that they would be able to cull some of the truth from the information they collected.

Detective Mary LeVeck was identified in this interview by her initials *ML*; Boris's responses were noted by *B*.

ML: *We're currently investigating the death of Constance Marie Terrell. Can you tell me what your relationship was with her?*

 B: *Yeah, we were close partners . . . friends . . . lovers.*

ML: *How long have you known her?*

 B: *Not long. Three or four years.*

ML: *I understand that she had moved all of her clothes and stuff into your house. How long ago did she do that?*

 B: *About two, three weeks ago.*

ML: *She's been staying there almost every night?*

 B: *Almost every night.*

ML: *Do you know where she stays when she doesn't stay with you?*

B: *I don't know where, but I see her out there, you know, doing . . .*

ML: *Picking up different guys?*

B: *Um-hum.*

ML: *When was the last time you saw Connie?*

B: *About four or five o'clock Saturday morning.*

ML: *You said earlier that you had an argument with her. A petty argument. Was that Friday evening or Saturday morning?*

B: *Saturday morning early. About eleven-thirty or twelve.*

ML: *And you said you punched her? Where did you hit her?*

B: *Head.*

ML: *On the right side of her right temple area?*

B: *Yeah, right there.*

ML: *Okay. Would you have hit her hard enough to leave a bruise? Did you slap her with an open hand or a clinched fist.*

B: *It might have been a bruise. But she had put makeup on.*

ML: *But you hit her with a closed fist? So there could have been a bruise left from it?*

B: *We was talking a long time, you know. I didn't see no bruise. But . . .*

ML: *Okay. Okay. So after this argument you had with her, what happened?*

B: *We sat down and made it up. 'Cause it don't make no sense arguing over something stupid.*

ML: *So this argument took place about eleven or twelve o'clock Friday evening. Did she leave at that time?*

B: *No. I left. And I came back, she was still there crying. And then we sat down and we talked.*

ML: *You left after you hit her? About how long were you gone?*

B: *I walked about ten or fifteen minutes.*

ML: *You came back and she was still crying?*

 B: *I let her finish crying. And then she got up and she changed clothes. She was in the bathroom. I was standing up there, and I wasn't saying nothing to her. She came on out and she sat in the living room with me and my brother. We sat down and we talked it over*
(Detective LeVeck asked about the clothes Connie was wearing when she left.)

 B: *The red T-shirt, that came out of the van. Now I know, 'cause she changed clothes in the bathroom. Had no sleeves in it. Okay, while I'm talking about this, it starts coming back to me.*

ML: *All right. Describe for me the socks she was wearing the night she left.*

 B: *Short white socks. They call them anklets. Like tennis socks.*

ML: *You're talking about they have like a ribbing in them?*

 B: *Yeah, these lines like here. (He indicates an area on his own socks.) And they weren't real long. Just like short.*

ML: *Do you remember what kind of shoes she had?*

 B: *A pair of white tennis shoes. Or they were beige. No, not beige, but they had holes in them. I believe they were white.*

ML: *What kind of pants did she have on?*

 B: *I believe they were dungarees. Blue. And a body shirt. No sleeves in it. A red one.*

ML: *Okay. Her jewelry—can you describe the jewelry she had on?*

 B: *Yeah. A golden color necklace. It came out to a point in the front. Like a little heart there. It was on a chain.*

ML: *A thick chain? A wide one?*

 B: *It wasn't thick. One of her rings had a little pearl*

in it. I can't remember the others. And a gold bracelet. Gold-chain thing.

ML: *So after she changed her clothes and you guys made up, what happened then?*

B: *She walked down the street. It was getting daylight, because the rooster was crowing. I asked her what time she was gonna be back and then I stood at the door and watched her walking the streets. That's when they called me back inside and I went back in there.*

ML: *Where do you think she was going at that time?*

B: *She could have been going to make a phone call or to meet somebody.*

ML: *Do you think she might have been going out to pick somebody up? Or somebody pick her up?*

B: *Yeah. 'Cause she said it's about time for her to go. It means somebody's coming, you know. She got to be someplace, to be picked up by somebody. She was telling me she wouldn't jump in nobody's car she didn't know. And she wouldn't jump in with no car full of people, more than one or two.*

ML: *So was this a prearrangement that she was being picked up?*

B: *Yeah. It was . . . you know. . . . She wasn't gonna be standing for any stranger to come pick her up. She had somebody that had an appointment pick her up. Or she had to be making a buy.*

ML: *And that was the last time you saw her? How did you find out she had died?*

B: *When they found her dead, I said to myself, "Don't you be lying and putting a bad mouth on nobody." See, I was already feeling bad. 'Cause it (the argument) was stupid. And I had punched her. I hurt her, in other words, you know. By hitting on her. 'Cause I [was] mad,* 'cause they beat me out of my paycheck. A whole day's pay for me. I had bills to pay, you know.

ML: Did Connie ever give you any money she made?

B: Well, I didn't ask her to pay no bills, you know. (At this point Boris is trying to justify the fact that he acts as Connie's pimp and that she gives him money she earns through prostitution.) If she walk out there, she likes to eat, you know. There always would be food. I'd say, "There's something to eat as long as you like, you know." I just tell her to buy her clothes. Get herself straight, you know?

ML: So tell me about the Wiley Simms, the guy Connie used to live with. Did she ever keep her clothes at his place?

B: He burned them up. Cut them up or something.

ML: When did he do that?

B: I don't know. I was in prison at the time he done all that. She used to drive his truck and she stayed out overnight or something, then took the truck back and left the keys in it and went on about her business. That's when he messed her clothes up. Because she stayed out too long.

ML: Do you know anything about his hitting her with a flashlight?

B: Wiley said he bopped her on the side of the head with it and she fell out.

ML: She fell out unconscious?

B: Same thing.

ML: Did you and he ever get into a fight?

B: Yes. I don't know what happened down on the street, but Wiley came back acting off, so I told him he wasn't coming in with all that noise. He sat down outside with Milton and they were talking. Then Connie came to the door and he got off of my face. I was drinking a little bit, you know, so I may not be accurate. But Wiley hit Milton, and Milton hit him with this little stick; then Wiley walked on down the road and I ain't seen him since.

ML: You told me that a couple of days before Connie was killed, there was a girl at your house that had made reference to her boyfriend trying to strangle her. What was her name?

B: Don't know. She had short black hair. On the thin side. A white girl. But I don't think she was no longer on the street.

ML: Do you know any other girls that had problems with any of the guys out there, men who were crazy or tried to hurt them very bad?

B: There's one girl told me that, but she didn't tell me the dude's name. Said he had her in a pickup and was taking her the wrong way. She said he had a pistol beside her head. Ms. Greenhalgh (another detective from the sheriff's office) and them came here. They was telling her to stop, get some nice job. They was going to get her a place to stay and put her in a drug treatment program. It ain't worth it, you know, walking the street. People on North City will kill us, you know. They said that other girl got killed, you know, she walked the street and she was white. Somewhere around here. These people trying to help her get off the street, go back to school, learn something. Stay around the house. Be a baby-sitter.

ML: Can you think of anything else that might help us? Anything I haven't asked you that you might know that would help us to investigate Connie's death?

B: Put me on the case. Let me find . . . I'll get locked up. I'll go to jail. (He is offering to be a jailhouse informant.)

ML: Don't want that to happen.

B: Oh, my God! This is on a tape recorder. You got

to erase that. Like I say, nobody didn't hate Connie. She got friends. People liked her and cared about her, you know. She was a nice person.

Another interviewee after Connie's murder was Lashawna Streeter, who would later become the fourth St. Augustine victim. She reported that shortly after Connie's death she had encountered a man she knew from having previously partied with him. "I was over town walking down the street passing by the Bull Pen (a local bar) when this guy called to me, so I stopped. I was very upset about what had happened to Connie. He seemed to support me very much. Then he turned on me and grabbed me and choked me. He said something about paying her (Connie) two thousand dollars, but he never said why. Then he kept saying, 'She deserved it.' Then he started dragging me and dragging me toward his car and tried to make me get in. He said, 'The bitch f . . . over me and I just paid out two thousand dollars.' All the things he said, he was referring to Connie."

Several informants suggested that Connie's murder might be racially motivated. "Some crazy trick that picked her up, somebody that was mad at her from St. Augustine. Because she grew up in the white world, now she's living in the black world."

In an interview with Sally Temple, Detective LeVeck learned more details of the woman's association with Connie. Again it is possible to interpret some of Temple's responses as self-serving or concealing her own activities.

Temple reported that she had known Connie since school days. "We grew up together. First grade, all the way through school—St. Agnes, Catholic parochial school, and St. Joseph's [not the same schools reported by Connie's mother]."

Asked when was the last time she had seen Connie,

Temple responded, "About seven months ago. Out on West King Street. If she was walking down the road or something, if she was by herself, I'd stop and offer her a ride. Everybody would be grabbing me and asking for a ride. I basically ran a taxi service for everybody. They'd pay me two or three bucks to drive them to here, to there. Easier to drive around in a car that nobody knows. That way the Nine, as they call police officers, don't know what they was doing. But I know and you know—running back and forth, from here to there. Which, at the time, I didn't give a damn what they were doing."

Asked if she assumed Connie was prostituting, she responded, "None of my business. Most of [the] time when I picked her up, it would be just around the block, just drop her off on the street. 'Cause she was, you know, hiding from the law or something like that. I'd drive her around the corner to keep her from getting busted. This one time I took her to a guy's trailer that she was . . . that she had a date with or whatever you want to call it."

Temple was unable to provide any further identification of the man Connie was meeting. "Just some old guy. The reason she took the ride that night, she was in a hurry. She was late. The business she was in, I couldn't very well hang on her (waste her time talking). It would cost her money."

Temple offered her own logic as to Connie's need to prostitute herself. "A lot of people didn't like Connie because she was out there with the black people. But people don't understand what you got to do to survive. She looked to make money, you know. She had a drug problem. You've got that problem; then you're doing what you got to do to survive. I don't knock anybody for anything that they do.

"I used to live with a black man, too," she volunteered. "So I'm trash now. I mean, there's white guys hanging out down in West Augustine, too, looking, you know, with the black girlfriends. But that's all hush-hush-hush. They're not gonna say anything."

Detective LeVeck asked if Temple thought anyone in St. Augustine might have been upset enough with Connie to kill her because she liked black people.

"I don't know," Temple said. "Everybody looks down their noses at her because of the business that she was in, her problem with drugs and all that. But as far as being a bad person, Connie wasn't. She was a real nice girl. But I happened to mention Connie to a friend at work, a redneck girl. Her daddy used to be years and years ago with the KKK and all that shit. She said, 'Yeah, that girl used to hang around out West. She got what she deserved.'"

As with other witnesses and suspects that the detectives interviewed following Connie's murder, none could offer specific information as to who her killer might have been. Once again the lifestyle of the murdered woman obscured the path to her killer.

Chapter 5

An Advocate for Victims and Their Families

While there is no way to ease the hurt that families suffer when a loved one is murdered, St. Johns County Sheriff's Office offered a unique service in the form of the Victims' Advocate Program. Early in Sheriff Neil Perry's tenure, he canvassed his staff as to what changes they felt might be beneficial to the department and to the community. He also asked individual staff members what responsibilities they might be interested in assuming. Through this process, he came up with an individual uniquely suited to the position of victims' advocate.

Mary Alice Colson began her career with the sheriff's office in 1985 as a switchboard operator handling long-distance calls. At that time the county offices were housed in downtown St. Augustine in what is now a luxury hotel, the Casa Monica. "Sheriff's office personnel worked in the area where the hotel's restaurant now is," Colson recalled. "At that time we were a small office, where everyone knew everybody." As long-distance operator, Colson handled all the calls made out of the local area, sharing duties with another operator, the two working either day or evening shifts.

Perry suggested to Colson that she might be interested in working with the juvenile division, but as the mother of growing children, she felt she would prefer something in another area. Perry then brought her a book containing information about a Victims' Advocate Program and suggested she look into the possibility of starting such a program in St. Johns County.

After reading the book thoroughly, Colson checked around the state for other such programs. She found one in Pinellas County, the first such program instituted in Florida. She went there for a week and studied the work of the three advocates employed by the department. She found that the advocates' duties varied but included an opportunity to be of help to people in time of great need. She returned enthusiastic about the possibilities. Sheriff Perry then applied for grants to fund a similar program within his department.

Mary Alice Colson was the only victims' advocate originally employed in St. Johns County and was on call twenty-four hours a day. Among the types of situations to which she responded were domestic violence calls, homicides (all deaths are considered homicides until proven otherwise), suicide (not considered a crime, but usually leaves victims in its wake whose needs must be met), auto crashes, and problems with elderly persons. As an advocate she often accompanied police personnel when it was necessary to deliver death notification to families. At that time victims advocates also handled court cases, a duty that has since been transferred to the states' attorney's office.

Colson explained that when a crime occurs, officers at the scene have specific duties such as traffic control, crime scene preservation, attending to the injured, interviewing witnesses, and notifying other agencies. Often they do not have the time or resources to attend to the needs of survivors or family members. The victims' advocate, on the other hand, focuses solely on offering such assistance to those who need it. Often they make living arrangements for survivors, help them with phone calls, and generally try to comfort the often-traumatized survivors. Colson notes that the most devastating effect on victims' advocates and police personnel are when serious crimes or accidents involve children.

The job is not without danger. Colson experienced a chilling episode when she was sent to notify a man that his wife's body had been found in a van in nearby Jacksonville. After she had been alone in the house with the man for some time, she received a phone call from a sheriff's deputy asking if she was all right. It turned out that police had discovered that the husband was the murderer.

Mary Alice Colson, with her outgoing nature and easy ability to relate to all sorts of people, was a particularly suitable person for her position. To better understand her job and what was involved in police procedures, she attended the police academy for nine months and became a sworn officer. Colson was in her forties at the time she went through the academy and attended classes at night while working during the day. She developed a close relationship with the younger cadets, to whom she soon became "Mom." She would encourage other victims' advocates to take the same training. "Even though they are around law enforcement officers, they don't really understand police procedures without the training," she said.

Victims' advocates were provided with the equipment they may need on the scene of crimes or accidents. In addition to a car, they have on hand a cell phone, beeper, child car seats, flashlights, blankets, and other equipment that may be required. A van was available to the advocate on call for transporting large numbers of people.

Colson became involved in the St. Augustine murders when Anita Stevens's body was found. She and Sheriff Perry made the death notification to the McQuaig family. This was particularly traumatic, as Colson had previously known Anita and her family and was aware of the extreme efforts the family had made to help Anita. She was also involved with the Bennett family after Connie Terrell's death. At that time she did not suspect how many more times her services would be needed before the killer was captured.

Chapter 6

March 1992: Lashawna Streeter-White

The man had been out of town for a while. Other places. Other . . . but he didn't allow himself to think too much about that. What had happened up there in Virginia . . . up there in North Carolina.

Now that he was back in St. Augustine, he knew exactly where to head. The pickings at Crack Head Corner were always easy. But this time he'd be more careful. No gun. Something about the way that other one died bothered him. There were better ways.

Guns and bullets could leave a trail

Around 4:15 P.M. on the first day of March 1992, a red four-door Granada pulled into the parking lot at Crack Head Corner. Twenty-seven-year-old Lashawna Streeter broke away from the half-dozen or so people clustered around a bench and walked toward the vehicle. Kind of an old dude behind the wheel. Plain enough what he was hunting for. With her most provocative grin, she leaned against the passenger-side door. "Lookin' for a date?"

He gave her the once-over before he answered.

"Maybe," he said. "But you won't do. I'm looking for a white woman."

Bastard! Still, if she played it cool, she might make a few bucks out of the old honky. She put on a fake smile. "I might could help you out, sugar . . . for the right price."

He pulled three $10 bills from his wallet, but he didn't hand them to her. "How's thirty sound?"

Lashawna considered for a minute. The man didn't look like a big spender—very likely $30 was as much as she could hope to get out of him. Enough for a few happy rocks. She opened the car door and got in. "Head up Volusia Street. White woman I know lives up that way."

She glanced down at the money that he'd placed on the seat between them. He saw her looking and took his hand off the wheel to clamp it down on top of the bills, letting her know he wasn't about to hand it over until she delivered the goods. Lashawna was offended. First the old fool had made it clear she wasn't good enough for him because she was black. Now he was suspicious that she was going rip him off. She decided that at the first opportunity she'd grab the money and bail out. No creepy old white man was going to "dis" Lashawna Streeter!

Her chance came when they reached the intersection with Four Mile Road. She signaled to him to make the turn; then, as soon as he slowed down, she snatched up the money and made a grab for the door handle. But the man, already suspicious of her intentions, was too quick for her—before she could jump out and run, he slammed on the brakes, throwing her forward into the dashboard. His rough hand grabbed the back of her neck and squeezed it in a tight, painful grip. Once, twice, three times he banged her head against the dashboard. As she struggled wildly to free herself, he forced her down onto the seat and began pummeling her with his fists. The last words she heard before she lost consciousness were "Dirty, cheating nigger whore!"

He shoved the woman's unconscious body to the floor of the car, then headed back toward King Street. He would have to find a place to dump her out of the car. She kept groaning from time to time. Well, she deserved to groan. But she wouldn't be making any noise at all by the time he finished with her. The more he thought about the way she'd snatched his money, the angrier he became. She deserved what she had coming.

He turned the car south on Pellicer Lane, then continued on down South Dixie Highway toward Moultrie. With each passing mile the uncontrollable fury was building tighter and tighter inside him. He felt as if gasoline were surging through his veins and the least spark would trigger an explosion.

At last he spotted what he was looking for. OLD DAIRY FARM ROAD, the sign read. He swung the Granada onto the little dirt lane, continued a short distance to a small clearing, then turned the car around. The spot was perfect—out-of-the-way, with little likelihood of other traffic.

Soon as he'd braked to a stop, the man leaped out of the driver's seat, circled to the passenger side and jerked open the door. Surging anger gave him almost superhuman strength as he reached down, seized the woman by her hair, and dragged her from the car. Her body was limp, but she was still moaning and feebly trying to resist. Again he started beating and kicking her. *Rotten rip-off bitch! Deserved what she got! Taking from me just like all the others did. Lying when she said she was going to get me a white woman, then stealing my money! Damned whore!*

His fury finally spent, he gave a last vicious kick, then stood back, panting. No more moans. No movement. Grabbing the woman's now-lifeless body in a chokehold, he dragged it several hundred feet into the woods, where recent rains had left the low-lying area saturated with standing water. He hauled the body toward one of the deeper puddles and dumped it, watched it splash into the mud and slime. He turned for a last look and realized he'd left it too exposed. He gathered some armfuls of underbrush and covered her. Again the man stood back. That took care of . . . . What was the bitch's name? She'd never mentioned it, and he hadn't asked. . . . Just another dead whore.

Previous to her murder, Lashawna had been living for two years with Curtis Glover, a food-service worker at Flagler College. The two of them shared a home with Randy Hodgkins, a prep cook at a local restaurant. Glover and Hodgkins were with Lashawna the night she disappeared; it was Glover who reported her disappearance to the St. Augustine police. In his missing persons report, Glover stated that he "believes Streeter may have run into trouble and could even be dead." He described her as having had on blue jeans, black shoes, and a green-colored army coat. He said she was a crack addict and a prostitute.

Detective Jeremy Masters investigated the missing persons report. He contacted the St. Johns County Sheriff's Office, the Jacksonville Sheriff's Office, and the Duval County Medical Examiner's Office to determine whether they had an unidentified body of a black female matching Lashawna's description. None of them reported having such a body. Masters also contacted Lashawna's mother, Nadine Jakes, who reported that she had not had contact with her daughter for approximately two weeks and did not know where Lashawna might be.

When Masters spoke with a manager of ARA Foods at Flagler College, where Lashawna had been employed, he learned that she had been fired a couple of days previously for not showing up for work. He also told Masters that she had not picked up her final check from work.

As he had done with Anita Stevens and Connie Terrell, the killer had disposed of Lashawna Streeter's body in a damp area near a borrow pit. Ten days later, on March 11, 1992, David McClure, a white male employed as a handyman and lawn-service worker, discovered her remains. McClure's gruesome discovery occurred as he was walking down State Road 207 to the railroad tracks on his way home, following a well-traveled trail which led onto Old Moultrie Road. When nearly opposite Flagler Hospital, he encountered a smell which he at first assumed came from a dead animal. The farther he advanced, the stronger and heavier the scent became.

He poked through the palmettos for the source of the smell and was shocked to discover a dead body covered with maggots. Shaking with terror, he ran to the hospital and told a doctor of his gruesome discovery. The doctor notified the Sheriff's Office. Detective Jennifer Ponce appeared and took McClure back to the spot where he had stumbled across the body. She confirmed that the remains were those of a human.

Detective Jennifer Ponce later interviewed John Pickens, the paramedic at Flagler West Hospital, whom McClure had encountered that afternoon. His report agreed with the information McClure had given detectives. He reported that McClure was quiet but visibly upset. "He stated that he had never seen a dead body before, other than his friend being shot under the bridge." Pickens also noted that McClure had returned to the hospital several times since, each time elaborating more on his relationship with Lashawna and claiming that she had propositioned him. He claimed, too, that he was having nightmares and that "her dead body came back to haunt him."

Deputy Joan Bleacher had been the first law enforcement officer to arrive in response to McClure's alarm. With Deputy Steve Brack, she secured the scene. Deputy Bleacher then proceeded to take McClure's statement. Meantime, a car was spotted in the area and Deputy Robert Snyder, who had arrived in response to the police bulletin, was assigned to interview the driver, who was considered at first to be a possible suspect and was read his Miranda rights.

The driver reported that he often came to this area, locally known as Quinney's Land, to drive his truck on off-road trails. On that particular day, he said, his vehicle had become stuck on a muddy trail for a short time. After he extracted the truck from the mud and finished exploring, he allowed the engine to cool while he smoked a cigarette. He was preparing to leave the area when he was stopped by the deputy's car blocking his path. The man was unable to supply any leads to Deputy Snyder, except that he had spotted a long-haired man at the beginning of the road.

This man, like the many others that detectives would question in the days to follow, proved to know nothing of the crime.

Detective Jennifer Ponce, of the St. Johns County Crime Squad, arrived at the scene at 6:10 that evening and met with the other officers on duty. She read over McClure's statement and briefly interviewed him. Shortly after, Ponce, along with Detective Mary LeVeck and now Lt. Elliott Gribble, followed Deputy Brack to the crime scene. In her report, Ponce noted:

> *The body was located under a palmetto thicket a
> short distance from the road. I observed a small pile
> consisting of bush debris and wood debris located
> northeast of where the body was laying.*

Ponce then went on to describe the position of the
body and the clothing the woman was wearing:

> *The body was badly decomposed with maggot infes-
> tation in the chest cavity, pelvic area, and inside right
> leg. The head and chest area were partially skeletalized.
> Signs of putrification were visible.*

Around 7:00 P.M. evidence technician Susan Biesiada arrived and videotaped the body. It was decided
to secure the area and leave it intact until the following morning in order to allow the FDLE to
process the crime scene. Detective Mary LeVeck also
made contact with Investigator Kenneth Moore from
the medical examiner's office to notify him of the
circumstances. She also contacted Sergeant David
Braddock, of the St. Augustine police, and obtained
information from him regarding the missing persons report on Lashawna Streeter, which had been
filed earlier. Braddock provided her with details
of his investigation and she advised him that they
would be in touch with him the following day.

After leaving the crime scene, Detectives LeVeck
and Ponce met back at Criminal Investigation Division (CID) with FDLE technicians, who would process
the crime scene the following day.

The following morning FDLE crime scene technicians Steve Leary and John Holmquist met with
detectives at CID and traveled with them to the crime
scene, where Officer Susan Biesiada and Lieutenant
Gribble were already on hand. The scene was videoed
and photographed and measurements were taken.

That same day Detective Masters, who had followed up on the original missing persons report, learned that an unidentified body of a black female had been located in a wooded area behind the Ponce de León Mall. He met with St. Johns County detectives at the scene and learned that the description of the clothing found with the body matched those Glover had reported Lashawna was wearing the night she disappeared. Masters noted that "the unidentified body was in such a state of decomposition that it would have been almost impossible to identify the body by having a relative examine the remains." (This speaks to the rapidity with which bodies decompose in the damp, humid climate of northern Florida.)

Masters then recontacted Lashawna's family and obtained photographs from them in an effort to determine if the body was indeed hers. Her mother and stepfather, Mike Millard, informed him that Lashawna had "large teeth, with a small gap between the two upper center teeth." He further learned that she was once married to a Willie Lee White. Their marriage license, obtained in St. Johns County, stated the bride's full name as Lashawna Falesha Streeter and her age as twenty-two. The groom, age thirty-four, had been born in Georgia and was twice divorced. The couple later separated and Lashawna never used her married name.

Nadine Jakes, Lashawna's mother, attested to the clothing Lashawna had been wearing:

> The pictures of the red socks, belt and jeans that Detective LeVeck showed to me, I've seen Lashawna wear and I know they are hers. The t-shirt Detective showed to me, I've seen Curtis (Glover, the man with whom Lashawna was living at the time of her murder) wear

before. Lashawna also had a tooth missing on the bottom, one of the pointed ones.

Lashawna's clothing was also identified by her stepfather, Mike Millard.

Later that day Masters reinterviewed Curtis Glover and obtained a more detailed description of the clothing Lashawna was wearing when last seen. Glover reported she had on a green-colored army jacket with a furry-type liner and that it had four or five letters across the back, although he could not remember what they were. He described other items of clothing consistent with those found with the body.

Masters concluded his report by noting: "It is my belief that Lashawna Streeter has been located. Case status: cleared, missing person located."

Later that morning LeVeck and Ponce met with Barnett Bank president Bill Young, whose office windows overlooked the area. Young stated that he hadn't noticed any vehicles in that area recently, but that it was frequented by numerous people over the years. Karen Johnson, who worked in Young's office, stated that one day the previous week she had returned from lunch at about 2:00 P.M. and noticed a white window van driving back on the dirt road. She thought it was strange because she never saw vehicles driving in that area. Neal Canada, who was interviewed by detectives, confirmed that the area in which Lashawna's body had been found was often used as a rendezvous spot for lovers. He said, "My brother was back there about two weeks ago and noticed a large party of young people. They had a big fire built back there." The discarded beer cans, cigarette butts, and food wrappers left behind by others made it very difficult for detectives to identify objects that may have been related to the murder.

Another informant gave a detailed report of a vehicle he had seen in the area several days before the murder:

> On March 6, 1992, between the hours of 12 noon and 1600 hours, I observed a black in color Jeep CT-7, approximate year model 1989–1992 with a gray soft top, factory rims and tires, Islander paint package, entering the woods off Old Moultrie Road known as "Queens Land." Jeep was occupied by a white male driver, and I believe white male passenger.

Dr. Terrence Steiner, the medical examiner, and Investigator Moore, from the medical examiner's office, arrived to examine the body. By that time the body was in an advanced state of deterioration with little more than a skeleton remaining.

In his report, the coroner noted that he had arrived on the scene at approximately 10:45 A.M. and followed the deputies several hundred feet off a dirt road to the area where the body had been discovered. He described the remains as those of a young adult black female, lying face-up. Her elbows and knees were flexed and a burgundy shirt and undershirt had been pulled up near her collarbones. Much of the skin over her upper body was missing and there was considerable maggot infestation. He also stated that while driving around he did not see anyone or anything suspicious except for a long-haired man at the beginning of the road, particularly of the soft tissues.

Her size seven blue Jordache jeans had been unzipped, pulled inside out, and were down around her ankles. A brown belt was unbuckled but still in the belt loops. She had on red socks, but no shoes. Her jeans and socks were removed and bagged as evidence.

At 11:45 A.M. the body was transported to the Medical Examiner's office, where the chest and abdomen were x-rayed.

In a report filed on March 12, 1992, by Dr. Steiner, Lashawna's cause of death was listed as "unnatural," and the manner of death as "homicide." This description of the death as a homicide would later become a critical factor in a court hearing regarding Lashawna's death.

Present at the autopsy were Detective Ponce, Sergeant West, evidence technician Susan Biesiada, Deputy David Flutz, Investigator Ron Moore, and senior crime lab analysts Steve Leary, and John Holmquist. Biesiada and Ponce took still photographs of the procedure and recovered the articles of clothing as they were removed from the body.

Further examination of the remains showed that the body was that of a black female, five feet six inches tall, weighing approximately one hundred pounds. A yellow hair comb was identifiable in her medium-length dark hair. Much deterioration had taken place and a number of body parts were missing, including a great deal of skin and her left ear. Various bones were exposed. Her fingernails were short in length and free of breakage. Small amounts of red nail polish remained on the fingers and thumb of her right hand and her left fifth finger. Fingerprints were taken for the records from her right hand.

The remains were reexamined later by Dr. William R. Maples, a forensic anthropologist from the University of Florida. No visual defects were discernible on the exposed bones. Although no dental history was available on the dead woman, her identity was determined by the fact that her left lateral incisor was missing and also by visual identification of her clothing by family members.

The sheriff's office sent out a bulletin requesting officers to field identify any possible johns in the high-traffic prostitute/drug areas, especially Lincolnville and the King Street region. The notice also listed possible suspect vehicles, including a small dark blue car similar to a Chevette, a blue van, and a CJ-7 or similar model Jeep.

David McClure became a suspect in Lashawna's case by virtue of having discovered her body. He was identified as a person who frequented Crack Head Corner and the drug and prostitution hangouts in Lincolnville. His long rap sheet included offenses such as burglary, grand theft, and violation of parole. One such offense involved his theft of food, cologne, and a belt buckle from the Circle K convenience store. When questioned, McClure claimed that Lashawna, whom he described as "pretty," had once solicited him for a date. He said he told her no and she walked away with another guy. However, his responses to detectives' questions about the relationship were inconsistent and evasive.

His behavior after finding the body led police to continue to pursue him as a suspect, especially since he seemed unduly curious about Lashawna's death, even offering to serve as an informant for the police. Months after her body was discovered, he was still intruding himself into the case. He had saved the newspaper article about her death and carried it with him in his wallet. He said he was distressed that the article mentioned his name because "he didn't want whoever killed her to come after him."

Later, on August 18, some five months after his discovery of Lashawna's body, McClure appeared at the St. Johns County Sheriff's office and asked to speak with one of the detectives assigned to the case. He then offered to work as an informant, claiming he had contacts with the drug dealers in Lincolnville.

The detective thanked him, but said that his services would not be required.

At that, McClure quickly changed the subject. "I heard they caught the guy," he said.

The detective asked what he meant by that statement and McClure repeated that he had heard that "the guy that did the murder" had been caught.

The detective told McClure he was not at liberty to discuss the investigation but McClure continued to push for information. He claimed that the police had tried to pin the murder on him and had brought him in for questioning in an effort to obtain a confession that he had murdered Lashawna.

When the detective refused to divulge any information, McClure again offered to become a confidential informant. He also informed the officer that he would be willing to buy narcotics for him. His services were declined.

After McClure left, the detective contacted Detectives LeVeck and Ponce and relayed to them what had transpired with McClure.

Ponce then interviewed McClure, who claimed to have been severely traumatized by finding the body to the extent that he was experiencing nightmares and other symptoms of post-traumatic stress disorder. He said he was seeking help from the church and from "mental-health specialists" for these symptoms. When questioned by Detective Ponce, he reported that he went to Trinity Chapel to talk to someone but only talked to the janitor.

In August 1992 detectives again interviewed John Pickens, the Flagler Hospital emergency room paramedic who had first spoken with McClure after the discovery of Lashawna's body. He reported that McClure had paid several repeat visits to the hospital, one of which occurred after he had been drinking for forty-eight hours or so and wanted to get some help.

At one point he called the police, threatening suicide. In spite of McClure's bizarre behavior, no convincing evidence was found that would connect him to the murder.

Curtis Glover and Randy Hodgkins, Lashawna's roommates, were also interrogated as possible suspects. Glover, originally from New Jersey, had felony convictions in various states for crimes, including burglary, larceny, possession of burglary tools, receiving stolen property, and obstructing the police. Randy Hodgkins described Glover as "pretty straight up, but light-fingered, and he has a crack habit." These two men, like most of the suspects in the St. Augustine murders, had extensive criminal records, if not for major felonies, at least for crimes such as drug use, DUIs, theft, various forms of assault, resisting arrest, or violation of parole.

Although they realized that Lashawna was crack addicted and supported her habit through prostitution, both men insisted that they did not object to her sexual activities because she shared the crack she obtained with them. Both were also aware that she had a reputation for ripping off her clients.

According to the account Glover gave Detective Mary LeVeck, Lashawna came home at around 2:00 A.M. on the evening she disappeared. She told him she had been at Bob Trotter's house on Washington Street, but when the cops came by she left. She told him she was planning to return there to meet a man in a blue van who had a lot of drugs. Glover said that Lashawna had brought a dime rock (crack cocaine) back with her and that they smoked it before she left to return to Washington Street. He said that the next morning when he woke up to go to his food service job at Flagler College Lashawna was not there.

Another informant interviewed by Detective Jennifer Ponce claimed to have seen Lashawna on

Sunday, March 1 in a blue van with a white man whom he estimated to be in his late thirties or early forties. He described this man as balding, with short brown hair, and wearing a white T-shirt and blue jeans. The informant said the pair had stopped him at the corner of Martin Luther King Drive and DeHaven Street and asked if he could get them some drugs. He got into the van and they drove around Lincolnville and stopped at a few places, but had no success in obtaining drugs.

The pair became impatient with him and two hours later took him back to the corner where they had picked him up. Before they left, he told them he could probably get them some drugs out on West King Street, but Lashawna said she had her own sources out there.

The informant insisted that there had been very little conversation exchanged during the time he was with Lashawna and the man and that although the man came into the area every week or so looking for drugs and girls, he could not identify him. As Detective Ponce was aware, informants are subject to convenient memory lapses when asked to identify potential suspects. In the interwoven society in which the pimps, drug dealers, and prostitutes operate, it is dangerous to relay such information to the police.

Another acquaintance of Streeter's was interviewed, and when asked what she thought happened, she replied, "She probably got into someone's vehicle and he took her out there and killed her. I knew Lashawna got into guys' cars for drugs, but I didn't think she would get into a stranger's car."

Lisa Streeter, Lashawna's sister, agreed with that analysis. "She probably got picked up by some crazy guy and he killed her."

Lisa also stated that a few weeks previously she herself had been approached by a suspicious-looking man driving a dark blue Jeep with a black lightning bolt decal on the side.

Further investigation by sheriff's department detectives revealed that Lashawna had been married in 1987 to Willie Lee White from whom she was divorced in 1992. She had recently completed a nurse assistant course. Although employed, she was getting food stamps. She, too, had had a number of arrests for assault, threats and intimidation, domestic disturbances, and intoxication.

Apparently Streeter's family was one in which there was considerable turbulence. Malvera Lucas who lived next door (her daughter, Cheryl, would later become another of the killer's victims) reported that frequently her neighbors' loud arguing could be heard throughout the neighborhood. Once, after Lashawna's death, Lucas reported she had had to confront Lashawna's mother and sisters who were outdoors, shouting and using foul language.

Randy Hodgkins, who shared living quarters with Glover, was also questioned in the case. He stated that he had met Lashawna Streeter and her boyfriend, Curtis Glover, through the use of crack cocaine. Although he declared himself to be friends with Glover and Streeter, he said he "did not trust them because of the crack habit." He also stated that neither he nor Glover had a problem with Lashawna prostituting because she would bring them crack. On the night of her disappearance, he said she had seen someone with whom it would be "prosperous" for her to hook up.

Curtis Glover suggested to police that a likely suspect in Lashawna's murder was a local drug dealer known as "Snakeman." Shortly after Connie Terrell was killed, Snakeman had tried to force Lashawna into his vehicle. Lashawna had described the incident to the police in a deposition given on June 13, 1989, three days after Terrell's death: "I was walking down by the Bull Pen (a local prostitute hangout) and a guy named James or Snakeman pulled me to his vehicle. He kept saying, 'She deserved it. Bitch fucked me over. I had just given her two thousand dollars.'" Lashawna could only assume the "her" Snakeman referred to was Connie Terrell. (Several other suspects in the St. Augustine murders used this type of "false confession," apparently as a means of intimidating prostitutes.)

Lashawna's sister Marsha Jakes later reported she had been subjected to the same threatening technique. She said a man told her, "Bitch, I'm the one killed your sister!"

Another prostitute, Dawn Johnson described a similar encounter. "Two years ago when I was pregnant, a man in a new model silver-gray truck picked me up. He threw the money on the dashboard and drove down a side road. He had me take my pants off. He then pulled a blade out and put it on my throat and made me have oral sex with him." Afterward, he apparently felt sorry for her and took her back to where he had picked her up. En route he told her that he threatened girls on the street to scare them so they wouldn't go back out. He left her with the warning, "I'd better not see you out again."

(Dawn later reported to police that she had spotted the man's photograph in the local newspaper. He proved to be a successful local businessman. Police questioned him, but he insisted that he had never been with any prostitutes, had never been on West King Street harassing prostitutes, and that he had never killed any prostitutes.)

In Lashawna's case, as often happens in the serial
murder of prostitutes, none of the leads or suspects
contributed to the identification of her killer. On August 19, 1992, an intelligence bulletin went out to law
enforcement agencies asking that anyone observed
dumping debris in the area of Old Dairy Farm Road
be reported:

> *Field Contact any traffic observed entering or exit-*
> *ing this road. Any information received should be*
> *forwarded to Detective Jennifer Ponce at the Persons*
> *Crime Unit of the Sheriff's Office.*

The bulletin also provided a sketch of Lashawna
Streeter and a map of the area where her body had
been found.

However, the bulletin, like other law enforcement
efforts, produced no viable leads to Lashawna's
killer. In a narrative summary that became part of
Lashawna's file, it was noted that "two similar type
cases occurred in 1988 and 1989. They both involved
the same type lifestyle. The general type area of location [of the body] was also a similarity and the
manner of which the bodies were disposed of and
their positions." This would seem to indicate that
at this point investigators were leaning toward the
theory of a serial killer.

The summary also noted that "the exception to this
case [Lashawna's], however, is lack of evidence. The
other two bodies were recovered in time to reveal
some evidence."

In fact, the resolution of Lashawna's case would not
come in time to save four more women from meeting
death at the hands of the same sadistic murderer.

Chapter 7

The Stalker and the Stalked: A Prostitute's Life on the Streets

I was just cleaning up the streets
   —Serial killer Peter Sutcliffe's explanation
      of why he killed helpless prostitutes

In the course of investigating the St. Augustine murders, detectives questioned many of the prostitutes who worked the same West Augustine territory as the slain women. That prostitution was rampant in the West Augustine area is confirmed by the fact that police had only to stake out the parking lot of the Pic 'n Save store or other nearby haunts to find informants, either prostitutes or johns looking for a date.

Often the women attempted to rationalize the fact that they were selling their bodies. While investigating one of the murders, detectives observed a known prostitute getting into a white four-door New Yorker. When questioned, the woman stated that the driver's wife was unable to have sex, which was why he picked up prostitutes.

While such information may seem to indicate that

prostitution is a victimless crime, other contacts that officers had with these informants provided a vivid picture of the trapped existence these women and others like them were leading. And—in almost every instance—the bait for the trap was crack cocaine. Once the drug's tentacles closed around them, the women lost not only the respect of their families and society in general, they lost the free will to escape to a better life. In the worst instances, they lost life itself.

A police report taken at about the time of Anita's murder provided vivid evidence of the kind of dangers these women faced daily. The report was taken by Sergeant John Jenner in the presence of Beth Farley, a victims' advocate from the state's attorney's office.

The victim Carol Thames said that she had been raped and beaten by a man who threatened to kill her if she did not perform as he ordered. She had met the suspect at the St. Augustine home of a mutual friend, whom she refused to identify. With her friend and two black males, Robert and Johnny J, they drove to a motel in nearby Orange Park (a suburb of Jacksonville), where they obtained cocaine and partied until the following morning. At some point the friend left, and Carol asked to be taken home, but Robert refused. Instead, he drove her to a dirt road in the vicinity of Green Cove Springs. The road ran between a swamp on one side and a graveyard on the other. While they were driving, Robert told her that since she refused to have intercourse with him, he was going to kill her. He bragged that he had just gotten out of prison for rape and murder, so she believed his threat.

As soon as he stopped the car, Carol tried to jump out of the vehicle, but Robert pushed the power door-lock button, locking all four doors. He then threatened again to kill her if she didn't submit to sexual intercourse. He also pulled from beneath the car seat what appeared to be a broken broom handle and threatened to "shove it into your vagina until it cracks your neck" if she didn't comply. "Take your clothes off," he told her. "You don't, I'll bury you in the graveyard just like the others."

Fearing for her life, she complied with his order and he raped her. During this episode he also sodomized her, which she said he described as "treating her like a man." He kept repeating a bizarre insistence that she was a man but had had a sex change and that he knew she couldn't have any babies because babies came from the stomach being cut open.

Later he shoved her out of the vehicle, dragged her by her hair, beat her with the broom handle, and raped her again on the grass. She kept begging, saying that she had two children and to please let her go. Instead, he began searching his car for a gun he claimed was there. While he was looking for the gun, Carol jumped in the creek and started swimming toward the opposite side. She thought she heard a splash behind her but was too terrified to look back. Totally naked and soaking wet, she reached the opposite shore and ran toward the nearest house she could find.

The officer, who responded to the resident's call, found Carol in shock and nearly incoherent. The only information he could get from her at this point was that she had jumped into the swamp to escape a man who had raped her. She said that the only name she had for the man was Robert.

Other police who responded found Carol's ripped clothing in the woods on the opposite side of the stream. They also collected nearby tire imprints and shoe prints, preserving them with labstone, a plaster-like substance used to preserve imprints, for future evidence. They also collected sunglasses and a card case that were lying nearby.

After Carol was treated at a local hospital and semen specimens were collected, she was able to identify for police the motel room where she and Robert had stayed. The bill had been paid in cash, so no information had been taken on the vehicle. However, from the description Carol had given of Robert and the car he was driving, investigators were able to locate the vehicle. Although the owner at first denied that his car had been driven during the previous two months, he was arrested and charged with the crime.

To police who respond to incidents involving prostitutes, the above scenario was all too familiar. The hunger for crack cocaine and the "partying" that generally followed led all too often to rape, abuse, and, in the worst cases, murder.

After the news spread that three St. Augustine women had been brutally murdered, fear—especially fear of the unknown—had a chilling effect on Crack Head Corner's prostitutes. For a time after each of the killings, they exercised greater caution, turning down dates with any johns who appeared suspicious or who had a reputation for brutality, or whose faces were unfamiliar.

Engaged in an occupation that was itself illegal, the women had only meager means of protecting themselves from predators. Only in the most extreme cases would they call upon the police for help. Most often they relied instead on a loose-knit grapevine to exchange information regarding the johns they dated.

Any unfamiliar man who appeared on the scene was carefully checked out, but since the johns frequently used aliases rather than their actual names, this offered scant protection. However, thanks to the grapevine, by the time a john had been to Crack Head Corner two or three times, most of the women knew what they would have to contend with if they got into his vehicle.

When asked if Fish Island, where Anita's body had been found, was the usual place where they took their johns, one of the women replied, "I don't go out that far unless I know the guy very well. I don't think Anita would have taken someone out there unless she knew them. Too far away from her rocks. The way most of us girls work is to stay pretty much in town."

Asked to describe her relationship with a former boyfriend who had often beaten her, the same woman stated that she was afraid to go back to him because he had a "tendency to fly off the handle. He throws you down stairs and beats you. He ties you up and takes advantage of you. He strangled me twice. One time I was knocked out. When I woke up, I was tied to a bed. He's a strange person," she reported.

In an interview with Detective Mary LeVeck following Connie's murder, one of the prostitutes revealed just how hazardous that occupation could be:

> It happened New Year's Eve. He picked me up on King Street by the Jiffy Store, King and Riberia. We went down to Little Links and when I got out of the car he just sucker punched me. I was looking down at his wallet for him to take out the money and all of a sudden, bam, I was laying on the ground. After, he took my pants off and got what he wanted. He told me to shut up or else he was going to hit me again. I was really scared because it was right after what happened to Anita. That just kept running through my mind. Afterwards he got in his car and left. I had a fractured cheek bone.

As time passed following each of the murders, those supporting a $100-a-day-or-more drug habit became less and less particular. Needing a fix, they once again jumped into any car or truck that slowed down. Ultimately, even the threat of death was not enough to prevent the women from returning to the streets, willing to take on almost all johns. This played directly into the killer's hands and made them easy victims. All he had to do was choose his next victim and wait.

That is not to suggest that the women were merely innocent victims of predatory males. They themselves were often the victimizers. Hollywood's interpretations of the oldest profession——*Klute* or *Pretty Woman*——aside, charity toward the johns has never been a priority with women who make their living on the streets. Among prostitutes, a john is rated not for his good looks or his sexual prowess but for his ability to pay or to provide drugs. Illustrative of this tough attitude was the approach used by an African American prostitute named Tenderoni. She stated, "If the john is somebody I don't know, I tell him, 'Look, buddy, you pay me upfront or I ain't touching you. I ain't even going to talk to you nice.'" If the man was one she had known previously and who paid well, it was "Oh, just be good to me. You know, get me what I want (drugs); then I'll go to the room with you, be nice to you some more."

Some of the females who worked Crack Head Corner were dangerously aggressive in their dealings with the men who bought their services. One woman, who was known to pull a knife on johns and rob them, bragged, "When I have a live one, about the time he's in the middle of getting his rocks off, I slip his wallet right out of his pocket. He's feeling so good in front, he don't know what's happening in back."

Obviously, ripping off johns in this manner was a highly risky business, especially since, in order to support their habit, the women were forced go right back to Crack Head Corner, often to confront the very tricks they had just robbed. Two factors accounted for the prostitutes' dangerous behavior:

one was obvious—the intense craving for cocaine. The other motive was vengeance for the humiliation and abuse they often received at the hands of the men to whom they prostituted themselves.

In the never-ending quest for their next drug fix, the prostitutes stole from and exploited anyone, including their own children. In addition to what they earned on the streets, some prostitutes tried to hold jobs, mostly in minimum-wage food-service jobs such as waitressing or kitchen help. They also collected food stamps, welfare checks, and SSI for their children. However, none of these side activities even began to yield enough income to support a "rock queen" or "crackhead whore," as the johns referred to them.

Many of the women on the streets ended up divorced and losing custody of their children as the result of their pursuit of drugs and prostitution. If ever any faint suspicion existed that theirs was a glamorous existence, the experience of one such woman dispelled the myth.

She related to detectives an endless saga of her hand-to-mouth existence. Following a divorce in which she initially retained custody of her three children, she was involved in a car wreck, in which she was injured. She returned from the hospital to find that her roommates had ejected her from the trailer they shared and that all her possessions were gone. With no place to live, she camped out on Anastasia Beach for a time. When she finally was able to find employment, she had no car and had to walk long distances each day to her job.

At that point, unable to care for her children and work at the same time, she sent them to live with their father and signed over their custody to him. Even then, she was unable to earn enough to sustain herself and her cocaine habit. When she failed to pay her utility bills, the electricity was shut off.

After giving up her children, the woman's situation continued to deteriorate, and her life became a trail of broken relationships, frequent moves, lost jobs, and ever-declining prospects for a better life. In desperation, she took up residence with a black man. "That's when I got labeled a rock whore," she commented bitterly. "All my white friends turned their back like I didn't even exist because I was living on the street."

To satisfy their need for money to buy crack, the prostitutes frequently became involved in a number of scams, one being the "food stamp shuffle." In this scam the women would use the food stamps they received to purchase legitimate items from a grocery store. Then they would have someone else return those items for cash. They then used the cash to buy drugs.

Another dilemma faced by the prostitutes was betrayal by their associates. Should they be arrested, the drug dealers, pimps, and prostitutes living on the fringes of the law are often subject to long prison terms for drug offenses or as habitual offenders. Faced with these kind of sentences, they are quick to turn one another in to the police. (Even longtime members of the Mafia, when facing fifteen to twenty-five years in the penitentiary on drug charges, usually informed on their friends despite the sacred vow of *omerta*, which demands utter silence at the threat of death.) As Lieutenant John Harrison, of Buncombe County, North Carolina, Sheriff's Department, noted, "Anytime we can nail one of them on a charge that will result in a sentence of six months or more, they will rat out the pushers, thieves, and prostitutes quicker than you can snap your fingers. But there's gotta be a payoff for them, too."

Vengeance, as well as pragmatism, enters into the prostitutes' dealings with the johns. It is understandable that the women attempt to retaliate for the type of physical abuse they frequently encounter. A devastating experience Diana Richardson (later another of the killer's victims) reported to police in May 1993 illustrates this:

> *It was about 1 A.M. These two white guys drove up and asked me to ride with them to Hardees and the Pic and Save. I said no, but one of them grabbed me and shoved me into the car.*
>
> *They drove me to a dirt road then ripped my clothes off and beat me in the face and stomach with their fists. They took turns having sex with me. One of them wanted straight screwing, but the other tried to butt fuck me. While he was doing that, the first one took out a knife. He said to me, "I'm going to cut your hair. I'm going to cut some more. See, you don't need five dollars for a haircut."*
>
> *I think the way they acted they had planned this. While they were raping me they kept making comments to each other like, "Don't forget, you can't come inside of her."*
>
> *After about an hour and a half of this they started talking about what they should do with me. One of them started to beat me and choke me, but he whispered, "Act like you're passed out." That's what I did. But then the one with the knife started stabbing me. I played dead and he finally stopped. I heard him say, "I killed the bitch." After that they dumped me out of the car, threw my clothes into the woods, took the fifty or sixty dollars I had in my purse. Then they took off, thinking I was dead.*

Later that night Diana was discovered near a city landfill, nude, bleeding from stab wounds, and moaning incoherently. A trail of blood led from the crime scene on Allan Nease Road, some three hundred feet away, to the spot where she was found. After being airlifted to University Hospital in Jacksonville, she informed police that her attackers were two blond males in their twenties. She was able to identify one of her attackers from police photos. Judge Richard Watson issued a search warrant for the man's vehicle, a 1981 Ford Fairmont. FDLE crime scene technicians processed the vehicle for evidence. In their search they found a box cutter, a paring knife, and long blond hair on the rear floorboard. They also obtained and photographed latent prints from the vehicle's interior.

The evidence police had obtained was sufficient to identify Michael Motes, the man whose photo Diana had identified, and his partner, Brian Madasci, as well. When questioned, Madasci at first stated he had been at home at the time of the attack and denied his involvement, but he later admitted to being with Motes when Diana was picked up.

Detective Pat Greenhalgh contacted Madasci's mother, who, after being told that her son had admitted to being at the crime scene, stated that he woke her up when he got home that night and told her he did not stab the girl or rape her. He said he was afraid to call the police because he was on probation and it was his knife that Motes used. The detective took possession of the knife and had Mrs. Madasci sign a property release.

At the time of this crime, Madasci was on probation. Motes had previous charges for stealing and for beating his wife. Both men were arrested and charged with attempted murder, armed robbery, and sexual battery. Detective Jennifer Ponce, who was assigned to this case, questioned one of the perpetrators all night. "He finally confessed after I ordered Burger King Whoppers," she recalled.

At the two men's trials, defense lawyers attempted to use the argument that since Diana Richardson was known to be a prostitute, she had not been kidnapped.

Instead, they claimed, she had been soliciting the men as customers and was a willing participant in their sexual activities. Both men were convicted on attempted murder, rape, robbery, and kidnapping and were sentenced to twenty years in prison.

Sadly, Diana Richardson survived this assault only to be killed two years later by another, even more dangerous predator. The fact that she would return to prostitution after a traumatic, near-death experience of this magnitude bore vivid testimony to how overwhelming an addict's need for crack can become.

Another example of abuse of a prostitute occurred at "the Cut," a hangout also known as "the War Zone," and "the Hole." Located in a wooded area near Lincolnville, it consisted of a few old car seats, a lot of broken drug paraphernalia, and used condoms scattered about on the ground. In this setting the drug dealers, prostitutes, and users bought and sold their wares, partied, and got high. One night Bonnie, a prostitute, arrived at the Cut crying and screaming that "some creep in an old red pickup truck tied me up and raped me with a hammer handle."

Shelley, another prostitute, heard Bonnie describe her experience. Shortly after, Shelley was picked up by a john of similar age and driving a similar pickup truck. When he asked if she liked being tied up, she jumped out of the truck and ran, probably saving herself from serious injury.

A racial motive often seemed to be behind the abuse. Andrea, a white prostitute, made the mistake of getting into a blue Ford pickup truck with one of the rednecks, a group that comprises a significant segment of the Crack Head Corner johns. They were on their way to his house when he told her, "The reason I picked you up is because I can't stand all you Crack Head queens going with niggers. I should take you out and shoot you, like I did the other one over on Fish Island." (His reference to Anita Stevens's murder was an obvious attempt to terrify Andrea.) Fortunately for Andrea, she was able to open the truck door, jump out, and run away before he could carry out his threat.

Despite the ever-present risks the prostitutes faced, they still went out night after night, still rode off to isolated areas with johns, who could, at any moment, turn deadly. And it was not sex or excitement the women were seeking, it was crack cocaine . . . or the money to buy crack cocaine. Trapped by their need for the drug, they put aside considerations of personal safety and exposed themselves time and again to danger and degradation. Another potential risk they faced was the very real possibility of contracting AIDS. At least two of the women murdered in St. Augustine were already infected with the virus at the time of their deaths.

As the atmosphere of fear and distrust generated by the murders of three Crack Head Corner prostitutes gradually began to fade, the killer was once more on the prowl for his fourth victim. Once again he would leave his lair in the nearby potato farming area of Hastings to slip into the jungle of Crack Head Corner's subculture. Once again he would kill swiftly and brutally.

Chapter 8

April 1993:
Donetha Snead-Haile

*The thing inside him was getting worse . . . wanting
more. He had to be careful. But he had a hunter's
smarts. It was the dumb ones who got caught.*
He was no dummy, even if Mama . . .

Although the similarity of Lashawna Streeter's
murder to the two previous ones focused attention
on the possibility that a serial killer was stalking local
women, by April 1993, those events no longer occupied the attention of either the press or the
public. On Palm Sunday that year, crowds gathered
along St. Augustine's bayfront, as they always had,
to watch the blessing of the fleet. The newspaper
reported that the planned space shuttle mission
from nearby Cape Canaveral had been postponed
due to blustery weather, and the local fight over
parking spaces in the downtown area was once again
in full swing. In short, life in St. Augustine had once
again settled into the familiar patterns.

Then, on April 23, 1993, Carolyn Snead reported to
the St. Augustine Police Department that her thirty-two-
year-old daughter, Donetha Snead-Haile, was missing.

Donetha, a five-foot-five-inch 110-pound attractive African American woman, was next-to-youngest of the eight children born to Carolyn Snead. Carolyn, a certified nursing assistant at Flagler Hospital, had raised her eight children basically alone. She owned her home, a side-by-side duplex on Calle Real Street, immediately adjacent to New St. James Baptist Church. (Donetha's younger sister Stacey Snead Craine and her family still occupy a large modular home at this location, although the original house burned in 1980.) Carolyn Snead ran a loving but strict household. "Mama never permitted any drugs or alcohol in the house," Stacey Snead reported. "When we children wanted to go out, we had to ask permission. Discipline was strict—Mama didn't shy away from the belt."

Carolyn Snead was adamant that her children attend both church and Sunday school. At various times they attended New St. James Baptist and the Church of God in Christ. On Sunday mornings she was up early to fix breakfast for her clan, a meal that always included fresh grits. Carolyn Snead was also determined that each of her children should get an education. Stacey, for example, was a graduate of Edward Waters College, with a background in criminal justice and sociology. She is currently employed at the Hampton Inn in St. Augustine.

Because "store-bought" clothes and the latest styles were beyond Carolyn's means, she sewed all her girls' school dresses. She would begin that task in summer, shopping for fabrics at Bee's Yardstick on Anastasia Island. "Each of us girls had five school dresses," Stacey said. "Mother was a professional designer."

Carolyn Snead also shopped carefully for food, often purchasing her week's groceries at Premier Foods, on Beaver Street, in Jacksonville. "We ate a lot of what you'd call soul food," Stacey said. "Fried chicken, collard greens, black-eyed peas, and such."

Donetha and Stacey were very close as children. "I was the baby, she was the knee child," Stacey said. "Donetha was the one pushed me to do things. If she wanted to get permission from Mama for something, she'd say to me, 'You ask Mama . . . she'll say yes to you.'"

Stacey described Donetha as a very sweet-tempered, loving person. "She was especially nice with older people," Stacey recalled. "She sometimes cleaned house for some elderly twin sisters, who lived nearby."

Like the rest of her siblings, Donetha attended the local public schools. While in high school she became pregnant and suffered a miscarriage. She later married Charles Haile, who provided well for his young wife. Donetha also worked at various jobs, but mainly to have her own spending money. Donetha was known as a hard worker and was, at one time, assistant manager of the Pic 'n Save Market on King Street. The couple had no children and they later divorced.

Sometime in the early 1990s, Donetha asked Stacey to take her to the St. Johns County Health Department to obtain the results of some tests. The news the tests conveyed was that she was HIV positive. "After that was when Donetha got on drugs," Stacey said.

Although the family was aware of Donetha's drug problem, they remained close to her. It was unusual for more than a day or two to pass when Donetha, who lived nearby, failed to visit her mother, who at that time shared the family home with Stacey and her husband. "She always came by for her favorite dinner of fried chicken and macaroni and cheese on food stamp days," Stacey said.

On Wednesday, April 21, at about 5:00 P.M., Donetha rode her bicycle to her mother's house and asked to borrow her mother's car. When she returned the car, she asked to borrow some money, so Carolyn Snead handed her $3. When Donetha left on her bike, she turned to her mother and said, "Go in the house and lock up. I love you."

The first hint the family had that something was terribly wrong came when Donetha's neighbors, Mr. and Mrs. Sam White, called on Thursday, to say that they had noticed that Donetha had not returned home for several days. As they were very friendly with Donetha, they were concerned and felt Mrs. Snead should know.

Troubled, Carolyn Snead got in her car and went to find her son, who sometimes stayed with Donetha. She asked if he had seen his sister. He told her that he had seen Donetha at the Cut the previous night. She had asked him for money, and when he told her he didn't have any, she went away angry. He said that when he got home, the door was locked and the light was on in the kitchen. He knocked several times but got no answer, so he left.

Accompanied by her son, Carolyn Snead went to check out Donetha's apartment and found the kitchen light still burning. They then rode around and asked several people that they knew if they had seen her. No one had.

On April 23, 1993, Carolyn Snead called the St. Augustine police to inform them that her daughter had not been seen since 9:00 P.M. two days previously. Officer Tim Willingham filed this as an information report, since Donetha had not been missing the necessary forty-eight hours to treat it as a missing persons case. He noted that at the time Mrs. Snead said she was not in great fear for Donetha's safety. The following day Willingham came to the house to obtain a photograph of Donetha.

When Donetha had not been heard from by April 29, and there was no further contact from the St. Augustine Police Department, Stacey Snead phoned the police department and was connected with Detective

Nolan Shapiro. She reported to Shapiro that it was highly unusual for her sister to be gone from home for so long a period and that it was even more unusual for her not to have contacted her mother during this length of time. Stacey also revealed that Donetha was addicted to crack cocaine and had a "potentially fatal disease" for which she was being treated at the St. Johns Health Department. Meanwhile, Carolyn Snead had checked her daughter's home to determine if Donetha's personal belongings were there. She found nothing missing except her daughter's medications.

In the course of his investigation of what now appeared to be a missing persons case, Detective Shapiro interviewed several of Donetha's neighbors and known acquaintances. Sam and Diane White, who had first alerted the Sneads to Donetha's disappearance, told the detective that they had last seen Donetha "going over the fence behind the house." They said that this was not unusual. According to them, she was wearing a red blouse, possibly with a pattern on it, a red scarf on her head, and blue jeans. They reported that on many previous occasions they had seen Donetha being picked up at her home by an "older" white male who drove a burgundy-colored car. Neither of the Whites knew the man's name or where he lived. They also indicated some other persons who might have information regarding Donetha's whereabouts.

When contacted, one of these informants verified that he had seen Donetha get into a burgundy-colored vehicle in the Pic 'n Save parking lot. He said the car was driven by "an older, gray-haired man," whose name he did not know. He said that this occurred on Tuesday, a day prior to when Donetha was reported missing.

Another informant described a woman dressed all in red and "acting demented," in the vicinity of the Rodeway Inn on North Ponce de León Boulevard.

Another offered the information that a young black male accompanied by a young black female had been seen pushing an aluminum rack with a black plastic garbage bag on it that appeared to contain "a body in a sitting position." These leads, like the others the detective followed, proved valueless.

Detective Shapiro did learn that Donetha was frequently seen near the Hardee's restaurant at the corner of King Street and Ponce de León Boulevard. He obtained a recent photograph of her from her mother and a set of her fingerprints from the St. Johns County Jail, along with a booking photograph taken in 1979. Teletype BOLOS were sent to the surrounding counties and cities noting that this was unusual behavior for the missing woman and that she was a drug addict with a potentially fatal illness. "It is reasonable to conclude that she may be endangered."

On April 29, after several calls by Stacey Snead Craine to the local police, Donetha was officially listed as a missing person. Later, television channel 4, WJXT in Jacksonville, aired a brief segment asking the public for information, and a reward of $150 was offered. This produced no results.

During this time the Snead family had become increasingly concerned that maximum efforts weren't being exerted by the St. Augustine Police Department on Donetha's case. (This is not uncommon in the early stages of a missing persons case when detectives are pursuing various leads and have little to report.) Stacey had flyers made up with Donetha's picture, which she and other family members posted in prominent locations around town. Relatives and other friends joined in the search as well.

Frustrated with the slow pace of the investigation, two weeks after Donetha's disappearance, Stacey enlisted the help of her pastor, the Reverend John Williams, in composing a letter to the St. Augustine

Police Department. In it she stated that she felt she had been given the run-around regarding the disappearance of her sister and that the police had failed to act promptly to declare Donetha missing and had also been negligent in failing to inform the family of developments in the case.

In the letter, Stacey also claimed that she had been treated in a cold and uncaring manner by a desk dispatcher at the department. Later, she said, she received an apology for the dispatcher's rudeness and was told that the officer handling the case was new to the area and unfamiliar with local procedures.

However, when police later failed to keep her informed, she threatened to contact the NAACP (National Association for the Advancement of Colored People) and the news media. In conclusion, Stacey stated, "In the two weeks since my sister's disappearance, my family and I have had absolutely no encouragement or sign of visible actions being taken by our police department."

In response to Stacey's complaints, the St. Augustine Police Department renewed its efforts to locate Donetha. Detective Jeremy Masters requested that the local TV stations air a photo and information about the missing woman. He also contacted the local newspaper, the *St. Augustine Record,* and requested that they rerun their original article on Donetha's disappearance. In addition, he sent out bulletins to the surrounding counties and cities as far away as Fort Lauderdale, where he had received some indication Donetha might have gone. He also pursued what seemed like several strong leads as to suspects, but none proved to have anything to do with the case. An off-line search through the Florida Criminal Information revealed that Donetha's name had not been run by any police agency from April

1 through the date on which her name was entered as a missing person.

On May 20, an article about Donetha's disappearance and her photograph appeared in the Jacksonville paper, the *Florida Times-Union*.

Shortly after, Carolyn Snead received a phone call from a family acquaintance, Merrill Short who claimed to have information about Donetha's disappearance. He told her he had heard "through the grapevine" that Donetha was buried in the woods and claimed that he knew the exact location. (Later in the investigation another informant would confirm that while he was fixing her car, this same man had told her he "was going to show the police where the body was supposed to be.")

However, when police attempted to interview Short by phone, he became evasive, not surprising considering that he had a police record that included convictions for accessory to murder, aggravated assault, and attempted aggravated battery. When interviewed, he gave the following explanation for the information he had conveyed to Mrs. Snead: "I used to live on the streets, so I know a lot of street people and prostitutes. I heard this bunch of men standing around out by the Fina gas station at West King and Volusia saying how Donetha was buried out there at Nassau and Duval Streets. If it was my daughter, I'd want her found and that's why I came forward. I figured as a good citizen somebody ought to tell Mrs. Snead where her daughter's body was."

When questioned further, Short admitted having known the Snead family for a number of years, but he denied any personal knowledge of Donetha. However, one of his neighbors indicated that she had seen Donetha visit Short's home often, an allegation that he vehemently refuted. He also denied any sexual relationship with the missing woman.

Following the lead Short provided, detectives
searched for Donetha's body at the location he had
indicated, but they found nothing. With no body as
evidence of murder and the alleged victim possibly a
runaway or someone who may have simply left town,
police investigators had few clues to go on and no cer-
tainty that a crime had been committed.

In Donetha's case, as in others involving a prostitute in which homicide is suspected but no body
can be found, law enforcement officials were uncertain as to whether the young woman had been
killed or had merely left the area and was possibly
leading a vagabond existence as many prostitutes
do. It was speculated that she could have taken off
with a cross-country truck driver, perhaps wound
up in a new community when the relationship
ended. This happens with some prostitutes who work
truck stops. Referred to by truckers as "lizards," they
often travel with truckers for days or weeks before
separating. There was also the possibility that
Donetha, like others in similar situations, may have
absconded to escape prosecution for criminal offenses or probation or parole violations. Regardless
of the reasons, Donetha had departed, leaving few,
if any, clues to her disappearance. Consequently the
investigation yielded few suspects, and less investigative time was committed to her case than those
in which the presence of a body indicated with cer-
tainty that a death had occurred. With no crime
scene to investigate, and no body to yield information, murder could only be presumed.

Three years later, in February 1996, the St. Johns
County Cold Case Homicide Task Force reopened
Donetha's case as a possible homicide. Detectives
again began their investigation into her disappearance by interviewing other prostitutes who knew
her. One, Leana Garret, said that Donetha often

hung out with a man called "Papa Jake" who lived in an apartment near Crack Head Corner. According to Robin, Donetha got money from him. Detectives who checked him out found no evidence indicating he had harmed Donetha.

It would be another four years before Donetha Snead's murderer would be revealed. Although he was able to identify the area where he had disposed of her body, no remains were ever found. In addition to his other crimes, the killer left another entire family not only mourning their loved one, but living for years with the slim, futile hope that she would some-day return. In many ways that torture equaled the actual revelation of her death.

Chapter 9

Red Bird

As in many high-profile cases, a particular name kept cropping up in police reports. In this instance, it was an individual known as Red Bird. This name appeared in several reports given by prostitutes to the detectives working the cases of the first several women murdered. However, he seemed only to have been one of the habitués of Crack Head Corner, not a viable suspect. He was known to frequent the fast-food restaurant where many of the prostitutes picked up their dates and was frequently seen driving in the area frequented by the prostitutes and drug dealers.

In December 1992, while riding around in his pickup truck, Red Bird confessed to an acquaintance, Wilford Ames, that he had killed Anita Stevens. Ames was later arrested and passed along the story to police. According to the story Red Bird gave Ames, he and Anita were planning to do some drugs and went to a property he owned, somewhere between Hastings and Palatka. When they got there, they had an argument about money, drugs, and sex. Red Bird said he hit Anita "many times" and choked her to make sure she was dead. Then he took her to a pond, took her clothes off, and put her in the water. "Everyone would think she was just another crack whore," he told

Ames. "No one will ever try to find out what happened because it was drug related."

After relaying this story, Red Bird threatened Ames, telling him never to repeat what he had just heard or "something bad would happen to him."

Ames promised never to tell. But after seeing a newspaper article about Anita's murder, the information began weighing on his conscience. Also, he saw a TV show about a murderer who had gotten away with his crime for a long time and then been caught. At that point he felt he should tell someone, as "Red Bird is guilty and should have to pay."

Ames's information was investigated, but no proof of what he claimed could be found.

Some months later, after Donetha Snead's disappearance, a waitress at a local fast-food restaurant reported to detectives that she had overheard a telephone call in which Red Bird told the person to whom he was speaking that Donetha was dead. According to the waitress, Red Bird claimed that Donetha had been "knocked in the head and put in a pond on Old Moultrie Road."

It is not known what follow-up took place, but several weeks later when Detective Jeremy Masters was on his lunch break, he encountered Red Bird at the same fast-food restaurant from which Red Bird had made the phone call. He asked Red Bird to tell him what he knew about Donetha's disappearance. Red Bird repeated that Donetha was dead, that he thought she had been knocked in the head and put in a pond. He described the pond as deep with lily pads around it. However, he was vague about the location.

A prostitute, Robin Holden, also gave information that seemed to connect Red Bird to the Snead case. She reported that near the time of Donetha's disappearance, she had seen her with an older white male who drove a red pickup truck. She knew him as Red

Bird and reported that the other prostitutes claimed he was violent. "All the girls are afraid of him," Robin stated. She also claimed that he liked to take nude pictures of the women.

Since Red Bird was known to use drugs and to be frequently intoxicated, it was likely the information he gave Ames and others was viewed with skepticism by the police. A check of his vehicle revealed that it was not the same as those described by several informants as having been seen at the time of the women's murders. It seemed probable that his wanting to display inside knowledge of the murders was a way of seeking attention and increasing his self-importance.

Chapter 10

June 1995: Cheryl Lucas

If you looked at it the right way, it was a good thing he was doing.
Cleaning up the streets.
After tonight, one less whore out there.

Cheryl Lucas, a thirty-two-year-old African American female, became the killer's fifth known St. Augustine victim. Unlike the others, she was not a St. Augustine native and had not been a longtime resident of the area.

Cheryl grew up in New York City in a family with two sisters and a brother. Like her handsome siblings, Cheryl had classic, distinctive features and a quick, ready smile. She attended public schools in New York and graduated from Walt Whitman High School. She and her sisters belonged to a Girl Scout troop and the family attended church regularly. Cheryl, also known as "Niecey," was a lively, athletic girl who loved physical sports and excelled at jumping double Dutch, a rope-skipping game played by children. Her mother, Malvera Lucas, had been a hairdresser and all three daughters seemed to have inherited her talent. Cheryl was particularly adept at weaving hair into fashionable braids.

As a high-school student, Cheryl became involved with a man by whom she became pregnant. After high school she attended college for a semester before withdrawing. Her mother, Malvera, claimed it was the man with whom Cheryl was involved who discouraged her from continuing her education. "He could talk her out of anything," Mrs. Lucas said.

Further pregnancies resulted, while, at the same time, both Cheryl and her boyfriend became heavily involved in drugs. For a time Cheryl entered a drug rehab program, but again the man she was with talked her out of continuing with it. Ultimately she gave birth to six children, five of them born after she became seriously addicted. Mrs. Lucas ultimately assumed custody of the children, as her daughter's addiction made her unable to care for them.

In 1994 Malvera Lucas, along with Cheryl's six children, who then ranged in age from four to fourteen, moved from New York to St. Augustine. Malvera could more easily care for her aging parents and a handicapped sister there. The grandparents, however, had warned her that St. Augustine was not a safe place, especially as Lashawna Streeter, daughter of their next-door neighbor, had recently been murdered.

The house into which the Lucas family moved, and where they still live, was a comfortable one-story frame home on Chapin Street, several blocks off West King Street. The front and side yards of the house were filled with flowers that Malvera nurtured. Roses and impatiens, cacti and azaleas, bloomed side by side.

At the time Malvera moved to St. Augustine, Cheryl and her boyfriend at the time, King, were still living in New York, where both had been arrested for drug offenses. Because there was also a felony arrest warrant out for King in Suffolk County, New York, the couple moved for a time to Bessemer, Alabama.

Then, in January 1995, Mrs. Lucas received a call from Cheryl asking her to come pick up Cheryl and King at the St. Augustine bus station. This move, Cheryl told her mother, was to be her fresh start, a chance to kick the drug habit, to go straight. "Cheryl tried to take care of her children," Malvera reported. "She would cook and clean for her kids and she took them places."

According to Mrs. Lucas, King was sincerely trying to help Cheryl get off drugs. "He had a good head on him," she said. For a time things seemed to be going well. Cheryl, who was receiving disability, was attending vocational school, caring for her children, and struggling to straighten out her life. A friend described her as "that skinny black girl who rides a bicycle around town."

But Cheryl's life fell apart once again when King was arrested and extradited to New York to face serious felony charges on the aforementioned warrant. Despondent and lonely, she relapsed into heavy use of crack. Mrs. Lucas pleaded with social service agencies for help for her daughter, but was faced with endless bureaucratic stumbling blocks.

To pay for her habit, Cheryl prostituted, generally working an area called "the Crack Hole," a few blocks from her home. According to one police informant, the petite woman sometimes dressed and made herself up to look like a little girl, a pose that was a turn-on to certain johns with atypical sexual preferences, including pedophilia. One of the places Cheryl often took her "dates" was the area under the 312 Bridge, the same spot where Anita Stevens had been murdered.

Another way Cheryl obtained money for drugs was by stealing from local business establishments. As Sandra Spinks, a fellow prostitute, later reported, "Cheryl was a thief and a good one." That was confirmed after

Cheryl's death when police searched her house and found numerous purses and other items with price tags still on them.

In the weeks just prior to her death, Cheryl was living with her mother. The relationship between the two was not a smooth one, with Cheryl constantly plaguing her mother for money. Malvera Lucas, aware of Cheryl's crack addiction and that she was prostituting herself to support her habit, continued to refuse Cheryl the "loans" she was begging for. On the day in mid-June 1995 that Mrs. Lucas last saw her daughter, she sensed that Cheryl was behaving abnormally. "She was acting kind of nervous," Malvera Lucas said. "She just kept at me for money."

Cheryl's final plea before leaving home that afternoon added to the uneasiness her mother was feeling. "Mom, do you have two dollars . . . five dollars . . . ten dollars? I *need* the money! I have to pay him." She was probably referring to a drug dealer to whom she owed money.

That same week, Mrs. Lucas was preparing to leave for a wedding in Athens, Georgia. When her daughter failed to return home on Wednesday or Thursday, she became increasingly worried. On Friday morning Malvera Lucas called 911 to file a missing persons report with the St. Augustine Police Department. She went on to attend the wedding, but she spent an uneasy weekend, concerned that Cheryl was in trouble.

During her final hours on earth, Cheryl Lucas was involved in the kind of activities characteristic of the prostitutes who frequented Crack Head Corner. She met and chatted with friends and fellow prostitutes. One of the women later told police that Cheryl had declared, "I'm gonna get me one of them Crackers tonight and make me some money." Shortly after that she was seen getting into a 1978 Firebird with one of her regular johns, "a guy who looks like Willie Nelson," a witness later reported. That same evening others saw her getting in and out of cars at Crack Head Corner between 8:00 P.M. and 1:00 A.M. Cheryl, wise to the ways of the street, knew these were the peak hours for making money, the time of night she was most likely to encounter white men—Crackers driving expensive cars and cruising for dates.

An intermittent drizzle had been filling the air throughout that evening. Around 2:00 A.M. Cheryl was standing at the corner of Palmer and King Streets near the Pic 'n Save store. With the rain and the late hour, few cars were on the road. Rose Harris, who lived in the neighborhood, watched Cheryl calling to various vehicles to "hold up!" When Harris went to her front door to tell Cheryl to go home, she saw her wave to a man driving a dark-colored pickup truck. She could not see the driver of the truck or how many people were in it. (Later police would try hypnosis with Rose Harris to see if she could remember any further details.)

Cheryl had been about to give up any hope of scoring again that evening when the man in the pickup truck cruised slowly by. She signaled to the driver, a middle-aged man. He pulled into the store parking lot and motioned to her to get in. She opened the passenger-side door and jumped in. "What you looking for?" she asked him.

The man shifted his vehicle into gear and prepared to exit onto King Street. He turned to look her over before answering, "How much you get for straight up?"

Cheryl was still considering what she could charge when she spotted some cash lying on the seat between them. Deciding it was much easier and quicker to rob the man than to engage in sex with him, she snatched up the bills and leaped from the slowly moving vehicle.

Realizing he had been robbed, the driver quickly slammed on the brakes. As soon as the pickup truck came to a stop, he grabbed the metal nail bar he kept under the seat, jumped from the vehicle, and set off in pursuit. He caught up with Cheryl as she raced along the railroad tracks west of Palmer Street, a short distance from where he had picked her up. She heard his heavy footsteps crunching on the wet gravel, paused for a second, and turned to look behind her. That brief hesitation enabled the man to catch up with her. Wielding the heavy metal bar, he swung it at her head. As the cold metal crunched the fragile bones of her head and face, Cheryl fell to the ground unconscious. Blood spurted from her wounds and stained the grassy area where she lay.

His fury unabated, the man continued to bludgeon her with fierce blows, three times, four times, more. Finally, seeing that she was no longer moving, he turned away and hurried back to his pickup truck. As he ran through the rain, he glanced around, fearful someone in the vicinity might have seen or heard what had taken place. But at that hour of the morning, and with the now heavy downpour, the area was isolated. He returned to his truck and backed the vehicle up near to where Cheryl lay. There he hastily loaded her body into the truck bed and covered it with a tarp before pulling back out onto King Street. Adrenaline still rushing through his veins as he racked his brain for a safe place to dispose of the body. Then it came to him—the boat ramp on Moultrie Creek, some five miles distant.

Fearful of being stopped and the body discovered, the killer avoided the main thoroughfares. Using his familiarity with the area, he slipped cautiously down deserted back roads and side streets. His most hazardous moment came when he had to cross heavily traveled US 1, but again luck was with him—there were only a few vehicles on the road and no police cars in sight. His tension eased a bit when he was finally on dark, winding Shore Drive, in the area known as St. Augustine South.

Shore Drive rambles for several miles, following Moultrie Creek's twisted path. The area between the roadway and the water forms a sort of linear park enhanced by live oaks and other foliage, with occasional picnic tables and benches. Houses line the side of the road opposite the creek.

The man glanced furtively at the homes he passed and was relieved to find that they were mostly unlit, with no sign of human activity. Off to his left, the tidal creek's waters glimmered blackly—the perfect dumping place for his grisly freight.

Reaching the boat ramp—a small public area with picnic tables and parking space for cars and boat trailers—he pulled off the road and carefully backed the truck onto a grassy area just north of the ramp, as close to the water's edge as he dared. He tried at first to slide Cheryl's lifeless body from the truck bed by grasping the waistband of her shorts. The wet shorts slid off in his hands. He seized the fabric of her shirt, tugging until it, too, pulled loose from her body. Finally, grasping her limp limbs, he managed to haul the body free of the truck and dragged it to the water's edge, where he left it facedown and partially submerged in the creek's tidal waters.

Several days later, Brenda and Eddie Stewart pulled into the ramp parking lot preparing to launch their boat. The moment their golden retriever, Pickle, was released from the car, she went racing toward an area of tall weeds some fifty or so yards away. The Stewarts followed her and made a grim discovery. The body of an African American woman was facedown in the water, her knees up, her buttocks in the air, and her panties pulled down. Shocked, the Stewarts hurried to a house opposite the ramp, where the homeowner, a Mr. Pacetti, called the police for them.

Both St. Augustine police and officers from the St. Johns County Sheriff's Office responded to Mr. Pacetti's call. Soon the boat ramp was a scene of intense activity as detectives examined the body and collected evidence. Detective Carl Bradley, one of the first to arrive on the scene, reported that the body was on the bank of the inlet, some fifty to one hundred yards north of the boat ramp, and appeared to be that of a black female. He noted that the rectal area appeared to have some damage, although it was not known if this was due to an injury, since the body showed signs of decomposition and insect infestation. A white T-shirt with the design of a shark on the front was recovered near the body.

Technician Susan Biesiada arrived along with St. Augustine police officers David Stark and Robbie Zukauskas. Biesiada proceeded to process the crime scene. She noted that the body had been found facedown, with the legs and arms splayed to the side. A mass of the victim's hair had separated from her scalp and was hanging from a nearby reed.

Sergeant Stark reported to Detective Bradley that the St. Augustine Police Department had issued a report of a missing black female named Cheryl Denise Lucas. Bradley returned to the sheriff's office and ran a criminal history on Cheryl Lucas but found no listing of any local offenses. Later he learned that Lucas had been arrested in Suffolk County, New York. He contacted the Suffolk County Police Department and obtained Cheryl's fingerprints and a photograph. However the faxed copy of the prints was not sufficient to make a positive identification. Later, the Suffolk County Police Department mailed hard copies of the prints, which were examined by fingerprint expert Rick Crews, of the Jacksonville Sheriff's Office. He felt the prints matched,

but he could not be sure. Later they were examined by
Ernest Hamm at the lab of the Florida Department of
Law Enforcement. Hamm reported the prints were the
same as those taken from Lucas's body.

Bradley also canvassed the surrounding area to
inquire if the residents had noticed any unusual activity at the ramp. One woman told him that every
night vehicles were in and out of the grassy field
north of the boat ramp at all hours. She also mentioned that she had noticed an odor coming from
the area where the body was found.

Cheryl's body was turned faceup and placed in a
black plastic bag to be transported to the county
morgue by Faircloth Transport Service. Upon examination the medical examiner noted extensive
decomposition with exfoliation of skin, marbling,
and bloating, as might be expected with a body that
had been left exposed and in water for several days.
Most of her hair was gone. At the time of her death,
Cheryl weighed 115 pounds and was five feet four
inches tall. Red polish was present on her toenails.

Investigator Kenneth Moore and Detectives Mary
LeVeck, Carl Bradley, and Jennifer Ponce were present
at the autopsy performed by Dr. Terrence Steiner, the
medical examiner. LeVeck photographed the autopsy
proceedings and Detective Bradley also took Polaroids.
Dr. Steiner found numerous fractures on the victim's
head and facial areas.

Dr. William R. Maples, a forensic anthropologist,
later examined Cheryl's skull and sketched the extensive trauma to which it had been subjected. He
concluded that a tool, probably a pry bar, had been
used to fracture the cranial vault and face of the
deceased.

Several days later on June 21, Glenn Lightsey, an
investigator with the state's attorney's office, contacted Bradley to say that an informant had called

and told him that the body located off Shore Drive was that of Cheryl Lucas. The informant also identified Wilbur Long, a black male, as her pimp. When interviewed, Long insisted that he and Cheryl were merely good friends, although they had recently had a disagreement and he hadn't seen her for a week or two. Long was not considered a serious suspect, as he was unfamiliar with the area where the body was found and depended only upon a bicycle for transportation.

When Mrs. Lucas returned home on Sunday from her cousin's wedding in Athens, Georgia, she received a call from Errol Jones, a social worker with the school district where Cheryl's children were enrolled. (Errol Jones is currently a St. Augustine city commissioner.) "When was the last time you saw your daughter?" Jones asked. Mrs. Lucas told him she had filed a missing persons report the previous Friday. He then advised her that she should get in touch with the sheriff's office.

She called, thinking that Cheryl had been arrested. She was told that someone would call her back. A short time later Detective Ponce and victims' advocate Mary Alice Colson arrived at Mrs. Lucas's door to inform her that a body had been found that was possibly that of her daughter. They showed her photographs of a T-shirt, which she identified as belonging to Cheryl.

Detectives Pat Greenhalgh and Mary Fagan interviewed Mrs. Lucas, who provided them with photographs of Cheryl and escorted them to Cheryl's next-door residence, where they checked her personal belongings. It appeared only one person had last slept in Cheryl's bed, as they found her bedcovers folded back on one side with a nightshirt lying on top. At the end of the bed there was a stack of mail and other papers, which appeared to have been dumped out of a purse. Malvera Lucas reported that Cheryl was always switching purses and tended simply to dump the contents of the one she had just used. Several purses were stacked alongside a couch in the living room.

As a means of confirming Cheryl's identity, Mrs. Lucas told the detectives that her daughter had scraggly teeth, a deformed fingernail, and a scar either under or above one of her eyes. She also gave them the name of the dentist who had seen Cheryl in New York. Malvera also reported that Wilbur Long, whom the informant had identified as Cheryl's pimp, had stopped by to inquire about her. He had seen the report in the newspaper and "hoped that wasn't her."

Mrs. Lucas also identified the location where Cheryl "got her goodies," i.e., bought her drugs. She didn't identify the dealer by name, but she said he was a handyman employed at some nearby apartments.

By this time the murders were piling up. The police, aware now that a serial killer was making his forays at Crack Head Corner, continued their frustrating manhunt for the elusive killer. The first inquiries police investigators made were among Cheryl's customers and her fellow prostitutes. Locating such individuals proved to be a difficult task, as she had been in St. Augustine too short a time to establish many relationships. The African Americans involved in the crack trade in West Augustine were reluctant also to reveal any information to police, even in a situation where one of their own was a victim.

At this time Detective Frank Welborn, who was heading the investigation for the sheriff's office, met with Pamela Mertins, a FDLE analyst, in reference to charting the prostitute homicides that had occurred in St. Johns County over the past several years.

Officers staked out the Pic 'n Save, where Cheryl had been reported last seen. They took down tag

numbers from cars stopping there and interviewed
some of the drivers and the women they picked up.
No leads were developed to the killer. One informant,
however, presented what later appeared a possible
clue to the actual killer. The woman said that about a
month previously Cheryl had dated a guy in a red-
and-white small Ford Bronco or Blazer who gave her
$200.

One man who was stopped pleaded ignorance and
said that he only had recently moved to St. Augustine and that he had been told that West Augustine
was "where all the excitement was." Other informants
passed along rumors about males Cheryl had been
seen with or vehicles she had been seen getting into
or out of, all of which had to be checked out.

Corinne, a prostitute, acted as a police informant.
She identified for the officers some of the vehicles and
drivers they spotted cruising the area and reported on
the men's sexual preferences and peculiarities. She
pointed out a male she claimed had taken her to a
cemetery and demanded anal sex. Another she claimed
"liked titties."

One possibly significant report that the detectives collected was from a man who stated that in early May he
was standing in front of his home talking to a friend at
about 11:00 P.M. when a black female ran up to them.
She was upset about "an older man that she thought
was harmless, but was not." She gave them her name as
Cheryl Denise and said that she lived on Chapin Street.
The man's wife called 911, but the girl said she didn't
want to talk to a deputy. The man and his wife then
drove her home. When she got out of the car, she asked
them to pray for her.

Thirty-year-old Bradley Wharton was briefly considered a suspect in Cheryl's murder. He reported that
he had met Cheryl at a crack party on Chapin Street
over Memorial Day weekend and had invited her back

to his boat. When she discovered he had $40 in cash, she issued the invitation, "Let's get stoned." The two of them went to her house to buy crack from an African American man, but what he sold them turned out to be soap.

Undeterred, the two took a cab to an apartment on Riberia and DeHaven Streets in Lincolnville, where Cheryl managed to extract $30 from her "uncle." When they arrived back at the boat, Wharton gave her his remaining $10. She rode off on his bike and came back with what she claimed was $40 worth of crack. "We smoked it up, drank some beer, and played Battleship," Wharton told police. "She kept telling me how desperate she was to get off drugs. Then she tried to get more money out of me. When I refused, she got mad and left walking. We never had sex and I never saw her again."

The dealer from whom Cheryl obtained the drugs they consumed that night may well have been Fabian Stiles. Stiles, a black man, came to St. Augustine after his release from prison. He maintained a house from which he sold drugs, arranged dates between johns and prostitutes, and provided a room that could be used for sex, all for a price.

Like all dealers, when prostitutes or others owed him money for drugs, he used intimidation and brute force to collect. For this reason Stiles was feared, but he was also sought after for the drugs he could provide. He demanded sex from the women he pimped and sometimes fell into an on-again, off-again relationship with one or the other of them. Such had been the case with Anita Stevens. In one instance he blackened her eye with his closed fist during a fight. Although he was investigated for Cheryl's murder, he was proved not to be involved.

Rose Harris, the woman who reported seeing Cheryl get into a pickup truck on the evening she was killed, submitted to a videotaped hypnotic session. While under hypnosis, she recalled coming home from work and entering her home. At about 1:00 A.M. she saw Cheryl Lucas in the parking lot of the Pic 'n Save talking to several other black girls in a small white compact car. As this car drove off, Cheryl began yelling at someone else. Then an older-model black Ford pickup truck drove in. Cheryl approached the truck from the rear passenger side. She said, "Hey, baby," and then got in. Harris then saw the truck go through the light at King and Palmer Streets. She recalled that its engine was rather loud.

While the pickup truck Harris described was never found, one of the deputies on duty in the vicinity of King Street remembered having seen such a vehicle cruising the back roads in the area. He said it was occupied by a white male in his forties wearing a "redneck-type" hat.

Questioning Cheryl Lucas's drug connections consumed considerable amounts of investigators' time. Another difficulty they faced was that Cheryl was known to attract both black and white clients, some of them rather well-to-do. One of Cheryl's daughters, said, "This white man and his wife had this real nice house right on the beach. Mom would go see him. He liked 'powder' (cocaine) and Mom took him all over town to get it. He drove a cream-colored Buick. His wife was lonely, so Mom stayed with her a few days once. The wife didn't know Mom dated her husband."

The daughter also reported regarding another of her mother's liaisons: "I seen a white man coming to Mom's house several times. He was in his thirties, medium build, and drove a red vehicle. Mom cleaned his house sometimes. He had lots of money. Once he came to Mom's with a white girl, about twenty years old, in the car. She looked like a crackhead."

Another factor created special problems for law enforcement—Cheryl had been a risk taker, often dating men known for their quirky sexual appetites and/or brutal behavior. Jellica, a fellow prostitute, reported having seen her with a man known to use the girls in sadomasochistic videos. "He came around Crack Head Corner in his brand-new Cadillac and picked Cheryl up. Later when she came back, she had a thousand dollars with her, but she was all bruised up."

At other times it was Cheryl who presented the threat; she had been known to pull a knife on her tricks and rob them. Driven to take reckless chances by her never ending need for drugs—or money to buy drugs—serious injury or death were ever present possibilities Cheryl faced not once, but many times over. In her case the ultimate risk proved to be death.

Another man suspected of having taken advantage of Cheryl's risk-taking tendencies was Dallas Porter, a white man whom she once described as "crazy, but he pays good." When questioned, Porter explained that approximately five days before Cheryl disappeared he had met her in a partially wooded outdoor area located at the end of Chapin Street.

Porter reported that on the night in question he arrived at the Cut, as the area was known, at about 1:00 A.M. with some beer. Cheryl and two other prostitutes—Diana Richardson (a later victim) and Missy Carpenter, were already there. He said he had offered Cheryl a ride home, but she declined. Although at first Porter claimed that these events took place on Saturday, he later stated they had, in fact, occurred several days earlier. His inconsistency regarding the dates added to detectives' suspicions that Porter might have been involved in Cheryl's murder.

David Holmes, an employee of a restaurant located near one of the off-ramps of Interstate 95, had dated

Cheryl. He became a suspect when it was learned that he spoke disparagingly of her as "a crackhead whore." However, no evidence was found linking him to her death.

As evidence of the investigators' willingness to explore any avenue, Detective Jennifer Ponce contacted a local psychic known as "Kaimora" and asked her to assist in locating Cheryl's killer.

Kaimora, whose actual name was Kay Blaisdell Mora, was born in Livermore Falls, Maine, and attended school there. After graduation from the University of Maine, she studied under spiritualist Bill Ellis and internationally known psychic Alex Tannous. She founded and served as reverend in the Metaphysical Mother Earth Church, an organization that emphasized personal growth and development through a holistic approach to life.

During her thirty-five years as a psychic, she had assisted police organizations in various states, as well as the FBI and the Crime Commission of the Virgin Islands. She regularly conducted psychic awareness classes at the University of Maine and Florida Junior College in Jacksonville. She also wrote a horoscope column for the *St. Augustine Record*. Detective Ponce learned about Kaimora through the Healing and Learning Center that the psychic conducted in St. Augustine.

On March 28, 1996, Ponce met with Kaimora at her residence and place of business on Vilano Beach. She explained that the task force needed assistance in a homicide case and gave Kaimora the shirt that was found at Cheryl Lucas's crime scene. She did not tell her anything else about the case.

After several minutes of meditation, Kaimora stated that the victim was young. She described the killer's shoes as sneakers with wide, thick toes. "He lives in a country-type setting," she said. She also saw a "waterway" and "big machines of heavy equipment around the suspect." She said that he was a white male with light or blue-colored eyes. "He has a ring on his finger, a big ring, but not necessarily with a stone."

She went on to describe numerous details of the crime, many of which proved totally irrelevant. Her most accurate comments, in addition to those mentioned above, were a "small truck," the initial "L" belonging to the killer's name, that the victim was not killed at the place where she was found, that drugs might be in the picture. She also mentioned several times the "issue of money" and that "money might be involved."

While it is interesting to speculate just how much valuable information psychics, like Kaimora, can supply to an investigation, even where the information is accurate it does very little to identify any actual suspect.

In all, seven prostitutes were interviewed in the police search for leads to Cheryl's murderer. One of them supplied the information that a local businessman, C. D. Lester, may have been Cheryl's pimp. However, despite extensive questioning, police failed to find evidence indicating that he had any connection to her murder.

Although both white men and African Americans found Cheryl attractive, Cheryl told a friend, "I don't like being around white people." Adding to the irony, when her killer was eventually found, he proved to be a white man. But in the meantime he remained a shadowy figure at the fringes of Crack Head Corner, using its women for his sexual pleasure, waiting for his next opportunity to kill.

Chapter 11

A Typical Suspect

At the time of Cheryl Lucas's murder, the killer had slipped undetected in and out of West Augustine for more than six years, choosing his victims and murdering them seemingly at will. Law enforcement efforts to apprehend him were stymied by the random method of the killings and apparent lack of motive. No fingerprint records or bloodstains were found that could identify the killer. Another obstacle was the very nature of the individuals the police were forced to look to for information. In Crack Head Corner there were not too few suspects, but too many.

Of the dozens of male suspects and witnesses questioned in the murders, a number were of the sort described earlier who tend to drift into relatively sustained relationships with one prostitute after another. Some of these are lonely men or those who are unappealing and rejected by most women. Unlike most of the johns whose association with prostitutes consists of a one-night stand or repeat customers who have no relationship with the prostitutes other than sexual encounters, these men tend to develop more long-standing relationships with the women. Their liaisons with prostitutes sometimes last for weeks, months, or, in a few cases, for

several years. Some of these men—because of their
atypical sexual desires, such as bondage and rough
sex—are unable to find women other than prostitutes willing to meet their needs.

Dallas Porter, who came under suspicion after Cheryl
Lucas's murder, exemplified many of the traits that
have been identified as those of a serial killer. He also
had an extensive criminal record. As one of the most seriously considered suspects in the Lucas killing, it is
illuminating to explore his history in greater depth.

For detectives searching for a murderer, Porter
fit the typical profile almost perfectly. By the middle of 1995, the investigation was focused almost
exclusively on him with hundreds of man-hours and
police resources being expended to track down his
history and his movements during the time the murders were occurring.

Porter, thirty-nine years old at the time, stood six feet
tall, with elongated features and short, somewhat curly
dark blond hair. Wearing gold-rimmed glasses, he
looked somewhat more like a middle-aged bookkeeper
than a potential serial killer. As the result of an accident, he was forced to use Canadian crutches. These
devices, also known as forearm crutches, provide mo-
bility for patients with leg weakness. A brace attaches
the crutch to the forearms and allows hands to be used
without dropping the crutches. They lent an awkward-
ness to his gait and contributed to his insecurity around
most women.

The voluminous information law enforcement collected on Porter illustrated the thoroughness with
which investigators tackled the difficult and intricate
task they faced in pursuing the actual killer. On July
28, 1995, Detective Mary LeVeck, of the St. Johns
County Sheriff's Office, appeared before Judge
Richard O. Watkins, of the Seventh Judicial Circuit of
Florida. At that time Detective LeVeck was assigned to

the Persons Crimes Section of the Investigation Division. The reason for her court appearance was to petition for permission to search a storage shed, where he stored some of his possessions, on property owned by Porter's mother.

The affidavit for search warrant, which was filed in St. Johns County Court, detailed the strange web of circumstances that had led detectives to become increasingly suspicious of Dallas Porter, especially after his name was mentioned by several informants in connection with the murder of Cheryl Lucas. It should be noted that permission such as Detective LeVeck was requesting from Judge Watkins can only be obtained by presenting detailed justification for the search, including relevant facts about the crime of which the person is suspected and the individual's possible connections to the crime. Very often corroboration must be obtained from other law enforcement jurisdictions. This demands painstaking investigation, numerous phone calls, and many hours of work by law enforcement personnel. The voluminous information gathered on Dallas Porter and the people with whom he associated gave evidence of exactly how tedious this task could be. Considering how much these data corresponded to traits that often indicate a serial killer, it was understandable that investigators felt justified in believing they may have located Ms. Lucas's killer.

The first suspicions of Dallas Porter as Cheryl Lucas's potential slayer surfaced when he voluntarily phoned director Mike Cochran, of the St. Johns County Sheriff's Office, on July 19, 1995, to say that he knew something about "the body that was found in St. Augustine South." This was not the first time Porter had phoned the police with reports of suspicious activities. On June 10, 1994, he had called to ask for a routine patrol at his mother's home. In September of that same year, he called from the apartment complex where he was working as a maintenance man in reference to some criminal mischief that had occurred on the premises. On January 9, 1995, he called again in reference to a stranded stingray on the beach. Then on April 19, 1995, he called twice, the first time in reference to there being sharks in the ocean and swimmers who would not listen when he told them to get out of the water. The second call was to report some property he had found.

All these activities made him seem like a possible "police wanna-be," the sort of person who likes the excitement of being involved, however peripherally, in crime and criminal activities. However, it was not uncommon for actual murderers to attempt to inject themselves into the police investigation of their crimes. John Wayne Gacy, Ken Bianchi, and Edmund Kemp are examples of well-known serial killers who fit this pattern. Thus, it was decided to question Porter further.

On July 21 and 24, 1995, Detective LeVeck conducted interviews with Porter after advising him of his constitutional rights. In questioning Porter, she learned that when he was living in California some ten years previously, there had been several prostitute murders in the area where he resided. "These girls were being killed in California ten years ago," he stated. "You all are behind the times here."

Porter admitted that while residing in Oceanside, California, he lived with Francine Chisholm, a cabdriver, and that during the time they were together, several prostitutes were killed in that vicinity. He stated that two of the victims were Chisholm's friends. He said that one of them had been "cut up in pieces and strewn over a mountainside" and that the other had been "pushed out of a vehicle in downtown

Oceanside." However, he claimed he had known the victims "only in passing."

Porter's account of the murders was confirmed by the Vista, California, Police Department. According to their report, there was a series of prostitute killings in the area during the 1980s, to which a task force had been assigned. Then, around 1988, it seemed the killings had stopped. In a statement to St. Johns County detectives, it was also confirmed that one of the victims had been cut up and was found on the side of a mountain in one of the Indian Reservations. Porter was identified as having lived in the area of this Indian Reservation.

Further investigation showed that Porter's on-again, off-again relationship with Francine Chisholm lasted for about fifteen years, although they actually lived together in the same house for only about four months. Their relationship resulted in the birth of a son, Michael, whom Porter helped support. During this time Porter was involved with a number of prostitutes, whom he picked up in the bar where he worked. Through these relationships he became severely addicted to methamphetamines, the drug of choice in California at that time.

Chisholm described Porter as a workaholic, saying he held two or three jobs at the same time. She also noted that he was very neat, a perfectionist.

A request to the San Diego Sheriff's Office for additional information on Porter's background revealed that his police records and crime reports had been purged from the files. However, court records still on file revealed that, in 1987, he had been charged with felony assault with a deadly weapon and felony battery upon a person. This assault occurred on the Rincon Indian Reservation in the Pauma Valley area of California. The charges in the case were ultimately dismissed due to insufficient evidence.

The California office also reported Porter had also been charged with possession of a controlled substance. These charges were reduced to a misdemeanor and Porter had received a sentence of sixty days in jail and three years probation.

Detective LeVeck learned that Porter had moved from California to Jacksonville, Florida, around 1989, where he lived with a prostitute, Jane Annette Craig. Further deepening suspicion against him was the fact that this placed him in the area at the time Anita McQuaig Stevens was killed. This happened on Fish Island Road in St. Augustine, near the State Road 312 Bridge. Seven months later Connie Terrell was murdered in the area of the borrow pits off Holmes Boulevard. (While police were still investigating Porter for Cheryl Lucas's murder, in March 1993 another known prostitute, Lashawna Streeter, was found dead in the woods on Dairy Farm Road, off old Moultrie Road in St. Augustine. This further fueled suspicions of Porter as the serial killer for whom detectives were searching.) When detectives from St. Johns County checked with the Jacksonville Sheriff's Office, they discovered that an unusual number of similar murders had also been occurring in Jacksonville during this same period.

Porter was also involved in a breaking and entering during this period. An elementary school in Orange Park was burglarized in March 1996 and a number of TVs and pieces of other electronic equipment were stolen. Porter's role in the crime was the use of his truck to haul the stolen goods. He was arrested and confessed and, because he had no previous criminal record in that jurisdiction (his juvenile record had been expunged), he received probation.

Sergeant Frank Japour, of the Jacksonville Sheriff's Office, stated that for about eighteen months around 1990 there were a number of prostitute murders in

Jacksonville. Sergeant Japour further stated that there had been talk of starting a task force to investigate the murders, but before that could take place, the murders stopped. This coincided with the time Porter left Jacksonville for St. Augustine.

By the time Porter moved from Jacksonville, he and Jane Annette Craig had separated. Porter told detectives he then met another prostitute, Sandra Noland and lived with her for about three or four months in St. Augustine. Detective LeVeck's interview with Noland's lesbian lover, Maria Gonzales, revealed that when Gonzales got out of prison, she found Noland and Porter living together at a bayside motel in St. Augustine. When Noland tried to leave Porter to return to the lesbian relationship with Gonzales, there was a physical confrontation, at which time Porter pushed Noland into a wall.

Porter's account of the incident to detectives was that he wanted a relationship with Sandra Noland, but "it didn't work out." Feeling victimized, he told detectives, "I've always tried to be protective of these girls and I always turn out to be the underdog. I always get stabbed in the back. My relationship with them had nothing to do with sex. I just tried to help them. They (the prostitutes) use me for money and then discard me. I'm a dirty word until somebody needs me."

In his statement to detectives, Dallas Porter said that in the fall of 1993 he began dating another prostitute, Addie Devlin, and that on Valentine's Day, 1994, they moved in together. "I took her off the street and took care of her," he claimed. "We'd been living together about a year and I had been paying all the bills when I found out she'd been bringing those black men to our house and having sex with them." He said Addie denied it, but he knew better.

Despite the betrayal he described, Porter claimed that the only time he was violent with Devlin was when he tried to prevent her from leaving him. "She went right back to the 'War Zone' (an area between eastern Chapin Street and the railroad tracks that was frequented by drug dealers, users, and prostitutes)," he told detectives. "I tried to get her to come back, but she refused."

But his next statements revealed more than just a rejected lover's unhappiness, they demonstrated his ambivalent attitude toward women in general and prostitutes specifically, a trait frequently exhibited by serial killers. "Addie is a user, she likes black boys. She's smart. She uses the KKK to kill you, white boys, too.

"She 'tweaks' me," he said. When asked what that meant, he said, "Psych 101. She's always watching me." He claimed that one day after he and Addie stopped seeing each other, he took Diana Richardson (later another victim) under the 312 Bridge. "Addie had been tweaking me and she showed up under the bridge with a trick who was a friend of mine. She had sex with the guy right in front of me to get back at me." (Devlin later denied to Detective LeVeck that she had ever been under the 312 Bridge with Porter.)

He told detectives, "Go check the names under the 312 Bridge, read them. (Apparently, some of the johns and prostitutes inscribed their names on the bridge abutments.) You'll see. Addie is a sick person, a wicked person." Porter stated that he'd been keeping notes on Devlin and also had pictures of her (presumably taken during sexual acts with other men). "I have the information on her and her tricks," he boasted.

On the evening of July 19, 1995, Porter gave Detective Pat Greenhalgh, from the St. Johns County Sheriff's Office, a gray address book with Addie Devlin's name in it. He also told Detective Mary LeVeck that in due time he would give her all his notes on

Devlin. "You've already got the address book and you ought to work on that right now," he said.

When Detective LeVeck interviewed Addie Devlin, Devlin confirmed that she and Porter had dated in a prostitute-john relationship for about two months before they began living together. She said that Porter had paid to have her teeth fixed, paid her student loans, helped with student expenses, and took her to the opera and ballet while they were living together. The reverse side of the relationship was that he was very jealous and accused her of sleeping around and bringing men back to their bedroom. She left him on several occasions before finally ending the relationship. She said that his accusations became so unbearable that life on the streets was more acceptable than the conditions he was putting her through.

She told Detective LeVeck, "Dallas smokes crack and picks up other prostitutes to get back at me for wrongs he feels I'm causing him." On the other hand, she stated that "he likes to take people whose lives are bad and tries to make them better." (This pattern of a dual personality—one trying to help the prostitutes, the other hating them—would surface again, this time when the true killer was found.)

Since it was the Cheryl Lucas murder that brought Porter to detectives' attention, their investigation concentrated most directly on his relationship with Lucas. Porter told detectives that a local drug dealer, Rodrick Laine, had introduced him to Cheryl Lucas and that he began dating her.

This was confirmed by Laine, who told detectives that he'd introduced them after Porter asked Laine to find him a trick. Laine stated that he saw Porter with Lucas about fifteen or twenty times during that spring. "Dallas Porter talks about the 312 Bridge a lot," Laine said. "He says he's slept under it and that he takes girls there sometimes." Laine also gave information that reflected Porter's conflicting feelings in regard to prostitutes—"He talks about how he's in love with Addie; then he says he doesn't want anything to do with prostitutes and that they shouldn't be living."

Laine also reported that although Porter had frequently come to see him before Lucas was killed, afterward he ended their association.

Porter admitted he sometimes visited Lucas's house, and frequently drove her around town, but he claimed the relationship was a platonic one. "We just drove around the west side or parked at Oyster Creek and talked about our problems and our nonfunctional families," Porter claimed. "Cheryl would talk about her five children and her mother." He added that they also discussed his tumultuous relationship with Addie Devlin.

However, in other interviews with detectives, his description of his relationship with Cheryl varied. In one interview he referred to Lucas as his "buddy and friend." Another time he stated, "That girl's just another whore." He admitted to having flirted with her, but once again he denied having had sex with her. "It's okay to know them (black prostitutes), but you don't bed them or you'll lose your stuff," he told the detectives.

Other general comments he made about prostitutes also raised a red flag. A local drug dealer, who supplied Porter with cocaine, quoted him as saying, "All prostitutes are scummy and bad. They all need to be shot. Me, I like rough women, the trashier the better. They call me the 'whore dog.'"

When asked what information he had about Cheryl's murder, Porter claimed in his affidavit that the last time he had seen Cheryl was on a night when he had gone to the War Zone looking for Addie Devlin. "That was either two or three days before Cheryl's body was found.

I parked my truck off King Street and walked into the War Zone. I didn't find Addie, but I knew she was tweaking me (spying on him). I saw Cheryl Lucas there and talked to her for a while and then we left together. About one A.M. we were walking behind the Pic 'n Save towards my truck, which was parked on the south side of King Street. She had five rocks of crack cocaine and needed money to pay for them. I told her I didn't have any money, so she left and crossed back over King Street. I offered her a raincoat because it was raining out, but she declined it." He reported that there was a northeaster blowing that weekend and it was rainy. (That statement coincided with reports of the weather on the night Lucas was killed.)

"I got into my truck, but I don't remember what I did after that," he told detective LeVeck. "Probably went home."

After hearing that statement, the Detective told Porter another witness had seen Cheryl Lucas get into a dark-colored full-size pickup like his at the Pic 'n Save around one A.M. on the morning of June 17, 1995. LeVeck asked Porter if he had circled around the block and picked up Lucas. He said that was a possibility, as he had picked her up at that location on several occasions in the past.

"If you picked up Cheryl Lucas, where would you have taken her?" Detective LeVeck asked him. He said under the 312 Bridge. "I didn't, though," he added. "When I walked out of the War Zone, I knew Addie was watching us. At that point I had a passing thought to take Cheryl Lucas under the bridge because I knew Addie would follow us. I knew it would really rip Addie's ass if she saw me screw a black girl under the bridge."

Then he added, "That girl (Cheryl Lucas) is just another whore, an embarrassment to her family. She was probably killed for jealousy. You need to look at Rodrick Laine," he said, fingering in turn the drug dealer who had introduced him to Cheryl and later reported his connection to her to detectives.

In addition to Porter's own statements, reports of other witnesses made him seem the most likely suspect in the murders. One witness reported that Porter had done cabinetwork for Lucas's mother, who lived next door to her daughter. Adding to the circumstantial evidence against him was the fact that a nail pry bar, a tool frequently used by Porter in his carpentry work, was suggested as the possible blunt instrument that had killed Lucas. Detectives collected five such pry bars and Dr. Maples, of the University of Florida's forensic laboratory, examined them for similarities to the wounds he had observed on Cheryl's skull. He had also made an overlay tracing of the wounds. Three of the bars were flat bars, which he ruled out. He said two were similar to what they were looking for. Dr. Maples was also shown a photograph of Anita Stevens's facial injuries and he felt one of the marks on her face appeared to have been made with a pry bar. However, he said it would be extremely beneficial to the evidence in the case if her body was exhumed.

While being questioned, Porter offered investigators the name of another man he said they should regard as a possible suspect. He reported that a Dan Howell was "all cracked up and bragging that he had killed Connie Terrell and Anita Stevens." There was enough basis for this tip to lead the sheriff's detectives to check out Howell thoroughly. However, there was no evidence he was involved. This made the officers all the more suspicious that Porter was trying to focus attention away from himself.

Another clue in Lucas's slaying that seemed to point to Porter was the deteriorated state of her body. The medical examiner said it appeared to have been kept in conditions similar to those inside an

aluminum storage shed, such as the one Porter had
at his mother's place. This is what led to Detective
LeVeck's petition to search the premises. According to her petition, the list of the specific objects for
which law enforcement officials would be searching
included: address books, letters, notes, papers, photographs or newspaper articles relating to Cheryl
Lucas and/or any other prostitutes and/or other
females. They would also search for such articles of
female clothing as shorts, skirts, bras, socks, gym
shoes, slip-on shoes, a black shoulder bag, and baby
clothing outfits. In particular, they would search for
any type of object with suspected blood on it that
could have been used to inflict blunt trauma to the
victim's head. In addition, they asked permission to
obtain any articles of Porter's clothing or shoes with
suspected blood on them.

On August 1, 1995, evidence technician Susan
Biesiada met with LeVeck at the shed and tested several areas, including the inside corner of the door
and a white chaise longue for bloodstains. She used
a Q-Tip dipped in water and did a control test on a
Hemostik, with negative results.

In the process of verifying Porter's whereabouts,
the investigators spent many hours compiling a precise and detailed timeline of his activities from 1962
to October 1995. In order to do this they examined
his educational history, his employment records, hospital reports, military records, rental records, arrest
records, alcohol treatment programs he attended, etc.

On July 28, 1995, when Detective LeVeck presented
her petition for a warrant to search Porter's property,
she made the following statement: "It is this Affiant's
belief that there is probable cause to believe [Dallas
Porter] is a suspect in the murder of Cheryl Lucas,
due to his admitting to being with the victim shortly
before she was killed, his frequenting the area of the

S.R. 312 Bridge, which is just north of where the victim's body was recovered and his strong dislike toward prostitutes."

As further reason for the warrant, her petition stated: "It is believed that the notes and photographs which he said he has kept on [Addie Devlin], and any evidence he has kept from the crime, are in his storage shed because he stated that is where he keeps his files and all of his personal belongings."

When detectives converged on the property, they found bloodstains inside, at the bottom of the shed door, and on a chaise longue that was stored inside. A search of Porter's car yielded a glove and a rag also with possible bloodstains.

Following the search, investigators drew up a list of probable cause for considering Porter a prime suspect in the case. Among the list were the allegations that he was obsessed with prostitutes, that various murders of prostitutes had occurred in different areas where he was living, that he had past history of violence, that he admitted to being friends with Cheryl Lucas, that a tool frequently used in his work may have been the murder weapon, that the decomposition of Lucas's body indicated it may have been kept in a car trunk or a metal shed, and that a search of the shed and his car had yielded items with possible bloodstains.

But for all the evidence compiled against him, investigators were unable to present enough proof to file for a warrant for Porter's arrest. Part of the difficulty was the inconsistency of his statements, which sometimes verged on the bizarre.

During one interview with Detective LeVeck, he insisted that he had helped "the federal government" solve the "Page Boys Case." (This was a case that drew national headlines. It involved a Maryland congressman, Robert Bauman, and possibly other legislators who were found to be sexually involved with congressional pages and child prostitutes in Washington, DC.) According to Porter's brother, this claim was the result of Porter's delusional thinking.

Porter's strange claims may also have been in part a result of brain damage due to his prolonged drug abuse. During his military service he was run over by a tractor-trailer and suffered severe trauma, including fractures of both hips, his shin, and severe head injuries. When released from the medical center where he had been treated, he was addicted to the morphine given him for pain during his extended hospitalization. The accident physically left Porter with pain, swelling, cramps, and needing special Canadian crutches in order to walk.

The accident had several direct impacts on the rest of his life: First, it left him permanently crippled, in chronic pain, and suffering from insomnia. Second, as already indicated, he became addicted to the morphine given him following the accident. Later addictions included methamphetamines, alcohol, crack cocaine, and combinations of these. Third, Porter was given a disability discharge from the U.S. Marines in which he served from 1974 to 1978 and received a sizable insurance settlement from the trucking company whose vehicle injured him. The insurance came to him in the form of a trust arrangement.

He blamed the accident for many of his troubles. "God took away my looks, my youth. My pecker is the size of my thumb. I can't have any more kids, and I'm angry." He also indicated his pain accounted for his frequent outbursts and attacks on women—"It seems sometimes I can't stop myself from doing the meanest, cruelest acts possible."

Much of Porter's anger was focused against prostitutes, apparently the only sort of women to whom he could relate. Porter's statements regarding being used and then discarded by these women was no doubt true. This behavior is not unusual among prostitutes and for understandable reasons, considering the treatment they get from most johns. It is no coincidence that by the time Porter made these statements, all the insurance money from his accident was gone. Thus, prostitutes had no reason to relate to him.

Other insights into Porter's character came from Robert and Jane Sachs with whom he lived for a time. Robert was a cabdriver who first knew Dallas as a good fare who tipped generously. From this start their friendship grew to the point where Dallas and his girlfriend moved in with the Sachs family for a few months. Sachs finally evicted him, claiming he was untrustworthy, paranoid, and had frequent temper tantrums with violent blowups about once a week. A further rift in the relationship developed when Porter reported the Sachses to the police, saying they were abusing their children.

Like almost everyone who knew Porter, Robert Sachs felt that he was a chronic liar. Sachs was also convinced that Porter was "psycho," noting that he often thought cars were following him and that the government was "after him." This was verified by statements from Porter's live-in companion Sherry Tate. She told detectives, "He had paranoid ideas about the government following him and monitoring him." Porter also told the Sachses that he had once served ten years for beating up a man who molested a child. No record of this crime was revealed in the investigation of his criminal history.

Sachs informed police investigators that during the time Porter lived with them, he owned an automatic pistol and bondage items, including a collar with spikes, hooks for chains, and a set of handcuffs, bondage items used by many serial killers in torturing their victims. He also said Porter had night vision goggles and listening devices, which he used to observe and eavesdrop on couples in motels, condos, and related settings. These objects offered strong proof to investigators that Porter was involved in voyeurism and sadistic sexual practices involving violence and probable criminal behavior. However, detectives were also aware that possession of these items was fairly typical of some johns whose relationships with women are mostly restricted to prostitutes.

Some of the prostitutes with whom he had lived for months or years expressed opinions in contrast to these negative perceptions of Porter. Sherry Tate said he stayed with her to help when she was sick. In addition, when one of her children was molested, Porter "nearly beat the man to death with a baseball bat." She noted, too, that he tried to give assistance to other prostitutes. She acknowledged that he had punched and slapped her. But then, reversing herself again, she added, "But usually I started the argument and deserved it." In one of their altercations, she admitted, "I bit off the tip of his finger."

Another woman with whom he had been involved characterized Porter as "a hundred-dollar trick who was harmless." She described his generosity (perhaps the reason he was sometimes known as "Valentine"). "He liked to take people whose lives were terrible and try to help them. Said he wanted to get prostitutes off the street."

Her further revelations, however, painted a different portrait. "He got jealous and tried to control me. When I stayed out overnight, he would accuse me of whoring. The only time he was violent with me was when I was leaving him. Then he shoved me into a bathroom to keep me from going."

But she stopped short of accusing him of serious physical violence. "He would rave, but he never hit me. Mostly, when he got mad, he would smoke crack and pick up other prostitutes."

One prostitute explained that when she was living with Porter, "I didn't have to turn any tricks. He brought me all the cocaine I needed, bought me jewelry and fancy dresses. He even took me to visit his mom twice."

Another girlfriend gave what was probably the most accurate description of Dallas Porter—"a lonely man who picks up girls for company and sex."

When Detective Brian Whitbread, of the St. Johns County Sheriff's Office, interviewed Francine Chisholm, the mother of Porter's child, Chisholm stated she did not feel Porter could kill anyone. "He is good-hearted," she noted. "All these years he's been helping the wrong people. He always gets involved with people that use him." She admitted that she became frustrated when Porter spent all his money on his friends and prostitutes while ignoring their son, Michael. "My son loves Porter, but I won't let Michael go back to visit him."

Dallas Porter was an extremely complex man. Very early in life he demonstrated strong antisocial traits characterized by breaking the law and associating with delinquent peers. As is true with a number of the men who turn out to be serial killers, Porter was the scapegoat of a family headed by a mother who treated him brutally and saw him as nothing more than a chronic problem. Although his accounts of his abused childhood were conflicting, it appeared his difficulties were compounded by early severe sexual abuse, including a rape in jail and being subjected during adolescence to serving as a male prostitute. According to records of the Orange County, Florida, Sheriff's Department, as early as age nineteen he was arrested for auto theft, aggravated assault, and fleeing with attempt to elude. For this crime he received probation on condition he make restitution and also included loss of his motor vehicle license for four years.

During the time he served in the U.S. Marines, his antisocial personality manifested in instances of going AWOL, as well as other difficulties. He was headed toward a dishonorable discharge when the injuries he received in the accident resulted in a temporary service-incurred disability leave and an ultimate medical discharge from the marines. During his convalescence, he started bartending in places where he soon learned to take advantage of the readily available drugs and prostitutes.

Anger and frustration with his situation led to his requesting a full discharge from the service although he claimed that his only ambition in life had been to be in the Marines. "My father was a Marine, his father was a Marine, and I'm the ninth generation of Marines going back to (my family's origins) in Europe," he stated in the letter in which he appealed for his discharge.

He noted that even after extensive treatment he still suffered from pain, swelling, aches, leg and toe cramps, and clumsiness—"not being able to hold things with my left hand and tripping over my own damn feet." He also felt that his injuries accounted for his temper outbursts and caused him to "do the meanest, most cruel acts possible."

After receiving a medical discharge from the marines on the grounds of permanent disability, he continued his drug abuse. This determined his life pattern for the next two decades. At various times he entered drug and alcohol rehabilitation programs, at one point managing to remain clean for nearly three years.

During these years he developed a lasting attraction for prostitutes, desperate women whose lives were dominated by their constant and ever-increasing need for drugs. Porter got gratification for his special sexual needs from them, as well as the companionship he craved. He felt genuine affection for some of the women, but he was also naive enough to expect them to be at least relatively faithful to him and to give up the lifestyle of street prostitution to which they had become accustomed, and upon which they were dependent for their livelihood. Instead of being faithful, driven by their craving for drugs, they exploited him. The hurt he suffered when they betrayed his unrealistic expectations led him to develop a love/hate attitude toward prostitutes, a mind-set also characteristic of many serial killers.

Two aspects of Porter's personality deserved special attention: Any man who possesses bondage paraphernalia—such as chains, spiked collars, and handcuffs—has sadism and/or masochism as a sexual preference. Porter's ownership of voyeuristic equipment, such as night vision devices and eavesdropping equipment, further indicated sexual deviance. Such deviance was not unexpected in a man with Porter's early sexual trauma. Nor are his sex practices as atypical as most people would like to think. However, they did bring additional attention to him as a suspect in Cheryl Lucas's death.

Whether or not Dallas Porter was a killer remains a mystery. He was an enigmatic figure—generous and cruel, helpful and abusive, both a user and one who was used. In many respects he typified a type of suspect that law enforcement must deal with when trying to track down serial killers. For investigators he proved to be a major distraction from pursuit of the actual killer.

Chapter 12

October 1995: Diana Richardson

He was on his way to his daughter's house in Ocala, but there was this woman in St. Augustine . . . someone he'd dated a few times before. He'd been thinking about her all the way down from Asheville. Plenty of time. Stop by her apartment. Suggest they go for a ride. The rest would be easy. . . .

Diana Richardson was at home. Alone. It took only a few minutes for the killer to settle on the service—a blow job—and the price—$50. She was prepared to take care of him right there, but he knew that would be too dangerous. Too much possibility of clues left behind. He suggested they go for a ride in his Monte Carlo sedan. He said he knew a good spot, down by Holmes Boulevard.

As they drove along Four Mile Road, Diana began rubbing the man's penis, causing him to have an erection. His excitement rising, he pulled the car into a small driveway area near the borrow pits off Holmes Boulevard. He unzipped his pants and was sitting midway on the front seat. Diana was on the passenger side, fully clothed. She was in the middle of performing oral sex when, for some unknown reason, she bit down hard on his penis.

Pain shot through him. His hair-trigger temper flared, and he struck her on the back of her head with his hand. That surge of anger—the exhilarating sensation he'd been waiting for—quickly erupted into greater violence. He began pounding her with increasingly brutal blows, not wanting to stop. For long moments he continued his assault until she was completely unconscious.

Realizing Diana was either dead or dying, the man exited the car. Lifting her limp body in a "fireman's hold," he carried her to the borrow pit and threw her into the water.

Afterward, he drove away and continued on to his daughter's home in Ocala.

On October 12, 1995, Dale Lyman, Diana Richardson's seventeen-year-old son, reported her missing to the St. Johns County Sheriff's Office. He said he hadn't heard from his mother for several days and that he had gone to the Cut asking for her, but no one had seen her. Diana's name was placed on the missing persons list. A number of leads were followed, but no one reported having seen or heard from her since that date.

Ironically, the killer's final St. Augustine victim was a woman who had been questioned by detectives investigating several of the previous victims' deaths. Shortly after Anita Stevens was murdered in November 1988, Detective Mary LeVeck interviewed Diana who was, at that time, incarcerated in St. Johns County Jail on a charge of issuing a forged document. She acknowledged having known Anita for over a year and a half. It was Diana who described Anita as a rock star and reported that Anita had taken advantage of a man she was living with and that her treatment of him had contributed to his suicide.

Diana named a number of potential witnesses and suspects with whom Anita may have been associated. Her knowledge of the johns, dealers, and pimps was extensive, indicating she had done business with many of them. In discussing one such man whom she considered dangerous, she revealed the power of her own addiction—"I'll play along with anybody to get high." She also admitted to having taken her dates to Fish Island Road, the area where Anita was killed. "It might have been a cabdriver I went down there with," she added.

Later in the same interview, she referred to Anita as "a bitch," "a conniving little snake," and "a bad person." Her anger at Anita resulted from an incident in which Anita had thrown Dale and Diana out of the house of the man Anita was then living with. "She called the cops while we were there," Diana stated. "And she told the cops that my son, Dale, stole something of hers. I knew my son hadn't taken it. 'Cause my son and I are together all the time. (This statement seemed ironic in view of the fact that Diana's current incarceration wasn't her first.) We're real tight."

One declaration Diana made during that interview provided a clue to her murder some seven years later—"If I ever turned a trick, it would be strictly somebody that I knew." At the time Richardson was being questioned about Anita's murder, it was possible she actually knew the killer but was unaware that he was a murderer. However, she never mentioned his name to investigators, perhaps for the very reason that she did not think of him as a potential killer.

Diana Richardson was something of an anomaly in comparison to the other women murdered in St. Augustine. At age forty-seven she was the oldest. She was the killer's third white victim; of the six, three (Stevens, Terrell, and Richardson) were white, three

(Streeter, Snead-Haile, and Lucas) were African American. With better education than most of the others, she had, at one time, worked as a bookkeeper and a legal secretary. Everyone who knew her described the five-foot-six-inch woman with blue eyes and blond hair as unusually attractive even after years of addiction and prostitution.

Her drug abuse started with the kind of partying many young, employed singles indulged in for a time before going on to more stable lives. But, in Diana's case, whatever stability she might once have known had long since deteriorated into addiction and, ultimately, prostitution. By the time she was interviewed by Detectives LeVeck and Greenhalgh following Cheryl Lucas's murder, the detectives reported her as appearing "high and extremely intoxicated." She was even turning to her son's friends for drugs and sex.

Diana was also a pro at the food stamp shuffle, although on one occasion that activity landed her in jail. She explained to Detective LeVeck how she and her son's girlfriend, Lisa, had planned it. "It was food stamp day and I said to Lisa, 'Lisa, if you want to get high with us today, why don't you come help me do the food stamp shuffle?' So we woke up and went and paid all our bills and we went to probation and all that. So we got our food stamps. We took a cab over to Pic 'n Save, Dale goes and buys some shit, and I go to return it and get the cash. Coming outside, a cop car is there. Great! Lovely! Lisa called and set us up on that one big-time."

Diana was born in Breckenridge, Texas, on December 23, 1947. Her name as listed on her birth certificate was Barbara Sue Slaughter. Her father, Myron Slaughter was a member of the Texas Highway Patrol and her seventeen-year-old mother was listed as "housewife." It was not known when she changed her name from Barbara Sue to Diana, but the Richardson was the result of an early marriage.

In her interviews with detectives regarding the previous slayings, Diana appeared streetwise, a safe assumption regarding a person with her lifestyle who managed to survive so long in such a dangerous occupation as prostitution. She had been arrested in Alaska for conspiracy to smuggle marijuana. In Florida she had numerous arrests for fraud, retail theft, dealing in stolen property, uttering forged instruments, possession of drug paraphernalia, failure to appear, and probation violation. Among the aliases she used in her various scams were "Jade Richardson," "Barbara Sue Richardson," "Barbara Sue Slaughter," "Heather Martindale," and "Diana Witham." Some of the charges were at the misdemeanor level and resulted in verdicts of not guilty, judgment withheld, released to community control, or dismissal. For the more serious offenses, she was sentenced to house arrest, time served while awaiting trial, or incarceration.

Although obviously intelligent, she was unable to avoid the same sort of abuse the other women of Crack Head Corner suffered, as, for example, the incident mentioned earlier in which two males beat, raped, and robbed Richardson, then left her for dead. On that occasion the abuse was so egregious that she was willing to file charges. When interviewed at the hospital, Diana identified her two attackers. A search of their vehicle turned up traces of the victim's hair, latent prints, and apparent semen stains. The two men were arrested and found guilty of attempted murder, armed robbery, sexual battery, and kidnapping and are serving twenty-year sentences.

Despite frightening, life-threatening episodes, Diana's crack cocaine addiction kept her on the streets and in high-risk situations. She was also known as a party girl, one who knew where to buy the drugs, where to get the girls—all for a fee, of course. She reported having been partying at the Cut with Cheryl Lucas and several other women shortly before Cheryl was murdered.

Diana was not particularly discriminating in her choice of sexual partners. She described one client as follows: "Elwood is kind of strange and likes to dress up in women's clothes. I think he hustles down in Daytona as a woman." Diana acknowledged using him as a supply source for her own drug habit. "I don't care as long as he gives me something to get high on. One time Elwood and me and three others smoked up two thousand dollars' worth of crack. Talk about a party! Two OD'd. One survived."

Being streetwise, Diana was also alert to the risk of AIDS, possibly another reason she managed to survive as long as she did. "Elwood wanted to go to bed with me, but I never did. Number one, he used drugs, and number two, he's gay. That's a high AIDS risk."

When interviewed regarding a man suspected in Anita Stevens's murder, she reported, "I stayed with Roland for the money, but I was too bored. When I would go back out on the street, he'd get mad."

Oddly enough, for someone so bright and gregarious in her relationships, Diana had a long-term liaison with Deland, a semiliterate forty-seven-year-old man whom she had met while hitchhiking. Deland, who was employed by St. Johns County, was a large, bearded man, rather sloppy in appearance. He claimed that although he had never before had sex with a woman, he and Diana had intercourse the same day he first encountered her. She soon moved in with him and they began a sustained relationship. She gave him sex. He, in return, provided her a place to live.

The relationship, according to Deland's statement, was a turbulent one: "She never paid any of the bills and she got me started on crack. (Later he admitted that she had occasionally contributed $20 or $30 toward their living expenses.) Then I had an accident and the county made me take a blood test. It came back positive for cocaine. The boss told me if it happened again, I would be fired, so I quit using. I tried to get Diana to quit, too, but she wouldn't. I got mad and told her to leave. Then I threw her out. I threw her clothes out twice, but she kept coming back."

The couple patched up their differences for a time when Diana agreed that she would not use crack in the house. But that arrangement was short-lived. "One day I came home and saw a guy leaving the house," Deland said. "When I went in, I could smell crack smoke and know they had been using. We got in a fight and I punched her in the face. She called 911, but then hung up. They called back and I told them everything was okay. But I knew she was bringing johns to the house for sex."

Detectives investigating Diana's murder discovered that there were police reports of Deland having beaten Diana several times. In one such report, filed in April 1993, Deputy Craig Davis stated he met with Diana Richardson as she stood on the road in front of Deland's trailer. She was crying and the right side of her face was red and swollen. She stated that she and her boyfriend, Deland, had been arguing. "I was cooking dinner," she told the detective. "I put the potatoes on the stove and the burners wouldn't light. I said, 'Are we out of matches?' He said, 'What for?' I said, 'Don't answer my question with a question.' That's when he came over and hit me in the mouth with such force it knocked me down. It knocked the bridge out of my mouth and busted my lip on the inside." (The dental bridge was the result of a car accident that had occurred in Orange County some sixteen years previously. On the police report of the accident, Diana was listed as married to a Michael Martindale.)

Historic Castillo de San Marcos, constructed by
the Spanish in 1672, stands as a symbol of St.
Augustine's historic past. *(Photo by Gili Lochner)*

At night this dilapidated area became Crack
Head Corner, the center for drug and prostitution
activities in West Augustine. *(Author's photo)*

A moldering entrance is all that remains of a college that once drew
African-American scholars to West Augustine. *(Author's photo)*

Anita McQuaig Stevens, seventeen in this photo, was brutally murdered by William Lindsey in 1988 – his first known St. Augustine victim.
(Photo courtesy of Mildred McQuaig)

Anita Stevens shares Halloween fun with her young son, Parke. *(Photo courtesy of Mildred McQuaig)*

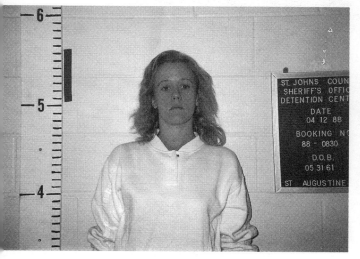

Anita Stevens, charged with driving with a suspended license, is booked into the St. Johns County Detention Center six months before her murder in November 1988. *(Photo courtesy of St. Johns County Sheriff's Office)*

Borrow pit on Fish Island where Anita Stevens's body was discovered.
(Author's photo)

Palmettos with razor-sharp fronds surround the area where Anita Stevens tried to escape her killer. *(Photo courtesy of St. Johns County Sheriff's Office)*

Constance Marie Terrell as a sixteen-year-old high school student. (*Photo courtesy of Nancy Bennett*)

Connie Terrell shares an embrace with her daughter, Kimberly. (*Photo courtesy of Nancy Bennett*)

Even as Connie Terrell battled crack cocaine addiction, she struggled to raise her infant son, Jackie. (*Photo courtesy of Nancy Bennett*)

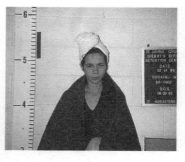

Already seriously addicted to crack cocaine, Connie Terrell was booked into St. Johns County Detention Center on a charge of retail theft. (*Photo courtesy of St. Johns County Sheriff's Office*)

Lashawna Streeter was one of three African-American victims Lindsey killed in St. Augustine. *(Photo courtesy of St. Johns County Sheriff's Office)*

In March 1992, Lashawna Streeter became Lindsey's third identified St. Augustine victim. *(Photo courtesy of St. Johns County Sheriff's Office)*

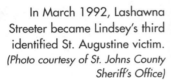

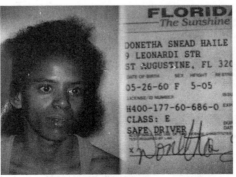

Police circulated this driver's license photo in hopes of finding Donetha Snead Haile, whose body has never been recovered. *(Photo courtesy of St. Johns County Sheriff's Office)*

In June, 1995, thirty-two-year-old Cheryl Lucas became the fifth St. Augustine victim. *(Photo courtesy of Malvera Lucas)*

Victim Cheryl Lucas as she appeared after her arrest in Suffolk County, New York on drug charges. She had only recently moved from New York when she was murdered in St. Augustine. *(Photo courtesy of St. Johns County Sheriff's Office)*

169181
5 28 90
POLICE DEPARTMENT,
...UNTY OF SUFFOLK, N.Y.

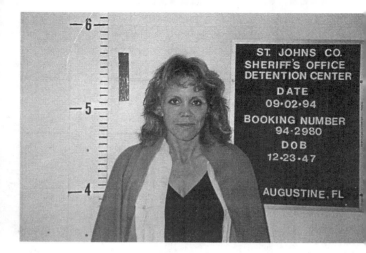

Murder victim Diana Richardson as she appeared when booked into the St. Johns County Detention Center on charges of retail theft and check forgery. *(Photo courtesy St. Johns County Sheriff's Office)*

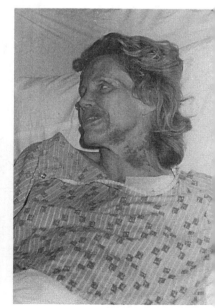

Hospital photo of Diana Richardson after she had been beaten, raped, stabbed, and brutalized by two men. She later became Lindsey's sixth and final St. Augustine victim. *(Photo courtesy of St. Johns County Sheriff's Office)*

Lucy Arnett Raymer. Her murder in Asheville, North Carolina in 1996 put law enforcement on the trail of a brutal serial killer who had eluded them for nearly a decade. *(Photo courtesy of Buncombe County Sheriff's Department)*

Lucy Raymer's body was found fully clothed in a small stream next to a culvert. *(Photo courtesy of Buncombe County Sheriff's Department)*

The area surrounding the spot where Lucy Raymer's body was found is roped off as investigators search for clues. *(Photo courtesy of Buncombe County Sheriff's Department)*

Borrow pits typical of those found throughout St. Johns County, Florida. The killer found these water-filled excavations convenient for disposing of his victims' bodies. *(Photos courtesy of St. Johns County Sheriff's Office)*

The killer abandoned several of his victims' bodies in the area of the State Road 312 Bridge in St. Augustine, Florida.
(Photo by Gili Lochner)

Lashawna Streeter's body was found in a wooded area, partially skeletonized and covered with brush. *(Photo courtesy of St. Johns County Sheriff's Office)*

Tire tracks left in the area of Anita Stevens's murder are measured and kept on record in the police files. *(Photo courtesy of St. Johns County Sheriff's Office)*

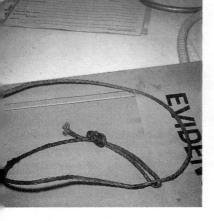

Noose used to strangle one of Lindsey's victims. *(Photo courtesy of St. Johns County Sheriff's Office)*

William Lindsey as a junior at Ketterlinus High School in St. Augustine, Florida. *(Ketterlinus High School yearbook photo)*

William Lindsey's adopted family: his sister Sue Alice *(left)*, mother Oleen *(center)*, and sister Verna *(right)* celebrate Sue Alice's wedding. *(Photo courtesy of Billie Sue Locke)*

William Lindsey relaxes at a family gathering during the time he was married to his second wife, Annie Laurie Lindsey. *(Photo courtesy of Agnes Marjenhoff)*

William Lindsey in February 1997, shortly after his arrest in
Asheville, North Carolina for the murder of Lucy Raymer.
(Left photo by Ewart Ball, Asheville Citizen-Times*; Right photo courtesy
of Buncombe County Sheriff's Department)*

Soft porn magazines found
in Lindsey's trailer in North
Carolina after his arrest by
Detective John Harrison.
*(Photo courtesy of Buncombe
County Sheriff's Department)*

Sheriff Bobby Medford. Cooperation of Medford's office in Asheville, North Carolina and his counterparts in St. Augustine, Florida, was critical in the capture and imprisonment of a serial killer who had plagued both jurisdictions. *(Photo courtesy of Buncombe County Sheriff's Department)*

Sheriff Neil Perry. During his twenty-year tenure as head law enforcement officer of St. Johns County, Florida, Sheriff Perry took his department from a small, local organization to national accreditation as a modern, highly trained police force. *(Photo courtesy of St. Johns County Sheriff's Office)*

The Cold Case Task Force investigating the St. Augustine murders was housed in this modest dwelling near the sheriff's office. *(Author's photo)*

Law enforcement officers celebrate the success of their collaboration in the Lindsey case. *Left to right:* Sgt. Frank Welborn, St. Johns County Sheriff's Office; Sheriff Bobby Medford, Buncombe County; a friend; Sgt. John Harrison, Buncombe County Sheriff's Department.
(Photo courtesy of John Harrison)

Detective John Harrison *(left)* of Buncombe County, North Carolina Sheriff's Department and Detective Frank Welborn *(right)* of the St. Johns County, Florida Sheriff's Office became fast friends as a result of their shared experiences on the Lindsey case. *(Author's photo)*

Detective Jennifer Ponce, formerly of the St. Johns County Sheriff's Office was involved in the murder investigations of the six women killed in St. Augustine. She was also a member of the task force that obtained Lindsey's confession to the murders. *(Photo courtesy of St. Johns County Sheriff's Office)*

As a result of his outstanding work on the case, Detective Sgt. John Harrison received his department's highest accolade, one of many awards he has earned during his long career in law enforcement. *(Photo courtesy of Buncombe County Sheriff's Office)*

Assistant States Attorney Maureen Sullivan Christine battled to put the confessed killer behind bars. *(Photo courtesy Florida States Attorney's Office)*

While Diana was being interviewed, Deland appeared at the door of the trailer, upset and sweating. "I just did it to shut her up," he explained to Deputy Davis.

At that point Deland was arrested, charged with simple battery/domestic violence, and booked into the county jail. Diana signed the complaint and also signed for a booklet on domestic violence.

This was one of several signal nines (domestic disputes) that had been logged in by the St. Johns County Sheriff's Office from Deland's address. Several times when deputies arrived, the residents claimed it had been a "misdial." At other times they found Deland throwing Diana Richardson's clothes out of his trailer onto the lawn.

On October 14, 1995, Deland reported Diana missing. He told Deputy Joseph Wells that his girlfriend had not been home since October 11. "Diana is up to her usual prostitution and cocaine use," he said. He added that it was not unusual for her to stay away for several days. However, always before if she was to be gone for two or three days, she would call and let him know. "I have lived with Diana on and off for the last eight years. We had problems, but we were still friends." Deland did not appear to be particularly upset by her absence and said there had been no recent arguments between the two. He said he had checked with Diana's other friends, but no one had heard from her.

One of Diana's fellow prostitutes, Sabrina Tanser, was her closest friend and the last person known to have seen Diana alive. She told detectives that on October 11, the day before Diana disappeared, the two of them were partying at Deland's house along with another friend. Diana had asked Sabrina to join her because she "hated to be home alone when Deland got there." When Deland arrived home, the two women and the other man left, went to Sabrina Tanser's house on Whitney Street, and partied some more. Early the following morning they called a cab and were driven to a house on Old Moultrie Road, where they bought more drugs. When they returned to Sabrina's apartment, she went inside, but Diana left. That, Sabrina said, was the last time she saw her friend.

Detective Mary LeVeck checked with the cabdriver, Dick Philips, who remembered picking up two girls and driving them to an auto body shop on Old Moultrie Road, then back to an apartment on Whitney Street. Philips said that one girl went into the house and the other left walking on foot. (As an illuminating sidelight to the role the cabdrivers played in the Crack Head Corner subculture, the same cabdriver came by Sabrina's house shortly afterward and asked her to trick. She told him she didn't do that anymore.) Obviously nervous about the questioning, Philips commented to the detective, "Yeah, and if she shows up dead, you-all will come looking for me because I was the last person who saw her." To which, Detective LeVeck replied that if he had been the last person to see her, she would definitely be talking to him again.

When the cabdriver admitted that it was possible Diana Richardson had not left on foot, but that he had dropped her off at another address, Detective LeVeck insisted he meet with her at the sheriff's office. Because he was reluctant to become involved, several phone calls to his home and to the cab company were required until he finally appeared. Philips brought his four-year-old son with him to the meeting and refused to be separated from the boy during the interview.

He gave LeVeck information about his background, including the fact that he had worked a number of different odd jobs, such as laying pipes for sprinkler systems, and had studied auto mechanics. He said he didn't like driving cabs, but it was a living. He agreed to sign a written statement about having given Diana and Sabrina a ride, but refused to give his address or phone number, stating it was nobody's business and he didn't want to be involved. Detective LeVeck explained to him that he was already involved and that the way he was acting made her wonder if he was keeping something from her. He insisted that he had merely forgotten having dropped Diana Richardson off at a second location until he had spoken again with Sabrina Tanser.

A check on Philips's criminal history came back with negative results.

Sabrina Tanser was also reinterviewed. In addition to the other information, she was also able to give detectives a description of the clothing Diana was wearing. "She had on an old nasty, dirty pair of white tennis shoes that had some pink on them. I think she was wearing jeans and a light-colored shirt. She also had an old light brown over-the-shoulder purse, medium size, with a lot of papers in it."

When asked if Diana was carrying any money when she left, Sabrina reported that Diana had $10 and that she had given her another $10 to buy drugs from Leslie, "a little black guy that sells drugs in the Cut."

She said that Deland had called on October 13, the day after Diana disappeared, to ask her to go to Jacksonville with him. After that, he continued to call her daily, begging her to move in with him. Terrified that he might have killed Diana, she refused his offer. Sabrina also claimed that some days before Diana's death she and her boyfriend had gotten into a fight. In tears she went to the trailer where Diana and Deland were living and told them she was going to leave. "When we were alone, Deland said to me, 'Well, if I got rid of

Diana, you could come and stay with me.' I thought he was joking. . . . Now I'm not so sure."

In view of this statement, Deland remained a suspect. When Diana had been missing for three weeks, Detective LeVeck called Deland into the sheriff's office for a follow-up interview. Due to his past violent history with Diana, she advised him of his constitutional rights before beginning the questioning. When questioned about his statement to Sabrina that "if he got rid of Diana, she could move in," he stated that what he meant was that if she moved out, Sabrina could move in, not that he was planning to kill Diana.

He denied knowing who had killed Diana or having any further information about her disappearance. He said he was "worried maybe one of those guys on the street got her and hurt her, like what happened in the past when she was stabbed and left for dead." When asked to make a written statement about his relationship with Diana, he said he could read and write, but didn't write very well. He allowed the detective to write the statement for him and signed it.

Deland also signed the rights form and also a permission to search form, which gave detectives the right to check his residence for Diana's personal belongings and for anything suspicious that might be found there. Detective LeVeck later met with Deland and his mother at Deland's house and inspected the personal effects in the bedroom that belonged to Diana. This included numerous articles of clothing, as well as her reading glasses and a prescription for Premarin. A check of the rest of the house did not reveal anything suspicious, except that the living-room furniture appeared to be quite new. When Deland explained that he had recently purchased the sofa and chair, and that the furniture store had removed the old furniture, Detective LeVeck visited the store to inspect the old furniture. Evidence technician Susan Biesiada was called in to test a stain on one of the cushions, but it proved to be merely dirt.

Dale Lyman, Diana's son, met with Detective LeVeck at the sheriff's office on November 1, 1995. Dale was accompanied by the man who had joined Diana and Sabrina at Deland's trailer the afternoon before she disappeared. Dale introduced him as being a good friend. Dale reported that he had first learned of his mother's disappearance when Deland phoned him at work to say she was missing. A day or so later, Sabrina Tanser had also contacted him because she was concerned. Dale reported that he had gone to Deland's residence, but he didn't see anything out of place, except that some of his mother's clothes were balled up on the floor in the corner of the bedroom.

On December 29 Detective LeVeck contacted Dale to tell him of the search they were conducting for any unidentified bodies and that a flyer about his mother's disappearance would go out to law enforcement offices all over the state. A flyer would also be handed out to businesses in the area. Dale said he was pleased with what they were planning to do.

Dale then called Detective LeVeck in mid-January to report that a man had called the Columbia Restaurant, where he was employed, saying he had some information about Diana. That information proved as fruitless as the others.

In January 1996, the sheriff's office sent out a missing persons report asking anyone with information about Diana Richardson's whereabouts to contact Persons Crimes detective Mary LeVeck. The report itself would generate no leads, but the riddle it posed—where was Diana Richardson?—would soon be answered.

Chapter 13

The Task Force

With the disappearance of Donetha Snead-Haile in April 1993, Sheriff Neil Perry felt there was a strong possibility the same killer was responsible for all three murders, especially as the missing woman had a similar lifestyle to the two previous victims. Since Anita Stevens's murder, his department's detectives had tracked down hundreds of leads, interviewed many suspects, and filed reams of reports on their investigation. They were still actively working the cases, but they had run out of leads.

In 1996 Sheriff Perry put together a special task force that would pull all the investigations together. He met with Special Agent Jack Wise, of the Florida Department of Law Enforcement, to enlist that agency's help. The FDLE is an agency established by former Florida governor Lawton Chiles. Its purpose is to provide statewide assistance to individual law enforcement entities within the state and to coordinate crime information into one central unit.

With the involvement of FDLE in the St. Augustine case, information obtained from all sources could now be coordinated under one central unit, while still giving local law enforcement broad latitude in the investigation. FDLE was also available to serve as a buffer if the case became political as sometimes occurs in high-profile cases. (While local sheriffs were elected and vulnerable to some extent to political pressure or public opinion, the FDLE investigators were not.)

Another important function FDLE filled was providing expert analytical help and analysis of criminal intelligence through access to databases and other sophisticated crime-solving tools. With statewide jurisdiction, the FDLE extended the effective range of the local investigators. This linking function was critical in tracking down serial killers, rapists, and child molesters. Without this pooling of information between jurisdictions, isolated crimes in different communities were quite often not recognized as having been committed by the same person. The lack of this kind of information sharing in many states was one of the major reasons why serial murderers often escaped capture for years or, in some cases, were never caught.

Sheriff Perry assigned detectives Frank Welborn and Jennifer Ponce from his Criminal Investigation Division to the task force, plus other resource staff when needed. Law enforcement agencies from adjacent areas were invited to participate, but they were mostly too small to commit their limited personnel full-time to the effort. Special Agent Allen Strickrott played a lead role as FDLE's representative to the task force. One of Strickrott's first functions was to discuss with all concerned parties the strict guidelines FDLE followed in reviewing cold homicide cases from other agencies. Together he and the local law-enforcement personnel discussed what resources would be available to them, what steps had already been taken in the cases, what evidence was available, and how valuable it might prove to be. They also reviewed the suspects and witnesses who had been identified and whether or not they were currently available. Another issue was the legal implications, such as whether the prosecutor involved agreed with reopening the case, and whether or not the statute of limitations might have expired.

Records from all the crimes were collected at task force headquarters and the painstaking job of rechecking informants and alibis began. Information on vehicles that had been spotted during the investigations was gone over. Additional interviews were conducted with the prostitutes and pimps who had known the slain women. Since it was suspected a single killer might be responsible for several or all of the killings, any similarities between the various cases were noted and recorded. Strickrott noted, however, that it was necessary for the investigators to keep an open mind as to whether they were dealing with a single perpetrator or multiple murderers.

The task force was based in a small house near the county office complex, but physically separated from the regular sheriff's office. Here, investigators would focus exclusively on the outstanding murder cases. Detective Jennifer Ponce, a member of the task force, recalled that she and the other detectives who worked in the small, cramped rooms were reminded of their mission each day as they faced photographs of the murder victims posted in their offices. NO CASE IS TOO COLD, a sign on the office wall read.

Detective Ponce, who would play a critical role in the killer's eventual confession, was an attractive, petite, blonde woman, who looked younger than her age. Before joining the task force, she had spent nine years investigating crimes against juveniles, including sex offenders. As a female law-enforcement officer, she had to work harder than the men to prove herself, and no concessions were made to her status as a female. On the other hand, she found that being a woman had some advantages in dealing with suspects, even male suspects. "Men trust women because of their mothering, nurturing aspect," she said. She admitted that she sometimes allowed suspects and witnesses to view her as a "dumb blonde" because in that role she was not an overpowering figure. She felt that another advantage she had as a woman was that "women are more intuitive and quicker to see the nuances in a situation. With men it's often either black or white, no in-between."

Agent Bill Haggerty, of the FBI, assisted the task force in developing a profile on the killer. A profile, like a police composite sketch, was a tool that was used more to eliminate unlikely suspects than to identify the actual perpetrator. Both can help to define investigative boundaries and thus allow detectives to focus on more likely suspects. If a suspect proved to be clearly outside the profile, less time was spent investigating that particular person.

In the six St. Augustine cold cases the profile did not provide much that was helpful. As Sheriff Perry later explained, "There are two types of homicides, and most are what we call smoking gun cases. These are homicides in which the victim and suspect are connected, such as bar fights that end in a death, domestic altercations that lead to murder, murders in which there are witnesses to the act, or there is strong evidence left at the scene. In those types of murders, investigators zero in on the most likely suspect within minutes, hours, or days, and arrests usually follow quickly."

What the St. Johns County Cold Case Homicide Task Force's investigators faced was what Perry referred to as the "Whodunit Homicides." These present far greater problems and, unfortunately, the prostitute cases fell into that category. While investigators could easily determine that a murder had been committed in those cases where they had recovered the victims' bodies, they had found little or no evidence at the scenes and nothing in the manner of killing that provided a significant clue. As the bodies were found partially clothed, it could be assumed that there was a definite sexual element to the crime. But these elements provided no specific connection between the victim and the perpetrator. Also the man had been careful—there were no witnesses.

One type of assistance the Florida Department of Law Enforcement provided to the task force was expert scientific testing. Evidence collected in all the cases was resubmitted for analysis. For instance, in the Anita Stevens case, they rechecked hair and fibers collected at the crime scene. The results of the testing proved inconclusive, as did the testing of the blood found on the leaves and debris at the scene. Anita's blood type O as well as B type from an unknown source were identified. The cost of the testing, for which FDLE used a private lab, Genetic Design, was $1,850. For a small local law enforcement agency, this was a significant sum.

At the time Anita Stevens was murdered, DNA testing was virtually unknown at the local police level. Although DNA, or deoxyribonucleic acid, was first discovered in 1886 and its basic structure determined in 1953, the technology was still in its infancy and was being used mainly in England. Its first use in an American courtroom was in 1986, shortly before Anita was murdered. At that time labs had not yet been set up in the United States. Even had such labs been available, techniques for DNA recovery were primitive at the time. Also, in order to use DNA effectively as a means of identifying perpetrators who may have been captured in jurisdictions other than the one where the crime occurred, national and international databases were needed. Such a database was started in the United Kingdom in 1995, and in 1998 the FBI launched its Combined DNA Index System (CODIS) database.

Basically, DNA is a code, which defines each individual. Every human being, except for identical twins, carries his/her own unique DNA pattern composed of pairs of molecules called bases. The four kinds of bases found in DNA and the manner in which they are arranged determines a genetic code, which is passed down through families from one generation to the next. A person's DNA pattern remains the same from infancy through adulthood. Every white cell in the human body contains DNA and the individual's DNA pattern can be determined from blood, semen, hair follicles, body tissue, saliva, urine, and bone material.

While DNA has currently become a powerful tool in the solution of crimes, such as those committed in St. Augustine, it is more useful at the point where a perpetrator has been identified. At the investigative stage, unless the perpetrator's specimen has been taken at a previous time and entered into a database, it is like fingerprints—valueless as an immediate tool.

As evidence of the thoroughness with which the task force conducted their investigation, a check was made to determine the source of two empty bags labeled FLORIDA TURF FOOD: 16-4-8, collected at Anita's crime scene. Detective Mary LeVeck found that the two bags were produced by Growers First Corporation and that the Ace hardware store on US 1 South was the only local distributor of the product. While this raised the remote possibility that the person who killed Anita worked in landscaping or lawn service, this, too, proved another dead end.

In questioning the murdered women's associates, many of whom were intensely averse to discussing their activities with anyone in law enforcement, task force members faced a massive roadblock. As one informant told Detective LeVeck, "If you live on the street, you associate with people who deal their drugs, which I know people who do. You don't say nothing, you don't open your mouth. You don't go around talking about who you're going out with tonight . . . who you're buying your stuff off of. You keep your mouth shut or you wake up dead." (In questioning people with knowledge of the crimes or possible involvement in them, the authors encountered the same problem.)

For the next several years, the task force would work as a cohesive unit, first to track down the murderer, later to follow the long and tedious investigative trail that would enable prosecutors to build their legal case against him. In the process they would endure long hours and undertake many tedious tasks. But their focus was always on their goal—get the monster off the street before he struck again.

Chapter 14

December 1996:
Asheville, North Carolina

On Thursday, December 26, Jack Shelton left his home on Chunns Cove Road in Asheville, North Carolina, heading out for his customary morning walk with his dog, Bowzer. The weather had turned cold, but no rain or snow was falling. Bowzer, a mixed-breed terrier, followed his usual pattern, stopping to sniff at every interesting scent along the way. Their walk took them toward where the road dead-ended, the regular route for their morning stroll. As they tramped along, the only sound besides leaves crunching underfoot was the tinkling murmur of the small stream that meandered alongside the roadway, ultimately passing through a nearby culvert that supplied water to a large duck pond, with gazebo-enhanced islands in its center.

On this particular morning as they approached the pond, something near the concrete culvert caught Bowzer's attention. He gave a sharp tug on his leash, forcing Shelton to focus his attention in that direction. Shelton spotted what he at first thought might be the tennis shoes and jeans-clad legs of a child trying to wriggle his way into the culvert. *Probably some kid fooling around,* he thought, and tugged Bowzer away.

But some backup instinct told him this was no youngster at play. He moved closer to get a better look. Whoever—or whatever—it was had not moved. Apprehensive, he stepped a bit closer to the culvert.

What he found stopped him in his tracks, too shocked at first to comprehend fully what he was seeing. Disbelief turned to horror when he realized the object in front of him was the motionless body of a woman. She was lying facedown in the stream, fully clothed. Her dark, wavy hair drifted down across the shoulders of her jean jacket and into the flow of the stream.

Soon police and emergency vehicles with sirens screaming shattered the morning peace as they raced toward the scene in response to Jack Shelton's 911 call. Detective John Harrison, of the Buncombe County CID, heard the announcement on his police radio that a woman's body had been found beside Chunns Cove Road. Harrison, who would become the lead investigator on the case, immediately headed to the location the dispatcher had indicated. Arriving there, he saw a fully clothed woman's body lying in the middle of a small stream that flowed through a culvert under the roadway.

A small crowd of neighbors gathered and watched anxiously as the area near the duck pond soon became a scene of intense activity. The North Carolina Highway Patrol, an ambulance, and crime specialists from the sheriff's office arrived with lights flashing. Emergency medical technicians quickly determined that the woman was dead and had been so for some hours. The roadway, culvert, and nearby woods were quickly cordoned off. Some of the law enforcement officers questioned Shelton while others knelt to sift through the leaf-strewn area surrounding the body.

Soon camera flashes lit the grim crime scene as investigators began shooting pictures of the body and the surrounding area. Crime scene specialists began collecting evidence, including impressions from tire marks that had been left in the muddy soil near the body.

After the area had been photographed and thoroughly examined, the body was removed from the stream and turned faceup. Wound marks on the woman's face and head raised further suspicions about the cause of death. Although there were no immediately visible signs of trauma, from the beginning it was suspected that the death was not of natural causes.

Initially it appeared that the woman was possibly the victim of a hit-and-run accident. The coroner's examination later indicated that she had suffered severe blows to the head and her neck had been broken. The injuries appeared to be as the result of a beating, rather than the type of trauma generally found in car accident victims. As soon as it became clear that this was a homicide rather than a traffic incident, the North Carolina Highway Patrol withdrew from the case.

Finally the ambulance bore the body away and the onlookers dispersed. But for Detective John Harrison, the work was just beginning, the painstaking task of linking a murderer to his crime.

The medical examiner's office determined that the woman had been killed late Christmas night or in the early-morning hours of the following day. A search of her clothing revealed her identity—an uncashed Wendy's payroll check in the pocket of her jean jacket bore the name of Lucy Arnett Raymer.

The mountain town of Asheville, North Carolina lay nestled between the Blue Ridge Mountains and the Great Smokies. In summer the area's cool climate of-

fered a welcome retreat for heat-weary Southerners
whose summer cottages and vacation homes dotted
the forested hillsides surrounding the town. Visitors
also flocked to the area for its natural beauty and
splendid opportunities for outdoor activities, such as
hiking, fishing, rafting, and golf. The nearby Blue
Ridge Parkway offered some of the most scenic vistas
in the eastern United States, and the Biltmore Estate,
a French Renaissance château that was home to
George Vanderbilt, has also drawn thousands of visitors each year. Arts and crafts abound in the area, and
it's an antique lover's delight.

But even this charming town, with its natural beauty
and its historic past, was not immune to the nefarious
influence of drugs and prostitution. And, as was true
in St. Augustine, these activities provided an ideal setting for a serial killer to find and stalk his victims.

The city of Asheville is the county seat for Buncombe
County. The county once encompassed a much larger
area than it now does, stretching from the South Carolina border to the Tennessee line. Today it consists of
646 square miles and is under the jurisdiction of the
Buncombe County Sheriff's Office, headed by Sheriff
Bobby L. Medford.

Serious crimes have been an anomaly here as compared to large metropolitan areas. Buncombe County,
with a population of 205,700, had only seven murders
in the year 2000, with the majority of crimes being larceny and theft. Nevertheless, citizens of the area
enjoyed the protection of a fully staffed professional
law-enforcement agency. When Buncombe County
sheriff Bobby Medford received word that a body had
been found on Chunns Cove Road, he immediately
activated the staff of his Criminal Investigations Division (CID). This division consisted of a captain, who
handled administrative tasks and made all final decisions, his assistant, a lieutenant, three sergeants, each

of whom handled a different area of criminal investigations, and sixteen detectives. In addition, there was support staff in the form of record and property clerks and office staff.

When Sergeant John Harrison, of the CID, received the coroner's report, it verified that Lucy Raymer had died from severe blows to the temporal area of her brain and the sinus areas of her face. As photographs taken at the crime scene revealed, her face was swollen and distorted from the beating she had received.

In checking with Donna Chandler, one of the dead woman's neighbors, Harrison learned that Raymer, although caught in the web of drugs and prostitution, had been a pleasant, generous person, well liked by those who knew her. Chandler described Lucy as an attractive thirty-two-year-old woman, with dark hair and a warm, ready smile.

Donna Chandler presented detectives with a touching description of her last visit with Lucy Raymer. She said that Lucy had arrived at her home on Christmas Eve, excited about the coming holiday. "This year we're going to have a real Christmas," Lucy told Donna, adding that she had spent $240 on presents for her children and her husband, Stan. Donna knew that Lucy's statement about a "real Christmas" was a reference to the year before when Raymer had used the money intended for her children's Christmas presents to buy crack cocaine.

At one point during her visit, Raymer handed Donna a package she was carrying, saying it was a present for Donna from Stan and herself. Donna protested that Lucy shouldn't have bought her anything, but Lucy smiled and insisted she open it. When Donna unwrapped the box, she found it contained a brand-new portable telephone. Half fearful of where Lucy had obtained the money to buy the phone, Donna nevertheless thanked her friend and gave her a warm hug.

Lucy then asked Donna if she might borrow a large kettle, as she was planning to make a pot of chicken soup. Donna put the gift phone down in order to search through her kitchen cupboards. She found the kettle and offered it to Lucy, who promised to return it the following day. Lucy wished Donna, "Merry Christmas," then picked up the kettle and headed out the door. "I'll bring the kettle back tomorrow," she promised. That, Donna Chandler said, was the last time she had seen her neighbor.

Chandler told detectives it was a puzzle to her how a person as pleasant as Lucy could allow herself to become hooked on a $100-a-day crack habit. Donna also noted that Lucy's drug use had created much turmoil, with trips to the emergency room the times she overdosed and revolving-door stays in drug rehab programs. She was also aware that when Lucy's craving got the better of her, she prostituted herself. "She got like that, she would hang out down on Lexington Street and pick up strange men," Chandler reported.

Investigators also learned from Donna that for the past couple of months Lucy Raymer had been trying hard to stay on the right track and seemed to be feeling better about herself. "She and Stan seemed to be getting along better," Donna said. She credited the fact that Lucy was holding a steady job at the nearby Wendy's restaurant as being responsible for the improvement in their relationship. Donna stated that for all her weaknesses, Lucy was a good neighbor and a kind and generous soul.

Accounts of the murder began appearing the following day in the local newspaper. In the meantime detectives had learned that Raymer, like most prostitutes and addicts, had a police record. Hers included twelve charges for crimes, including forgery, shoplift-

ing, and false identification. They also inquired of
local taxi drivers if they had any knowledge of who
might have committed the murder.

On Sunday, December 29, at 10:30 A.M., four days
after Lucy Raymer's death, a call came into the sheriff's office from a taxi driver, John Pearson. Pearson
told Detective Harrison he had read about the murder in the paper and wanted to discuss it. Immediately
Harrison had him come into the station. Pearson explained that he had recognized Lucy Raymer's
newspaper photo from previous times he had had her
as a passenger in his cab. Furthermore, on the night
of the murder, he had driven Lucy to a small trailer in
Taps RV and Mobile Home Park on Tunnel Road in
the nearby town of Oteen. On the way Lucy had told
him that she and her husband weren't living together
(an obvious lie) and that she stayed at the trailer park
with a man named William Lindsey. Pearson said that
when they arrived at the trailer, Lucy asked him to
wait while she went inside to get cab fare for him.
When she returned, she gave him the money and
kissed him on the cheek. He wished her a merry
Christmas and left.

After noting Pearson's information, Harrison took
the informant to Taps RV Park in his police car.
There, Pearson pointed out a small travel trailer
parked near the entrance and park office. He indicated that was the location where he had dropped
Raymer off the previous evening. Leaving Pearson
in the parked police car, Harrison approached the
trailer. As he did so, a man emerged from its door.
The frowzy-appearing middle-aged man at first
stared suspiciously at the officer. Harrison noted
that his clothing was rumpled and his graying brown
hair was uncombed. The detective identified himself and the man admitted to being William Lindsey.
Harrison explained that he wanted to talk to him

about Lucy Raymer. Lindsey seemed unperturbed and agreed to accompany Harrison back to the station. Upon entering the police car, Lindsey did not appear to recognize Pearson, who was in the passenger seat. However, when they arrived at the station and he spotted Pearson's cab in the parking lot, he suddenly put two and two together. Harrison recalled that at this point Lindsey's ashen countenance made it obvious he realized he was in serious trouble.

Harrison administered Lindsey his rights as contained in the Miranda warnings. In a 1966 case the U.S. Supreme Court ruled that any person suspected of a crime must be informed before his arrest that he had the right to remain silent, and to be represented by legal counsel. He must also be told that anything he said may be used against him in court. This was particularly crucial as the suspect later admitted to the crime in question. Without previous advisal as to his rights, the confession could have been declared invalid and any evidence obtained as a result of the confession ruled inadmissible in court. Where the Miranda left a gray area was in responses a person made *before* he/she was considered a prime suspect. In the Lindsey case this would later become a critical issue.

While the wording of the Miranda waiver varied from one jurisdiction to another, the one the Buncombe County Sheriff's Department used with Lindsey included the standard clauses:

1. You have the right to remain silent and not make any statements.
2. Anything you say can be used against you in court.
3. You have the right to have an attorney and have him present during questioning. (Note: Fourteen-to-seventeen-year olds have the right to a parent, guardian, or custodian present during question-

ing. Thirteen-year-olds or under *must* have a parent, guardian, or custodian present.)
4. If you cannot afford an attorney, the court will appoint one for you before questioning if you wish.
5. If you decide to answer questions now without an attorney, you still have the right to stop answering and remain silent, or consult an attorney.

Below the line reading, I HAVE READ AND UNDERSTOOD MY RIGHTS, OR HAVE HAD THEM READ AND EXPLAINED TO ME, AND I KNOW WHAT I AM DOING, Lindsey signed the form. He signed a second time under the line reading, AFTER HAVING BEEN ADVISED OF MY RIGHTS, I NOW KNOWINGLY WAIVE MY RIGHTS AND I AM WILLING TO MAKE A STATEMENT. NO THREATS OR PROMISES OF COERCION HAVE BEEN USED AGAINST ME TO INDUCE ME TO WAIVE MY RIGHTS.

Following the Miranda procedure, during two hours of interrogation, primarily by Sergeant Harrison, Lindsey confessed to disposing of Lucy Raymer's body. However, he attempted to portray her death as an accident.

According to his account at that time, Raymer had arrived at his trailer between 5:00 and 5:30 P.M. She asked for money to pay the cab fare, and he reported that he gave her $15, $11 for the fare and $4 for a tip. After the taxi left, Raymer asked Lindsey to take her to buy more dope. He said that he took her to a housing project near Mission Memorial Hospital and gave her $100 for Christmas and another $100 to have sex with him. According to him, she spent the entire amount on crack cocaine.

After their return to his trailer, Lindsey claimed they sat and talked for a few minutes, then went into the bedroom and had sex. Afterward, Lucy smoked some crack. Lindsey said he went to bed about 9:30 and she came into the bedroom between 10:00 and 11:00 P.M. They both went to sleep, but he wakened around 2:00

A.M., rolled over, and put his arm around her. "She was very cold and I could not hear her breathing," he told the detective. "I thought she was dead and I got scared." He explained away her obvious injuries by saying, "When I picked her up to take her to my van, I dropped her." After putting her into his blue Ford Bronco, he drove to the end of Chunns Cove Road—"the first road I could find." When he reached the road's dead end, he turned back and dropped Raymer's body near a duck pond.

Following Lindsey's admission to having disposed of Raymer's body in that fashion, a search warrant was issued for his trailer. Among the evidence collected there was a crudely drawn map showing where he had left Raymer's body.

Detective Harrison showed Lindsey explicit photographs of Raymer's autopsy, but the man displayed no emotion or remorse. However, with evidence collected at the crime scene, including blood samples, Harrison felt there was ample reason to hold him for further investigation.

Twelve days after the murder, at 11:25 P.M. on Monday, January 6, while incarcerated in Buncombe County Detention Center, Lindsey asked to talk to Sheriff Bobby Medford. At that time he changed his previous statement. He now claimed that Lucy Raymer stole $200 from him and would not give it back, although he asked her for it several times. When she refused, he got angry and punched her in the face. "I didn't think I hit her that hard," he said. "I didn't mean to hurt her that bad."

That December morning when Detective John Harrison of the sheriff's department, knocked on the door of William Lindsey's 1992 Hy-Line trailer, he had no idea that he had come face-to-face with a vicious serial murderer, a man who had managed for several decades to kill and kill again without being identified or caught. Nor did he know that the trail of bodies the killer had left behind would stretch from Asheville, North Carolina, through Tennessee and Virginia, all the way to historic St. Augustine, Florida, some six hundred miles to the south. For Harrison, deeply involved with his home community of Asheville, this case would be the capstone of a distinguished career in law enforcement. It would also be the beginning of a lifelong friendship with two fellow officers he had yet to meet.

For the man who had killed Lucy Raymer, the shroud of anonymity that had allowed him to prey undetected upon countless other women was about to unravel.

Chapter 15

Christmas Card Redux

On the day Lucy Raymer's body was discovered, Fred Thompson was driving through Asheville on his way home to Marshall, North Carolina. The flashing lights of a group of police cars and emergency vehicles caught his attention. With his law enforcement background—he had been a part-time deputy when he lived in St. Augustine, Florida—he was unable to resist the urge to find out what was happening. He followed the vehicles to Chunns Cove Road and the site where Lucy Raymer's body had been discovered. After observing the police action at the scene for a time, he continued on home.

Some days later Thompson read in the *Asheville Citizen Times* that a murder suspect in the case had been arrested and charged with the crime. The newspaper's biographical sketch of the suspect indicated he was from St. Augustine, Florida, and that his name was William Lindsey.

By an odd coincidence Anita Stevens's parents, Melvin and Mildred McQuaig, had kept in touch with Fred Thompson and his wife since they had moved from St. Augustine. Some years after Anita's murder, the McQuaigs had visited with Fred and Marie Thompson at their home in Marshall, North Carolina. During the course of the visit, the McQuaigs discussed their daughter's murder and their frustration that her killer had never been found.

When Thompson spotted the article about Lindsey's arrest, he was struck by the similarity of Lucy Raymer's killing to that of Anita and the other St. Augustine victims. Consequently, when he sent out his annual Christmas card to Sheriff Perry, he included the clipping. But it is doubtful that at that juncture even Thompson realized the massive police investigation that would be set into motion by this bit of newsprint.

Chapter 16

The Task Force
Meets the Killer

In early January 1997 Sheriff Neil Perry, head of law enforcement for St. Johns County, Florida, finally found time to read his Christmas mail. When he slit open the envelope with a North Carolina postmark, he expected to find the usual Christmas greetings from his former deputy Fred Thompson, now living in Marshall, North Carolina. But when he opened the card, with its bright holiday design, a piece of newsprint fell out, a clipping from the *Asheville Citizen Times* regarding a murder that had been committed there. In the last paragraph of the article, the reporter noted that the perpetrator, a William Darrell Lindsey, had once lived in St. Augustine.

At this point eight years had passed since Anita Stevens's murder, with Sheriff Perry's department continuing to struggle through a morass of investigations that seemed to lead nowhere. Five more women had fallen victim with no solid leads to their killer. The Cold Case Homicide Task Force had followed up eight hundred tips and interviewed fifty people in a total of eighty separate sessions without producing a viable suspect. The crime scenes had

yielded little physical evidence, and no witnesses
had come forward.

And now the sheriff held in his hands a few scant
columns of newsprint that offered only a vague suggestion of any connection to the killer his office had been
pursuing for so long. Aware that this could be just another blind alley in the investigation, Perry nevertheless
decided the information was worth following up.

He immediately contacted Sheriff Bobby Medford
in Asheville and received from him more detailed
information regarding the Lucy Raymer murder.
Recognizing that the similarities between that case
and his own unsolved cases might be more than co-
incidental, Perry relayed this information to
Detective Sergeant Frank Welborn, of the St. Johns
County Cold Case Homicide Task Force.

Welborn, a seasoned police officer, was a man who
thought and felt a lot more than he talked. He had
the looks and some of the characteristics of the
movie sheriff, the "good guy" who rides into town
and cleans out the viper's nest of "bad guys," all the
while maintaining a cool and stoic exterior. From
childhood Welborn aspired to be a policeman. He
started as a volunteer with the Jacksonville Sheriff's
Office, remaining in that capacity for three years
before transferring to the St. Johns County Sheriff's
Office. Now as coleader of the task force, he was
being offered the first clue to the mysterious killer
who had evaded the law for so long.

The first step Welborn took was to run William
Darrell Lindsey in the computer and obtain his criminal history. That history revealed Lindsey's arrest
for aggravated assault in 1974 and reported his having been the victim of car theft and burglary from
1993 to 1996. He was also listed as a suspect in a battery charge filed by Yvonne Burnett Brooks. This
seemed a rather slim criminal record for a possible

suspect in seven murders. However, Welborn followed up by contacting the Buncombe County Sheriff's Department and asked to talk with the officer handling the case, Sergeant John Harrison. At the time Welborn and Harrison were unaware of how close their professional and personal relationship was about to become.

The two officers discussed details of the murder of Lucy Raymer in Asheville. Harrison also told Welborn that he was looking at Lindsey for several other murders in the Asheville area.

Their discussion revealed considerable similarity between these crimes and the murders the Florida task force had been investigating. It was decided there was enough suspicion of Lindsey to justify sending the task force's two lead investigators, Sergeant Welborn and Special Agent Allen Strickrott, of the Florida Department of Law Enforcement, to Asheville to interview Lindsey. The fact that Detective John Harrison had successfully elicited a confession from Lindsey in the Lucy Raymer case assured that Lindsey would be confined in jail indefinitely and therefore available for questioning and additional investigation regarding the killings in Florida.

Following his confession to Lucy Raymer's murder, Lindsey was incarcerated at Buncombe County Detention Center in Asheville. This structure, new in 1994, allowed the jail to be separated from the courthouse. The 149,000-square-foot detention facility, located in downtown Asheville, was designed to house up to 356 inmates. Lindsey was held on the fourth floor, an area reserved for inmates accused of serious crimes.

While held there, Lindsey was served breakfast at 6:00 A.M., lunch at 11:00 A.M. and dinner at 4:00 P.M. During the six hours per day that inmates were allowed out of their cells, he could watch television, shower, or talk with other inmates. He was allowed to have up to five visitors on specified visiting days. A commissary store, open on Sundays, gave him the opportunity to purchase such items as aspirin, crackers, and sodas.

On January 13, 1997, Welborn and Strickrott arrived in Asheville, North Carolina, cautiously optimistic that they might find some answers to the murders they were investigating. Before meeting with Lindsey, the investigators spent most of a day reviewing and comparing all the cases that Detective Harrison and Sheriff Bobby Medford had unearthed. Two detectives from Virginia were also there, since in addition to the Raymer case, similar murders had occurred in Virginia and Tennessee as well as in Florida. Detective Harrison told the assembled investigators that Sheriff Medford had established good rapport with William Lindsey and that he would speak with Lindsey and find out if he was willing to talk with them. At about 4:00 P.M. that day, the group adjourned to the Buncombe County Jail.

The detectives from Virginia went in first and completed their questioning. At about 6:00 P.M. Welborn and Strickrott had their first meeting with Lindsey. Sheriff Medford had Lindsey brought to the conference room, introduced the detectives to him; Lindsey, dressed in prison garb, appeared outwardly calm, although the detectives perceived a hidden wariness. Medford asked Lindsey if he needed anything. Lindsey requested coffee and it was brought to him, then Sheriff Medford left the three men alone.

The investigators' first step was to read Lindsey his Miranda rights, which he stated he understood and signed. They also warned Lindsey that he was not to discuss the North Carolina case with them.

Strickrott and Welborn had agreed that their first step should be to try to prove Lindsey innocent. While this may initially seem an ironic approach, it was, in fact, an effective way to rule out innocent suspects in order to focus on the guilty individual.

The goal in the initial interview with Lindsey was to get some idea of his personality and to establish a rapport with him. To achieve this, they began by asking seemingly innocuous questions about such areas as his family history, his marriages, places of residence, past jobs, education, vehicles he had owned, and other such data. Lindsey spoke freely about his two marriages, his children, and his second wife's death from cancer. He stated that he was born in Palatka and also gave details of his childhood in St. Augustine, his adoptive family, his schooling, including his years at Ketterlinus High School, and his subsequent work record.

He mentioned his early employment at Pulling Typewriter Company and the various jobs he had held over the years. He told of having moved to Virginia, then back to Palatka, Florida, in 1989, and of his work for Barron Oil Company and Davey Tree Company, among others. He also discussed his frequent moves back and forth from Asheville to Palatka, with side trips to visit his children in Ocala. The detectives noted in particular that he had moved frequently, and he had never held any job for very long.

When Welborn and Strickrott focused on the weekend of October 14 and 15, 1995, the time of Diana Richardson's murder, Lindsey claimed he had been visiting a Missy Lake, who was incarcerated in jail in Ocala at that time. He claimed that he had driven straight from his trailer in Oteen, North Carolina, to Ocala, visited Missy twice, spent the night at his daughter's house in Ocala, then drove straight home to North Carolina.

In gathering this information, the investigators were obtaining facts and establishing times that they planned to check and verify when they returned to St. Augustine. In this way they could establish whether or not Lindsey was being honest with them. This also gave them the opportunity to compare times and places the women had been killed with Lindsey's whereabouts at those times. In addition, they could compare evidence and witnesses' statements with his account.

Throughout the interview Lindsey insisted adamantly on his innocence, asserting that he had no criminal history, "not so much as a parking ticket in Florida.

"I was brought up to do the right thing," he told the two detectives. "If I made a mistake, I would generally own up to it." He appeared cordial throughout the interview, and, on the surface, cooperative. The following day he signed a statement to the effect that he had been informed he was the subject of a criminal investigation in St. Augustine, Florida, involving at least four females. He also acknowledged that he had been informed of his constitutional rights to an attorney, which he waived. In addition, he gave permission for a licensed practical nurse from the Buncombe County Detention facility to draw a blood sample for DNA testing by Florida's Department of Law Enforcement.

In a statement that would later prove crucial, he declared that Special Agent Allen Strickrott of Florida Department of Law Enforcement and Sergeant Frank Welborn of St. Johns County, Florida, Sheriff's Office had properly identified themselves as sworn police officers in taking his statement.

The document was signed by Lindsey and witnessed by Sheriff Bobby Medford, Detective Frank Welborn, and Jennifer Parkham, the LPN who drew the blood sample.

During the time Welborn and Strickrott were in Asheville, the Buncombe County Sheriff's Department had obtained a search warrant for Lindsey's travel trailer. The warrant was served at 7:00 P.M. on January 15 at Tapp's RV Campground on Tunnel Road in Asheville. Several items obtained in the search were given to Welborn and Strickrott as possibly relevant to the Florida cases. These included miscellaneous business papers, personal letters, income tax returns, employment records, vehicle purchase records, and firearms purchase records. In comparing these records with some of the statements Lindsey had just given to the investigators, it was evident he had not been entirely truthful in the interview.

By the time Strickrott and Welborn left Asheville, they had accomplished their goal of establishing a rapport that would allow further questioning without arousing Lindsey's antagonism. They felt cautiously optimistic that they had perhaps found the killer they were looking for, but they withheld judgment on that issue until they could check further into Lindsey's background.

Chapter 17

A Long Investigation Begins

An air of cautious excitement filled task force head-quarters. They were a long way from a conviction, but at last they had something they could get their teeth into—plus a mountain of work to be accomplished before that end would be achieved.

With a suspect in mind and samples of his blood, the investigators were now in a position to reexamine the evidence collected from the crime scenes of his suspected victims. For instance, the pink shorts Anita Stevens had been wearing at the time of her murder had shown evidence of bloodstains. They were sent along with other evidence, containing blood samples such as fingernail scrapings, palm fronds, leaves, grass, and tree branches, to Florida Department of Law Enforcement's Crime Laboratory's Serology Section for analysis. When compared with Lindsey's blood, the shorts and vegetation yielded a positive presumptive result, although the semen test conducted on them was inconclusive. The vegetation, especially the palm fronds, were tested for the presence of flesh from Anita, who had clung to the fronds and underbrush as she tried desperately to elude her killer.

In similar fashion evidence from each of the crime

scenes was rescreened and reevaluated. Unfortunately, some of the materials had deteriorated with time, making them useless for analysis. It appeared that if investigators were to build a solid case against William Lindsey, they would have to delve deeply into his background and his movements over the past decade. To this end they began putting together a meticulous timeline, detailing his jobs, his rental records, his vehicle registrations, his telephone records, income tax returns, bank records, pawnshop tickets, and any other recorded evidence of his whereabouts. With these data they could reconstruct a picture of where he had been and when. This difficult undertaking would consume members of the task force for the next several months.

In addition, they faced the major undertaking of putting together Lindsey's family history. A critical question that is always raised in regard to a serial killer is where and how his aberration began. Is a murderer born with the instinct to kill or is he shaped by the circumstances of his upbringing, his environment? In the case of William Darrell Lindsey, it would seem that fate played a significant role, beginning in infancy when a bizarre accident snatched him from his natural parents.

Lindsey, investigators discovered, was born in Palatka, Florida, on March 18, 1935, to William and Mabel Armstrong. Twenty-eight-year-old William Armstrong was a roofer and his wife, the former Mabel Fowler, was a homemaker. Five months after their son's birth, on August 18, 1935, the Armstrongs were driving in their car with their infant son in the backseat when, for unknown reasons, their car careered off the roadway and crashed. A Clay County deputy cruising the highway on routine patrol near the town of Palatka noticed the wrecked vehicle partly hidden by underbrush. He stopped his car and walked over to peer through the shattered windshield of the small sedan. He saw two badly mangled bodies there, a man and a woman. Neither was moving. After forcing the door open, he checked for vital signs, aware even before he did so that both of the car's occupants were dead.

The deputy returned to his patrol car, intending to report the accident to headquarters when he was shocked to hear what sounded like an infant's cry. He raced back to the wrecked vehicle and found a tiny baby on the floor, wedged between the front seat and backseat. Except for some slight scratches and a bruise or two, the infant showed no visible evidence of serious injury.

By a strange coincidence, in the nearby town of St. Augustine, another couple, Cecil and Olean Lindsey, had recently been grief-stricken by the loss of an infant son. Hearing of the orphaned Armstrong child, they applied to adopt him. Their application was approved and the adopted infant was given the name William Darrell Lindsey, called Billy.

The Lindsey family lived in St. Augustine on Sylvan Drive, in an area of town referred to locally as "North City." North City consisted at that time of mostly modest homes, except where the streets extended to the Tolomato River; the waterfront residences were usually more imposing there. The Lindseys' house, a story-and-a-half frame bungalow located on a narrow lot, was one of the smaller, less impressive ones.

In addition to their newly adopted son, the Lindseys had three other children—James, Sue Alice, and Verna. Cecil Lindsey, Billy's adoptive father, was a large, gregarious man, well liked by those with whom he worked and socialized. In his early career Cecil was employed as an appliance salesman and the driver of a laundry truck, but the job he held longest—and enjoyed most—was playing the role of the Spanish explorer Ponce de León at St. Augustine's Fountain of Youth, a nationally known tourist attraction. The fountain purports to be the mythical source of eternal youth, which Ponce de León was seeking in his expedition through Florida. Cecil Lindsey, fully costumed in the military regalia of the period, would delight tourists with tales about the explorer and assurances that a sip of the vile-tasting sulphur water from the fountain would insure that they would remain forever young. Cecil's engaging manner made him a favorite of both the tourists and his coworkers.

Olean Lindsey, Billy's adoptive mother, was a complex and deeply pious woman, her personality the antithesis of her husband's friendly, outgoing nature. Her Calvinistic convictions included belief in the total depravity of man and that humans possess no will of their own. Her religious piety manifested itself in her puritanical views and intolerance for human frailty. She viewed normal childish misbehavior as sinful and saw it as her religious duty to punish the perpetrator. She persistently used the threat of hell and eternal damnation as a way to control her children. Whatever the situation, she self-righteously proclaimed her viewpoint to be correct and rarely admitted any failings or fault on her part.

Those who lived near the Lindseys and knew them well spoke highly of Cecil during the authors' interviews with them. However, when asked about Olean, without exception their comments were negative—"She was a hellion, mean as a snake. Thought everyone was no good." "Meanest woman I ever knew in my life." "She was tough—a screamer and a yeller."

Every Sunday the entire family attended nearby Ancient City Baptist Church. They arrived early and, with Olean in the lead, took seats in the front row. When the sermon ended, they left immediately, assuring that everyone would notice their presence as they departed. When at home from her job as a practical nurse at Flagler Hospital, Olean would pace through the house singing hymns. When her daughter Sue Alice took piano lessons, she was allowed to play nothing but religious music.

It was very possible that Olean sincerely believed that her pious pronouncements and stern child-rearing practices were in accordance with God's will. During this period many parents, especially those reared in the Fundamentalist tradition, adhered to such Calvinistic principles of parenting. However, even by those standards, Olean would have to be judged as a physically and emotionally abusive parent.

The Lindsey home, which Billy entered as an infant, was run like a prison, in many respects, with frequent beatings and extreme restrictions imposed on the children's activities. During their preschool and elementary-school years, they were limited to playing only in their own yard, despite the fact that the modest, small-town neighborhood was quite safe, with no heavily traveled streets nearby. Other children were rarely permitted to come onto the Lindsey premises during these early years. Later, when the Lindsey children reached adolescence, a cowbell hung on the front porch was used to summon them home. Failure to return immediately when it rang resulted in punishment.

Olean was quick to administer harsh physical penalties for even small infractions. On at least one occasion, Billy was beaten so badly by his mother that he had welts all over his body and had to remain home from school. His punishments included beatings with everything from a frying pan to a leather strap, as well as having his hair pulled and being pinched.

Unfortunately for little Billy Lindsey, the family he

had entered was a matriarchy headed by Olean, with Cecil assuming a more subservient role. As a consequence Billy's adoptive mother assumed complete control of the child rearing and all matters involving the home, while Cecil's attention focused on his job and other community activities. If Cecil bore any responsibility for the treatment of the children, it was not because he participated but because he did not intercede on their behalf.

James, the oldest child, was Olean's favorite. She took great pride in the tall, good-looking youngster; consequently he escaped much of the abuse she inflicted on her other children. James went on to become an air traffic controller and is now retired and living in Orlando.

Sue Alice, one of the two girls in the family, was also an attractive child. However, she was more resistant than James to her mother's puritanical rules. As she grew into her teens, Sue Alice rejected her mother's efforts to dominate her. During this period Sue Alice took a liking to a young TV repairman. Since her mother strictly forbade her to date, she would wait until her mother was out of the house, then break the TV in some small way so that the repairman would be called to fix it. Carrying her rebellion to the ultimate, Sue Alice became pregnant out of wedlock as a result of a liaison with a sailor from nearby Green Cove Springs. A friend, not aware of this, once asked Olean how Sue Alice was doing. "I have no daughter named Sue Alice" was Olean's abrupt response. Sue Alice later married the sailor. She died of cancer while still a relatively young woman.

Verna, the youngest of the Lindsey three natural children, coped better than Sue Alice with Olean's restrictions and harsh discipline. Verna strongly resembled her mother physically, which probably endeared her to Olean. A compliant child, she received less abuse than Billy and Sue Alice. Of the four children raised under the Lindseys' roof, Verna and James followed the more conventional paths in adulthood than those Billy and Sue Alice adopted.

Billy became a sort of male Cinderella, a scapegoat who bore the brunt of the punishment his mother so readily administered. Small and thin as a child, he was not strong enough to protect himself from his mother or, later, from bullies in the neighborhood and at school. Sue Alice often felt sorry for him and did her best to divert her mother's anger, but to little avail. Billy thus grew up terrified of the woman upon whom he was the most dependent.

In the opinion of those who grew up near Billy and attended school with him, he had average to low-average intelligence, a C student. Lacking self-confidence as a teenager, his manner was one of meekness and obsequious efforts to please others. He had no close friends and was a loner, often teased by his peers. Unlike most other boys in the neighborhood, he played no high-school sports and showed no interest in athletics or other extracurricular activities. Consequently many who grew up near him were hardly aware of his presence and few of his schoolmates even remembered him.

High-school yearbook photos show Billy as a pleasant-appearing, neatly dressed young man. His shyness and his family situation prevented his participating in much of the social life of his teenage peers. Like all the Lindsey children, he held a job during his teen years, in Billy's case as a busboy in a local restaurant. Because he was a bit slow in school, he had been held back several times. By age twenty-one he still had not graduated, although he was in his senior year.

Two disturbing reports surface from his early years: he was said to have killed one cat and tortured others, and he was also rumored to have set fire to a hut that a group of neighborhood boys had built. Cruelty to animals and fire setting are behaviors frequently seen in the histories of serial killers. The physical and emotional abuse Billy received from early childhood through his teens and the teasing he endured from his peers are other factors prevalent in the backgrounds of many, if not most, serial killers.

Considering his overall treatment in the Lindsey household, it was understandable that Lindsey inevitably developed into someone with a huge reservoir of pent-up anger and hostility toward women. Although many young men who endure such childhood trauma do not become serial killers, a disproportionate number of such killers display the same history of abuse and abusive behavior that characterized Billy as a teenager. However, no one who knew him at the time or even later in life ever predicted he would be violent, much less a serial killer.

At age twenty-one Billy experienced one of the most traumatic episodes of his entire life. At that time he came into a significant inheritance from his deceased natural parents, assets that had been held in the form of a trust for over twenty years. It was only then that Olean informed him he was not her natural son but had been adopted. Stunned by the revelation that Cecil and Olean were not his natural parents, he was further astounded by her demand that he must use his inheritance to repay her for all the years he had lived in her home. When he refused to give her the money, a tumultuous scene occurred, during which she screamed at him, "Well, what do you think I adopted and raised you for anyway?"

Devastated and furious, Billy struck Olean for the first time in his life. Soon after, he left home.

Once freed from the repressive environment of the Lindsey household and in possession of some money,

Billy began to evolve, like Sue Alice, into an adult who totally renounced the values Olean had attempted to drill into him. Although as an adult William Lindsey certainly did not lead what could be termed a religious life, the concepts so deeply ingrained in him as a child stayed with him, even though they had little direct influence on his behavior. At various times during his adult life, he attended church. When he and his family were in debt, he often appealed to the church to help feed and clothe his children. It is unclear whether his church attendance was motivated by his religious faith or the financial benefits he sought from the church or both.

In 1956 at age twenty-one, Lindsey left Ketterlinus High School and St. Augustine. After a short period of employment by Pulling Typewriter Company, he moved some twenty-eight miles away to Palatka, a small farming community on the banks of the St. Johns River. This town of seven thousand to eight thousand residents was where he would meet both his wives, and where he would spend most of his adult life, punctuated by shorter periods of time when he lived in Virginia, Tennessee, and North Carolina. It was also from this town and nearby Hastings that he would later make his forays into St. Augustine in search of prostitutes.

Palatka has had an interesting history. Its name comes from the Seminole Indian word, *Pilo-taikita*, meaning "cow ford" or "cow crossing." In 1774 William Bartram, a naturalist, arrived by boat at an Indian settlement on the banks of the broad St. Johns River. He found that the Native Americans had taken advantage of the area's rich soil to grow corn, beans, potatoes, pumpkins, squashes, melons, oranges, and tobacco.

The fertile soil and dense forests of the surrounding region soon attracted farmers and other settlers. In time the town developed as a small trading center. The establishment of a ferry service across the St. Johns River provided access to North Florida's coastal regions, including the town of St. Augustine, twenty-five miles to the east. By the early part of the nineteenth century, both steamship and railroad service connected the town with major cities up and down the Atlantic Coast. In the post–Civil War era, Palatka flourished with new hotels and tourist accommodations for visitors from the North, who swelled the town's population each winter.

This period of growth and prosperity ended abruptly with the Great Fire of 1884, which destroyed much of Palatka's business district. In that same period unusually heavy winter freezes wiped out the citrus crops and damaged agriculture. The inclement weather also had a devastating effect on the tourist business. Shortly thereafter, Henry Flagler bypassed the town in the process of extending his railroad to cities farther south along Florida's east coast. With that, Palatka's hopes for recovery were doomed. By the middle of the 1950s, there was little to attract newcomers or tourists to Palatka. Many of the stores along Main Street had closed, and the one surviving hotel had fallen into disuse.

The remaining bright spot in Palatka's future was the Wilson Cypress Company, the largest cypress sawmill in Florida and the second largest in the world. From the company's eighteen-hundred-foot pier on the St. Johns River, cypress lumber was shipped all over the world. However, the timber that the mill required had run out by the 1940s and the factory closed its doors, another huge blow to Palatka's economy. In 1947 Hudson Pulp and Paper Corporation became one of the town's major employers. It was here that young William Lindsey found employment upon moving to Palatka.

As a center for the surrounding agricultural and manufacturing industries, Palatka had its share of bars and restaurants. In one of these establishments— the Sip and Nip Bar—Lindsey met an attractive young woman, Willa Jean Willis. Willa Jean, eighteen at the time, was accompanied to the bar by her younger sister. Lindsey was also with a friend, Joe Taylor. After sharing a few drinks, Lindsey and Willa Jean left the bar and rode around for a while in his car. When she admired his white turtleneck shirt, he took it off and gave it to her. Willa Jean was favorably impressed by the clean-cut, solicitous young man she encountered that day.

The couple started going steady. At Christmas that year Lindsey gave her a pearl-and-diamond ring. Then, on New Year's Day, he gave her an engagement ring. The two families met and soon wedding plans were under way, with Lindsey's parents handling the arrangements. The couple was married on February 15, 1958, at the Ancient City Baptist Church in St. Augustine. Although both contracted flu on their wedding day, they were able to enjoy a brief honeymoon in Daytona Beach. Upon their return they lived for a time with Lindsey's parents on Sylvan Drive, in the home in which William had grown up. Apparently, during his absence from the family home, the rift between Lindsey and his adoptive mother had healed. Although he would carry a deep-seated anger toward her throughout his life, he also struggled to win her approval. His marriage may have seemed like such a step to him. Later the young couple rented a one-bedroom house on Rohde Avenue in St. Augustine, several blocks away from the Lindsey home. That same year Willa Jean gave birth to their first child, Beverly.

In all, five children would be born to the Lindseys during their marriage—daughters Beverly, Tina Marie, and Robin, and sons, Cecil and Billy.

The honeymoon period of the Lindsey's marriage was brief. Willa Jean's employment as a waitress in a Jacksonville restaurant during the early years of their marriage enflamed her husband's suspicions and led to his accusing her of infidelity. Like many other young men in St. Augustine at that time, Bill enlisted in the Florida National Guard. He began staying out drinking after National Guard meetings, coming home drunk, and beating Willa Jean. She later reported, "Bill would start using a lot of profanity and slapping me around. He was jealous of me and he'd yell even if I was only going to work. When we were fighting he'd yell, 'I'll kill you! I'll kill you!'"

After these episodes, Willa Jean would leave Bill for a time, he would swear the abuse would end and beg her to return, she would come back. For a while their relationship would be on a more even keel, but in time the pattern of abuse, separation, and reconciliation would repeat, not uncommon in marriages involving spousal abuse.

Later, Special Agent Allen Strickrott, Detective Frank Welborn and others offered the opinion that this turmoil early in the marriage reinforced Lindsey's tremendous anger toward women and his inability to perform sexually unless the act was accompanied by violence.

When interviewed after Lindsey's capture and incarceration, Beverly, Lindsey's daughter, told investigators that she remembered "vividly" her father beating her mother many times.

According to his own statements, during the 1960s Lindsey became a heavy user of heroin, but he quit after six months. At this time he would have been in his thirties. No proof exists that he became a serial killer at this time, although based on what is known about serial killers, the majority do start this activity in their twenties or thirties. While it is still not known if Lindsey was seeing prostitutes during these years, having access to heroin and using it heavily, as he acknowledged doing, would certainly suggest that he was associating with dealers and probably with prostitutes during this period.

Investigators noted that in addition to his chaotic home life, William Lindsey changed jobs frequently and was often fired for stealing and/or poor work habits. Family members report that his credit was bad and he was always broke. There were frequent periods of unemployment during which he turned to them for support. This pattern was chronic, persisting throughout his entire adult life. Most of the work he was able to obtain was unskilled or semiskilled labor in construction, roofing, or setting up mobile homes. In later years he did seasonal farming work, which was available at the huge potato-and-cabbage farms that occupied the surrounding area. As a mechanic in the National Guard, he had acquired the skills to repair heavy machinery, which he used at this stage in his career to repair farm machinery. Periodically he would return to his work at the Hudson Pulp and Paper Corporation. In between he had extended periods of unemployment.

Bill Lindsey and Willa Jean always rented their living quarters and most often resided in trailers, usually in Palatka or nearby Hastings. However, in 1970 they moved to Tennessee, where Lindsey found work in a steel mill. The marriage continued to deteriorate. During the two years they lived there, Bill claimed Willa Jean was behaving bizarrely, that "she called the president on the phone and tried to kill the children because they had rabies." He claimed, "She tried to shoot me up with a shotgun and I had to tie her up."

Willa Jean, in turn, claimed he was drugging her after she found containers of phenobarbital in his closet. This drug, normally used as a treatment for epilepsy and other conditions, has also been used by addicts. How Lindsey obtained it and why he took it is unknown. His wife knew of no medical condition he suffered that would require its use.

In 1974, a year prior to their final separation and divorce, Lindsey was under tremendous stress. He wrote a seven-page suicide letter addressed to Willa Jean. She showed it to the police and Lindsey was Baker Acted, or involuntarily committed, to a psychiatric hospital for two weeks. Willa Jean left Bill, took the children, and moved to Ocala, where she rented a trailer. They stayed there for a time. Then, after his release from the hospital, Bill asked to have the children for a weekend. He took them for a drive and wrecked the car, causing three of the children to be hospitalized, two with concussions and one with a broken leg. Willa Jean felt this was an attempted suicide/murder, but this was never proved or investigated by the police as anything other than a car wreck.

After the wreck the couple reunited once more. One day shortly thereafter, Lindsey told Willa Jean he was going fishing with a friend. "I had cooked dinner, and when it was time for the men to be back, I decided to go look for them," Willa Jean reported. "I went to Rodman Dam, but they weren't there." She did find him, however, at the same Sip and Nip Bar where they had first met. This time, though, he was with another woman, Annie Laurie Langley.

During one of their frequent separations, Willa Jean took the children; Bill had her arrested. "Bill had me fired from my bartending job 'cause I was always talking to him to keep the kids together," said Willa Jean. When she came to his trailer to talk to him, he slammed the door in her face. Angered, she put her fist through the window, cutting her hand, and again he had her arrested.

Throughout his first marriage Lindsey's strong tendencies to sadism were clearly evident in his abuse of Willa Jean. Other traits were also present, such as his Jekyll and Hyde personality, his jealous possessiveness, his volatile temper, and his refusal to accept no for an answer, all of which escalated in Lindsey's later years.

Willa Jean, the recipient of his cruelty, summed up her marriage to William Lindsey, saying, "I lived a nightmare with Bill."

In July 1975, after more than seventeen tumultuous years of a marriage punctuated by separations, physical violence, and infidelities, the couple divorced. By convincing the court that Willa Jean was mentally unstable, Bill was given custody of all five children, whose ages at that time ranged from about six to fifteen. According to Willa Jean's sister Joanne Willis Forsyth, this "pushed Willa Jean off the deep end and she was never the same again."

A month after his divorce from Willa Jean, Lindsey married Annie Laurie Langley. Lindsey's second wife was born Annie Laurie Smith in Waynesville, western North Carolina. This gave him a family connection to that area where he would commit at least one murder later.

In addition to the five children, ages six to fifteen, he brought to the marriage, Annie Laurie had two children she had adopted during her first marriage, both of them teenagers. After their marriage Lindsey adopted these two boys. With these responsibilities, the low-level jobs Lindsey could obtain, and his frequent periods of unemployment, life was anything but easy for the family. At various times he found work as a roofer, tree trimmer, setup mechanic for several mobile home companies, maintenance worker for Rent-A-Maid, laborer for a construction company, and oil change and grease job mechanic. He frequently jumped from job to job, again often being fired for poor work habits or for theft of company property.

When interviewed after Lindsey's arrest, Tim Langley, the son whom Annie Laurie had adopted during her first marriage, confirmed that the marriage had had its ups and downs: "Mom and Bill had a hard time with Bill's ex-wife. Anywhere from arguing with Willa Jean to her taking the kids. Me and Bill got along good, except three or four times when we got into bad arguments that Mom stopped."

(In one of the case's unexplained ironies, Detective Mary LeVeck had spoken with Tim Langley on March 10, 1989, seven years before Lindsey's capture. At that time investigators were collecting information regarding one of Anita Stevens's acquaintances. Langley reported that that man had assaulted him with carpenter's tools, a trowel, and a level. Langley reported that he had been treated at the hospital for his injuries and that the doctor had found a mark on the back of his neck; he felt certain it was a bite mark. Unfortunately, this information provided no clues to Anita's murder or to her murderer—Langley's stepfather.)

According to Lindsey's sister-in-law Lucille Lawson, he tended to procrastinate and never completed what he started. "Once, they bought a rundown house he never finished remodeling." Lawson also felt that he was selfish, as he spent money on himself, but not on Annie Laurie. "Even when she was ill, he bought an eagle for his collection of hunting artifacts and an expensive train set."

During the seventeen years Lindsey and Annie Laurie were together, their life was nomadic, especially after the children married or moved out to be

on their own. At various times the couple lived in
the Florida towns of Palatka, Ocala, Hastings, Belle-
view, and St. Augustine. At other times they were in
Asheville, North Carolina, and the Virginia communities of Ashland, Lynchburg, and Hanover.
Often they returned to live in the same town several
different times, Palatka and the nearby town of Hastings being their primary locations and the ones to
which they returned most often. As Annie Laurie's
niece reported, "He lived like a gypsy."

Detectives Welborn and Harrison both suspected
that he often moved immediately after his murders,
and this accounted for his constant change of address. Their hypothesis was borne out by the timeline
they had developed on Lindsey, which indicated a cor-
relation between his moves and his killings and
suspected killings.

Financially the Lindseys were always hard-pressed
to make ends meet. For instance, according to his
income tax returns, in the four years from 1991 to
1995, his average annual salary was only a little over
$15,000. Annie Laurie's family was often called upon
to help them out. At times Lindsey would take one
of his many guns to the Super Pawn and Gun Shop
in Palatka for a temporary loan. He was always trading one used car or truck for another, hoping to
pocket a few dollars on the transactions. The same
pattern had been present when he was married to
Willa Jean. During that first marriage Willa Jean's
sister Joan Forsyth and other family members helped
them with food and money.

Oddly, while Lindsey had described his marriage to
Willa Jean as "terrible," he would later refer to his second union as "about as good a marriage as you can
get." Annie Laurie died before Lindsey's capture and
conviction, so there are no statements directly from her
as to her view of the marriage. However, judging from

the testimony of her sister Agnes and others, she would have described her relationship with Bill Lindsey in far less favorable terms, especially during the period after which she was diagnosed with terminal cancer.

Family members and acquaintances, when questioned after his arrest, presented widely varying views of Lindsey's second marriage. Among the fifty people that detectives from Buncombe County, North Carolina, and St. Johns County, Florida, questioned, those who only knew the couple on a superficial social basis painted a far more positive picture than those who had a close relationship with them. Lindsey, like many psychopaths, could be very likable when he chose to be, a social veneer that caused him to be liked by people who knew him only casually.

Johnny Bugg, a North Carolina relative of Annie Laurie Lindsey's, said that he had known William Lindsey for about twenty years and had always found him to be polite. His wife, Cynthia Bugg, stated that William had helped them put in a water line to their new home. She also mentioned to investigators that they had shared cookouts and weekends at the lake with him and that he sometimes bought candy for their children.

Paul and Joyce Bugg, also relatives of Annie Laurie's, had gone out with Bill and Annie, fished with them, and visited them in their homes off and on over a twenty-year period, at one point living in a camper on their property for a month. The Buggs insisted they saw no evidence of discord or violence. Joyce Bugg said, "I never saw him violent with Annie. He was loving and caring. They had seven kids. I saw him drink beer, but there was no substance abuse." Her husband, Paul, a crane operator, stated, "I felt Bill and Annie were happily married. Never saw him mean to her. He was good to all seven kids and never hit them or Annie." Edith Farmer, a distant cousin of Bill's with whom he had lived for approximately a year in 1994, gave a similar description. "I never saw him drunk. Never saw him mean to his wife or kids."

Randy Doll, Lindsey's son-in-law, described Bill as "not close to the family, but a decent, nonviolent person until Annie Laurie died." After that, Doll said, Lindsey became more isolated. It should be noted, however, that Doll had never lived with Lindsey or been particularly close to him.

Those who had closer relationships presented a dramatically different picture. Lucille Lawson, Annie Laurie's sister, actually lived with William and Annie Laurie for two years in the 1980s. "Although at times he could be very nice, he had a bad temper and was easily angered," she said. "He would throw his food on the floor and Annie Laurie and I would have to pick it up."

Lawson was witness to episodes where Lindsey became both verbally and physically abusive toward his wife. "Once, I saw him hit her and knock her down," she said. According to her account, these rage episodes occurred about three times a week.

In another context Fred Marjenhoff, Annie Laurie's nephew, reported behavior on Lindsey's part that would hardly be characteristic of a caring person. Marjenhoff experienced a graphic demonstration of Lindsey's potential for cruelty: He and Lindsey came across a dog that had been struck by a car and was critically injured. Marjenhoff offered to go get his gun and humanely shoot the animal to end its misery. Lindsey stopped him and proceeded to beat the dog to death with rocks. Appalled by the viciousness of Lindsey's behavior, Marjenhoff refused to have any further contact with him. (This kind of senseless cruelty in a mature adult is considered pathological sadism of the same sort that was manifested in his treatment of the women in his life.)

Rose Werkheiser, Annie's niece, confirmed Lindsey's violent temper in an interview given to a reporter for the *St. Augustine Record:* "He had mood swings real bad. He would go through spells. Sometimes he'd be okay. Other times if he got mad at you he would completely blow up. That went on throughout their marriage."

Equally disturbing was Lindsey's insecurity and obsessive jealousy toward both Willa Jean and Annie Laurie. "He wanted no one close to her," Lucille Lawson, Annie Laurie's sister, reported. Joan Forsyth, Willa Jean's older sister, described the same sort of behavior on Lindsey's part.

One person toward whom Lindsey was particularly antagonistic was Annie Laurie's sister Agnes Marjenhoff. In the beginning of their marriage, Agnes was called upon frequently to help the Lindseys financially. "I gave them money all the time when he was between jobs," she stated, adding that he was often in that state. As time passed, however, she turned against her sister's husband. "Lindsey was the most hateful man you could ever know," she stated unequivocally. Speaking to reporter Diane Rodgers of the *St. Augustine Record,* Agnes said, "He hit my sister. My sister told me and I seen the marks on my sister."

So strong was the antipathy between Agnes and Lindsey, that when Annie got out of the hospital following treatment for her colon cancer, Bill put a restraining order on Agnes and her children, forbidding them to see Annie. This separated them from Annie during the last three months of her life. Agnes felt very strongly that Bill was not taking proper care of her sister, even to the point that he was using her medicine and not feeding her adequately. This view was shared by others, including Sandra Sullivan, who frequently visited Annie Laurie during the terminal months of her life.

By the early 1990s Annie Laurie's cancer was rapidly

progressing into its final stages. Paradoxically, although Agnes was forbidden to see Annie Laurie near the end, their sister Lucille Lawson continued to visit and became very close to Bill. During this period Lawson and Richard Langley, one of Annie Laurie's adopted sons, sided with Bill Lindsey in the care of Annie Laurie. Agnes and Annie's other adopted son, Tim Langley, did not.

Investigators learned from Tim Langley that in November 1990, after his mother had been diagnosed with cancer and told she had about two years to live, she revealed to him that she was "thinking of how they could get away from William and he not being able to find them." Tim Langley became especially perturbed when he noticed bruises on his mother. When he quizzed her about these marks, she always told him that she had fallen down. But two days before she died, they had a talk in which Annie Laurie admitted to Tim, "Bill has been beating me the past few years." But even at that extreme moment, she asked Tim "not to say anything." She also confided that Lindsey was having an affair with a Sandra Sullivan. She said he had returned home with a new rifle and told her that he had bought it for $10 at a garage sale, but she knew that Sullivan had given it to him.

There was also suspicion that Lindsey was using the prescription drugs given to his wife for her pain. Sandra Sullivan later supported this supposition in her interview with investigators. She reported that Lindsey told her he needed a lot of pain pills because he had a brain tumor.

In addition to the question of whether or not Lindsey was confiscating Annie Laurie's medications for his own use, the more serious issue was that he may have hastened her death in order to benefit financially. This was especially significant, as on November

6, 1992, Lindsey filed papers declaring his indigence, i.e., his debts exceeded his assets.

In interviews with St. Johns County detectives following Lindsey's capture, both Agnes Marjenhoff and Tim Langley alluded to the possibility Lindsey committed fraud regarding an insurance policy on Annie Laurie's life. The policy originally named her sister Lucille Lawson as beneficiary. On October 15, 1992, the beneficiary was changed to William Lindsey and the policy was increased from $5,000 in death benefits to $25,000. At that time Annie Laurie was in the terminal stages of the cancer that claimed her life a month later on November 17, 1992. Because no charges of fraud were ever filed, the suspicion that it occurred is speculation, although Lindsey went on a spending spree shortly after, as detailed in the police timeline of his activities. Annie Laurie's son Tim Langley also noted that immediately after his mother died, Lindsey bought 10 to 20 new guns. Receipts found by detectives verified those transactions as well as a number of other sizable expenditures totaling about $25,000, the amount of Annie Laurie's life insurance.

In spite of his suspicions, for several years after his mother's death, Tim Langley maintained contact with Lindsey. During that time Lindsey related to Langley a story about someone robbing him and tying him to a tree for five days. "I thought that was weird!" Langley told Detective Welborn. This may be one of the many lies Lindsey was noted for telling. Or it may have been a consequence of one of his transactions with the pimps, drug dealers, and prostitutes with whom he was interacting at this time of his life.

Whatever the impetus for his story, it did not deter Lindsey from pursuing his next victim.

Chapter 18

Lindsey's Sexual History

Most psychosexual disorders are the result of an aberrant fantasy system fueled by traumatic childhood and adolescent experiences.
—E. W. Hickey, *Serial Murderers and Their Victims*

The task force investigators, knowing that at the heart of a serial lust killer's pathology is an atypical expression of his sexuality, conducted numerous interviews that focused on Lindsey's sexual preferences and behavior. What they discovered confirmed that he was a man who required sadism and torture in order to achieve sexual satisfaction.

During the interviews Lindsey claimed that his initial marriage had been to an ex-prostitute, although he was not aware of her past at the time they wed. Second, he reported that he had trouble satisfying Willa Jean sexually. During the six months he was in psychotherapy with a psychiatrist, he was recommended to use a dildo as one way of resolving the issue. According to Willa Jean, this did not work. Third, he said that he and Willa Jean were in a swingers' group, comprised of couples who exchanged partners while engaging in sex. This practice reflected a desire for sexual variety and perhaps a lack of satisfaction with more conventional sexual routines. Some people can only experience sexual arousal under the stimulus of this kind of activity with its suggestion of kinkiness and the forbidden.

It appeared Lindsey may also have had extramarital affairs in addition to those occurring in the swingers' group. This was evidenced by the fact that while they were still married, Willa Jean had caught him at a bar with Annie Laurie, an event that triggered their divorce. It has not been determined whether he was involved with prostitutes during this time, but in view of what was learned about his swinging activities, his heavy drinking, and his sexual difficulties, this seemed a distinct possibility.

Although Lindsey claimed his second marriage was "a good one," his wife, Annie Laurie, felt different about it, and for understandable reasons. His unpredictable temper, his selfishness, and the frequent beatings he administered not only had her fearful of him, but planning to leave him. After she was diagnosed with colon cancer and given just a year or two to live, Annie Laurie gave up this idea. According to Annie Laurie's sister Agnes Marjenhoff, Lindsey and Annie Laurie had stopped having consensual sex a year or so prior to Annie Laurie's death.

During Lindsey's seventeen-year marriage to Annie Laurie, which ended with her death on November 17, 1992, he was sexually active with prostitutes. By then, he had already murdered Anita Stevens (11/29/1988), Connie Terrell (6/10/1989), and Lashawna Streeter (3/1/1992); other evidence suggested he may have been frequenting prostitutes and possibly killing them even earlier, during his marriage to Willa Jean. For instance, daughter Beverly told of one occasion when her father returned home with his shirt covered with blood after an evening out.

St. Johns County detectives Frank Welborn and

Mary LeVeck and Asheville detective John Harrison conducted numerous interviews with prostitutes and other women with whom Lindsey was known to have been involved. One of the more interesting of these relationships involved Sandra Sullivan. Sullivan first met Lindsey through his wife Annie Laurie. (Further adding to the convoluted situation, when Annie Laurie was still married to her first husband, James Langley, he and Sandra became sexually involved. The affair ended when Sandra became pregnant and Langley cut off their relationship, leaving Sandra to raise the child.)

Years later, when Sandra learned that Annie was sick with cancer, she went to see her to apologize for having had the relationship with Langley. It was at that time that she met William Lindsey. The two of them began a relationship, which Sandra described as "platonic." Sandra told Detective LeVeck that Lindsey was "good to her and her kids." However, she was aware of his brutal treatment of Annie Laurie. In fact, Lindsey admitted to Sandra his cruelty to his dying wife. Sullivan also noticed that he was taking Annie Laurie's prescription for morphine from her for his own use, either as barter for sex with prostitutes or else to get high on.

Sullivan herself experienced Lindsey's violence and unpredictable temper when, during a visit to his trailer, he attacked her without warning.

A North Carolina prostitute, Chanelle Barnes, had a somewhat similar incident with Lindsey. She was standing at the corner of Broadway and Elizabeth Street in Asheville, an area where prostitutes often pick up their johns. Lindsey stopped and asked her if she dated. After agreeing on a price, Barnes got into his vehicle. At some point during their assignation, she made an effort to con him out of his money, but she failed. Later, as they were driving back toward

Broadway, out of the blue Lindsey picked up a baseball bat and began bludgeoning her about the head
and face, almost killing her. Then, in an about-face
typical of his postrage contrition, he apologized to
her. When released from the hospital, Barnes told
Asheville detectives, "He needs mental help because
people who do what he did are not normal people."

In examining the behavior Lindsey exhibited with
Sullivan and Barnes and others, investigators developed a profile of a man with an intensely strong
desire to maim or kill women, yet one who did not
fully understand why these compulsive urges came on
him. To some extent he seemed to feel remorse about
them, a dichotomy that is true of some, but not all, serial killers. For instance, Jeffrey Dahmer, whose
killings included torture and necrophilia, spoke the
following words of regret: "I know how much harm I
have caused, but I tried to do the best I could after the
arrest to make amends."

However, there is always a question as to how genuine such sentiments are. As Dr. Drew Ross noted
in the book *Looking into the Eyes of a Killer:* "Sociopaths are masters at faking emotion, even
remorse." He also observed: "They are able to ruth-
lessly enact murder and smile about it."

In 1996, when Lindsey was jailed for the murder of
Lucy Raymer, he told Buncombe County detective
Butch Oxner that during his most recent stay in
Asheville he had picked up ten different girls, on a total
of twenty-five occasions, from the strip around Broadway and Elizabeth Street. This suggests a rather active
sexual life for a man who was sixty-one years old.

Another view of Lindsey's relationship with women
came from a pimp and drug dealer, Dale Chambers,
who, with his father, owned a house where some of
the Asheville prostitutes occasionally stayed. For a $10
fee, he also provided a room johns could use to have

sex with a prostitute, get high, or both. Chambers reported that Lindsey was at the house three or four times a week seeking girls. He told investigators Lindsey was usually dirty with oil and grease on him. "But he kept his vehicle clean," Chambers added. Others have commented on Lindsey's neatness—both with his car and his home, although not his person.

According to Chambers, Lindsey was free with his money in his dealings with the prostitutes. "Sometimes he gave the girls as much as a hundred-dollars tip. Some of them he let use his car." The detectives learned that others lived with him at times and in some cases their children moved in as well.

While most of Lindsey's sexual encounters at Chambers's house were one-night stands, according to Chambers, he also developed some longer-term relationships. "He used the room with Selica, a prostitute who lives here," Chambers said. "He claimed to love Selica. Sometimes he took her out, kept her with him for two or three days. When Selica had her baby, she named it Bill."

Lindsey offered Chambers an ostensible reason for his involvement with crack-addicted prostitutes— "I was on drugs before, and I know how it is, but I got straight. That's why I kind of help the girls out by dating them and giving them money." Lindsey failed to mention the other half of the story—that he tortured and killed some of them.

Following Lindsey's arrest for the seven murders, detectives interviewed Tonya Nichols, another crack-addicted prostitute who once lived with Lindsey. At the time of her interrogation, she was incarcerated at the Gadsden Correctional Institution in Quincy, Florida, the first such privately owned facility in Florida to house female offenders. A minimum- and medium-custody facility, Gadsden offered its inmates substance abuse programs and vocational programs, such as cosmetology, nail tech, data entry, commercial cleaning, and business administration.

Nichols stated that she first met Lindsey in 1995 when he picked her up on the street and took her to a bar. Shortly after that, he bought her $100 worth of crack, which she smoked as they rode around. Lindsey, she said, did not use any of the drug. They met twice more and on the third occasion she went with him to his trailer on Cracker Swamp Road in Hastings, Florida. Not long after, Nichols and her daughter moved in with him. In addition to allowing them to share his living quarters, Lindsey also gave them money and the use of his truck while he was at work. Nichols described Lindsey as being a quiet man who would often get depressed and who talked a great deal about his late wife and her death from cancer. Often he told her, "You remind me of my wife." She also said he made her crack pipes out of the vials in which the morphine he was taking was packed. She said he was never violent with her and the only unusual trait she saw in him was that he was "too nice," a description given of him by many others who knew him only casually.

According to Tonya, Lindsey claimed that he had cancer. This may have been true because by the time he pleaded guilty at age sixty-four, he had been diagnosed with colon polyps, a possibly precancerous condition. (This illness proved to be a factor in his plea bargain and sentencing.) His living arrangement with Nichols continued for three weeks, during which they had only one sexual encounter. She reported that at that time Lindsey was unable to get an erection, but he continued to fondle her.

Stephanie Lowell was another St. Augustine prostitute with whom Lindsey became involved. She said, "Lindsey was a regular client of Diana Richardson (murdered by Lindsey in 1995). He paid Diana for sex and gave her twenty-dollar finder fees to get him other girls." Lowell said Lindsey seemed only to want to talk with her, whereas "most men preferred me for sex over Richardson." About five days before Richardson was murdered, she brought Lindsey to Lowell's place. "This time he offered me one hundred fifty dollars to go to his trailer for the night," Lowell reported. "I got in his truck, then started to feel uneasy, so I jumped out and ran away." Lowell may have saved her own life by trusting her feelings and employing her "street smarts" and intuition to spot and escape being another victim of serial killer Lindsey.

In 1995 Karen Swift was walking "the Strip" in Ocala, Florida, looking for johns. She approached a car parked beside the road with a single man inside. When she asked if he wanted a date, he motioned for her to get into the car. The man was William Lindsey. That night he bought her $100 worth of crack. After that, she began seeing him weekly.

Later she was arrested. "When I was in jail, Lindsey visited me and gave me money," she told investigators. "He also gave money to my friends who I introduced him to. Those who were not in jail, he gave both money and drugs." How Lindsey obtained the funds for this kind of giving to women, both in and out of prison, remains an enigma.

While Swift was incarcerated, also at Gadsden Correctional Institution, she and Lindsey corresponded regularly. In his many letters to Swift, Lindsey often signed himself as "Crazy Bill." Lindsey's letters to her were extremely sentimental, in an adolescent fashion, and often included drawings of hearts and other romantic symbols. The language he employed was naively romantic, and grammatically confusing. In them he declared his intention to marry her when she was released from incarceration and counted the days and minutes until this happy event would take place. He said that although she had told him he was "next to Jesus" he modestly denied that claim. In a remarkable contrast, considering the nature of the crimes he had committed, one would assume from Lindsey's prose that his life was filled with nothing but religious sentiments—"I thank God for you all the time. I feel good about Him sending you by. God bless and keep you."

However infatuated Lindsey was with Karen Swift, he never meant more to her than a cocaine fix when she was out of jail and money while she was incarcerated. This became clear when she was released from jail in June 1995 and informed him that she was ending their relationship, that she was a lesbian and was returning to her female lover. She also reported to detectives that she and Lindsey had had only one sexual encounter and that Lindsey was unable to perform.

Through his contacts with Swift, Lindsey met other prostitutes in the Ocala area. One of these was Selma Wilson who was incarcerated along with Karen Swift. Lindsey frequently supplied Wilson with money and visited her in jail at the same time he was proposing and promising eternal devotion to Karen. Selma wrote him long letters that always included passionate proclamations of love, interspersed with equally passionate requests for more money. She complained that because of his failure to send her the promised cash she was unable to buy provisions from the jail commissary. "I was not able to get any shoes on Thursday and now tonight everyone is ordering food and personal items and I cannot order either of these."

Wilson also accused him of lying to her after having sworn that he would always be "honest." "Are you messing around with someone else?" she demanded. "Don't take me for a fool."

A few lines later she changed her approach and assured him that when they are together she is going to do everything she can for him, including getting their debts caught up. Throughout the letter her tone alternated between pleas and complaints. "No money, no visits, not even a birthday card," she complained. "My whole world is falling apart."

Her final P.S. reverts to an accusatory tone: "I hope some whore isn't using you and screwing you over! I hope even more that I never find out who she is!"

Marisa deSanto was another prostitute who remembered Lindsey well. She, too, was a lesbian. She recalled an incident in which Lindsey picked her up on King Street in St. Augustine. "He paid me ten dollars for a blow job but couldn't get an erection," she said. "He was nice . . . just another john."

The manager of the RV-trailer park in Asheville, North Carolina, where Lindsey had his small travel trailer parked, reported that Dorrie, a local prostitute, had lived there with Lindsey for a while, along with her child. Tonya Nichols and her daughter had a similar arrangement with him in Florida.

In addition to allowing them to know where he lived, Lindsey also told the prostitutes where he worked. Consequently they would frequently phone him at work. Some visited him at his workplace. On one occasion six of them showed up at the same time at the Ace Equipment Company, where he was employed. They became so aggressive they even entered work areas specified "For Employees Only." Their visits, coupled once again with Lindsey's poor work habits, led to his dismissal from the company, one of the best work situations he ever had.

When investigators looked at the evidence amassed from his two marriages and his multiple liaisons with prostitutes, two traits became clear: One, he was a sexual sadist, a man who got sexual pleasure from rough sex and brutalizing women. The brutal manner in which he murdered his victims gave further proof of his sadism. Some of these victims were raped; in other cases sperm found at the death sites suggested masturbation. Whether or not necrophilia was involved is not known. In at least one instance, he shoved broken tree branches into the vagina and anus of his victim, leaving her body to be discovered in this state. In other murders the bodies were nude and posed in obscene positions.

A second conclusion drawn from his relationships with women was that he was a lonely man, especially after Annie Laurie's death. Evidence of this was he allowed numerous prostitutes, often with their children, to live with him, off and on, over the years. This was in spite of the fact that they were crack addicts desperate for cocaine, and that many of them ripped him off. For example, Tonya Nichols robbed his trailer of $1,450 worth of jewelry while staying there as his guest. Her daughter, also a guest, stole his truck. Karen Swift and Selma Wilson pretended to care for him while in jail in order to get money, but they dropped him immediately upon being released.

Lindsey had been around crack-addicted prostitutes enough to know that their desperation for drugs would inevitably lead them to steal from him. But his loneliness was such that he exposed himself to this risk, whereas the typical john's encounters with street prostitutes are brief and limited to just sex.

One of the most important clues to understanding William Lindsey was the rage episodes he experienced, during which he bludgeoned and shot the women who triggered his anger. He did apologize to those who survived, as in the cases of Chanelle Barnes and Sandra Sullivan. Others were not so fortunate—

they died terrifying and brutal deaths. This rage and his desire to hurt and kill women were uncontrollable at times, especially when he felt he was being taken advantage of or denied sex.

One puzzling aspect of Lindsey's sexuality was the number of situations with women during which he was impotent. Several prostitutes reported that at times he was unable to get an erection. Willa Jean Lindsey stated that he could not satisfy her. On the other hand, Dale Chambers, the pimp/drug dealer who supplied Lindsey with prostitutes, observed that Lindsey came to his place for women three or four times a week. In addition to this, he was picking up prostitutes on the street.

Another factor stood out in trying to unravel the complexities of Lindsey's mind and the factors motivating his sadistic serial rapes and murders: under the seat of his vehicle he carried a short rope fashioned into a noose, which he used to strangle and subdue Connie Terrell, his second St. Augustine victim.

The only logical reason for having such a device would be to use it as a weapon in choking someone. Such ropes are standard equipment in the "rape kits" many sadistic serial killers carry in their cars when they prowl the streets looking for victims. This indicated to investigators that Lindsey was probably constantly on the lookout for victims and was quite premeditated in his murders.

Lindsey also had in his vehicles the guns with which he threatened and, in at least Connie Terrell's case, murdered his victims. While the weapons certainly played a part in Lindsey's killing spree, in a culture in which guns were prevalent, as they were in the areas in which Lindsey lived, it was difficult to pinpoint this as typical equipment only for a serial killer.

Chapter 19

A Pattern for Murder

One way in which William Lindsey attempted to justify his criminal behavior was by referring to himself as a dual personality, "Good Bill" and "Bad Bill." At one point Special Agent Allen Strickrott asked Lindsey point-blank, "Realistically, how many women has Bad Bill killed?"

"Quite a few," Lindsey replied.

"Ten?" Strickrott asked.

"Oh, no. More than ten."

"Twelve?"

"More."

Eventually Lindsey admitted he may have killed as many as twenty to twenty-five women around the southeastern United States. Strickrott thought this answer was honest and accurate, and he did not doubt that there were other unsolved cases that could be attributed to Lindsey.

Strickrott stated, "I firmly believe that when Lindsey left his residence to go out on the streets and pick up prostitutes, he did this with the intention of killing them. On some of these occasions, Good Bill would be the woman's rescuer. But, like an addict needing a fix, Good Bill could only fight his craving to rape and kill for so long. That's when Bad Bill would surface."

The fact that Lindsey carried with him in his car the iron bar, noose, and gun that were used in his various killings was proof of Strickrott's theory.

During the course of their investigation into William Lindsey's background, it became clear to investigators why he had been such an elusive killer. While detectives were searching fruitlessly and interviewing numerous suspects in the case, the man himself was constantly on the move. Because farming in Hastings and Palatka, both huge potato-and-cabbage-growing areas, offered only seasonal employment, Lindsey frequently sought jobs elsewhere in the off seasons. Police records collected subsequent to his capture showed him living at times in Ocala, Florida, and at other times in Hanover and Ashland, Virginia, in Asheville, North Carolina, and in Lebanon, Tennessee, then back to the vicinity of St. Augustine, usually occupying a trailer in nearby Hastings or Palatka. As indicated earlier, this peripatetic lifestyle may also have been dictated by his desire to escape detection for his crimes.

Although some moves were precipitated by the seasonal nature of farmwork, others resulted from his dismissal for poor job performance or theft. The timeline carefully compiled by the task force through Lindsey's credit card data, telephone records, income tax returns, vehicle license records, and other recorded data enabled them to pinpoint where Lindsey had lived and when. Based on the timeline, it appeared that Lindsey often moved right after a woman's murder had been committed in the area he left.

Thus, his peripatetic lifestyle also opened the possibility that Lindsey had committed more murders than previously suspected. In fact, before he was assigned a public defender, Lindsey admitted that he had killed between twelve and twenty women in four southeastern states. Detectives Welborn and Harrison felt that this was an understatement and that his killings began much earlier than those to which he had admitted. Their view was consistent with what is known about the ages at which most sadistic serial killers begin their murders, which is in their twenties or thirties.

Based on this, it was also possible that Lindsey's St. Augustine murder spree started even earlier than the slaying of Anita Stevens in 1988. At that time he would have been fifty-three years old, an age at which serial killers rarely start their murders. Before he confessed to the first St. Augustine murders, the FBI profilers had ruled Lindsey out as a serial killer suspect based on his age. As it turned out, the FBI made a serious error in taking this position. But Lindsey's case is either an exception or else he committed earlier murders that remain unsolved.

An interesting sidelight to this issue is that after Lindsey was charged with the St. Augustine murders, Canadian profilers called to learn the details of his crime and his background in order to incorporate them into their database. (In the United States it is generally believed that the FBI started and developed the idea of profiling and are the authorities on the subject. However, there is strong evidence that profiling actually originated in Canada.)

Strickrott theorized that Lindsey began his killings after his divorce from Willa Jean, his first wife. If Strickrott is correct, this would mean Lindsey was about thirty-seven at the time of his first murder.

When investigators began comparing Lindsey's movements over the years with unsolved murders in the areas where he had lived or traveled, one of the cold cases they looked at was that of Lisa Foley, possibly his earliest St. Augustine victim. Her body was found in a borrow pit in St. Johns County in October 1983. Lisa, a petite blond-haired blue-eyed woman, had been married and divorced and had a four-year-old daughter. At the time of her death, she was working as a barmaid at the Speak Easy Lounge, a strip club in Jacksonville, about a forty-minute drive from St. Augustine. The club's clients were a mixture of bikers, rednecks, and government workers. Employees of the bar were reported to act as prostitutes, a common occurrence in topless bars.

Lisa drank heavily, used cocaine, and was involved with a motorcycle crowd. Often she would hitchhike and disappear for a day or two. Lisa also reported having been raped several times. Her employment record was an erratic one in which she seldom lasted more than a year in any job. In her free time she frequented the Scarlett O'Hara and Tradewinds Lounges in St. Augustine as well as bars in Jacksonville.

A friend, Connie Travis, described Lisa as "naive," and as "someone who always aspired to make something of herself, but who was living the opposite of what she wanted."

The night of her murder, Lisa finished work at 9:00 P.M. She and her live-in boyfriend, Tram Borden, then started drinking and did not leave the Tradewinds until 1:00 A.M. On the way home they stopped at a convenience store to buy some beer. When they arrived home, Borden went into the house, but Lisa left, never again to be seen alive by anyone but her killer.

Five days later, on October 14, 1983, her severely decomposed body was found in a borrow pit. She had been brutally beaten about the nose and face and died of asphyxiation. The hyoid bone in her neck was fractured and the thyroid cartilage damaged, indicating she had been strangled. An investigation followed, but no credible leads developed as to her murderer. To this day her murder remains unresolved, even though Lindsey had admitted that he may have been her killer.

When detectives from St. Augustine interviewed

Lindsey following Lucy Raymer's murder in North Carolina, they brought with them photographs of local women who had been murdered during the 1980s and 1990s, as well as photographs of nonvictims. From these sets of pictures, Lindsey picked out the six women he later pleaded guilty to killing, along with one of Lisa Foley.

With regard to Lisa, he stated, "I picked her up in the Tradewinds Lounge. She told me she had been a topless dancer. When we left the Tradewinds, we drove to the A Street ramp and down onto St. Augustine Beach. Then we parked. We had intercourse and she wanted three hundred dollars. I said fifty dollars is all you're going to get. This started us fighting. It was a hell of a fight. I finally knocked her out. Then I strangled her and took her body down to Pacetti Road and dumped her in a borrow pit down there."

When investigators from the St. Johns County Sheriff's Office escorted Lindsey to the various sites where he claimed to have killed his victims and abandoned their bodies, Lisa Foley's name surfaced once more. Lindsey indicated a marshy area at the west end of Pope Road, where he claimed he had disposed of one woman's body. As evidence of the multiplicity of Lindsey's killings and their random nature, he could not recall if this woman was Lisa Foley or some other woman he had killed and dumped at this spot. However, the method of the homicide, the way he disposed of her body, and the overall nature of the incident that led to the murder were in keeping with his other killings.

Lisa Foley's case was never prosecuted, possibly because there was insufficient corroborating evidence and the fact that it had occurred sixteen years before Lindsey was brought to trial. Older cases are usually harder to prosecute because witnesses may have died or are unable to be located, evidence may be lost or deteriorated. It is not uncommon for prosecutors, in trying serial killers, to focus on the cases where the evidence is strong enough to secure a conviction and a sentence that will insure the killer will either be executed or spend his remaining life imprisoned. The expense of proceeding with litigation when the case appears weak will often lead to a decision not to prosecute, especially when the suspect is already in prison on a death sentence or a long term.

For these reasons a number of other murders for which Lindsey was a suspect have never been brought to trial. For example, On April 4, 1997, Lindsey admitted to Sheriff Bobby Medford that in 1987 he had kidnapped a woman from the Asheville Mall in North Carolina and shot her. Police records on file in Sheriff Medford's office indicated that twenty-three-year-old Pamela Michele Murray was abducted from the mall that year and murdered. Murray's body was found on a deserted road in Oteen, the same North Carolina town in which Lindsey was living when apprehended, and not far from where Lucy Raymer's body was later discovered. Murray had been shot in the head and back. Her case has not been brought to trial, although Lindsey remains a suspect in view of his confession.

Police in Asheville and Buncombe County also identified three other murders in that area that remain unsolved and show similarities to those to which Lindsey has confessed. Beverly Ann Sherman, seventeen, was found shot to death, her body disposed of in a wooded area of Buncombe County. Valerie Maxine Holloway was discovered beaten to death in a wooded area near Asheville. Cynthia Diana Tolbert's body was found in an Asheville cemetery, her throat slashed. All three cases bore similarities to murders to which Lindsey confessed and/or pleaded guilty.

In addition to these unsolved cases in North Car-

olina, strikingly similar murders took place in the
Richmond, Virginia, area at a time when Lindsey
was known either to be living there or traveling
through the area. In May 1994 the body of twenty-
seven-year-old Paula Faye Haden, a known prostitute,
was discovered on some rocks next to a culvert in
Hanover County, some twenty miles north of Richmond, where Lindsey was then living. Sandra
Sullivan, with whom Lindsey had been involved during his marriage and whom he once attacked,
received a letter from Lindsey in September 1994.
In it he stated "I need to tell you something . . . that
happened to me in April of this year." He further
stated that this information could not be told in a
letter but only face-to-face.

Investigators speculated that the letter may have
been the result of guilt Lindsey was feeling over a
crime he had committed, although this supposition
was never proved.

Two years later, in August 1996, twenty-two-year-old
Wendy Radcliffe's body was found in a secluded spot
some four miles from where Haden's body had been
located earlier. While investigators were unable to link
Lindsey directly to the murders, those were localities
near where he had lived at times and with whose
topography he would have been familiar.

Detectives from Virginia interviewed Lindsey after
his capture in North Carolina, but no charges were
ever brought in the two Virginia cases. Apparently,
North Carolina's case involving Lucy Raymer was so
strong that the Virginia authorities felt Lindsey would
be convicted on those charges and either executed or
imprisoned for life. Since their own cases were weaker
in some respects, it would have been futile to spend
countless hours of detective work and the expense of
a trial in their state.

In two instances Lindsey almost killed women who

barely managed to escape his attacks with their lives. In these cases he seemed able to restrain himself from the ultimate act of killing. The first incident occurred in 1993 and involved his late wife's friend Sandra Sullivan. While visiting him in his trailer, Sullivan was looking at some family photos when Lindsey suggested they go into the bedroom so that he could show her a photo of his daughter. When she declined, he went alone to the bedroom, returned with the photograph, then went behind her chair, leaned over, and dropped the picture in her lap. While she was looking at it, without warning he struck her in the back of the head with a vicious karate chop which bowled her over onto the floor. She tried to get up, but he forced her back down. Confused and terrified, Sullivan nevertheless managed to shove him away and stagger to her feet. Realizing the danger of her situation, she immediately started talking, hoping to calm him. Undeterred, he grabbed her hands in a tight grip and told her, "I have to do this. When I kill you, it will be like this." (This bizarre behavior and strangely worded threat suggest a man for whom killing met some deeply repressed need.)

Then, as Sullivan was struggling to free herself, Lindsey's expression changed abruptly. The maniacal rage that had distorted his face disappeared. At the same time his manner went from one of homicidal intent to one of conciliation. Relieved, Sullivan's only thought was to escape. But Lindsey told her, "You can't leave until you calm down. Then I'll walk you to your car."

After some time passed, he allowed Sullivan to go. She immediately reported the incident to the sheriff's office, filed a complaint, then went to Flagler Hospital to get checked out for her injuries. Later she dropped the complaint against him. About a year later, after Lindsey had returned to Asheville, he wrote Sandra Sullivan a letter asking her to come visit so he could explain in person what had happened. She declined to answer the letter and never heard from him or saw him afterward.

Jennifer Simms, another victim of Lindsey's rage, suffered a beating that nearly took her life. Again, as had happened with Sandra Sullivan, after having attacked her, he apologized. Another prostitute who had a similar experience was Christy, whom Lindsey often used for sexual purposes and had usually treated quite generously. After she experienced one of his rage attacks, she became absolutely terrified of him and refused to have further contact with him.

While it appeared to be generally true that Lindsey chose his victims indiscriminately and was not always acquainted with them previous to the killing, in at least one of the St. Augustine murders it appeared he did know the woman he planned to kill. In his confession Lindsey confirmed that he had known Diana for some time. "I met her on one or two occasions (at another woman's apartment) on Masters Drive in St. Augustine. Later I went to her house a few times when I was on my way to Ocala."

Additional evidence indicating Lindsey's lifestyle might have allowed him to kill more victims than he had been charged with came from two family members who independently observed the same phenomenon. In October 1983 Rose Werkheiser, Annie Laurie Lindsey's niece, was living with the Lindseys. In an interview with reporters Nancy Mitchell and Thomas Nord of the Jacksonville *Times Union*, she recalled, "One night Bill left the house and did not return until the next morning. When he came in, he had blood splattered all over his shirt." His explanation was that he had cut his hand, but she never believed him. This occurred around the time of Lisa Foley's murder.

Everyone who ever lived with Lindsey for any period of time would describe his frequent temper explosions, which often involved throwing objects or lashing out physically.

Dennis Bittner, Lindsey's cellmate in the St. Johns County Detention Center, informed detectives that Lindsey had confided to him that he murdered the St. Augustine women, but he also boasted, "They can't do nothing to me." Lindsey told Bittner, "I killed people all over the country and the FBI is looking for me. All of them were crackhead whores. I could go to any crackhouse and pick one up." In speaking of Lucy Raymer's murder, Lindsey told Bittner that he had done the killing, but, in contrast to the other murders, he had thrown Lucy's body where it could be found easily.

Such information as Bittner supplied to the police is generally considered weak evidence, as people who are incarcerated will often say anything in order to incur favor with the police or in hopes of reducing their sentences. There is no indication, however, that Bittner was offered any favors.

Another path that was explored in attempting to determine Lindsey's character was a handwriting analysis. (As information is not available as to who submitted the analysis and how much information about Lindsey that person may have had in advance, the findings, while interesting, must be viewed with caution.) Among the characteristics identified by the handwriting expert were poor organizational skills, instability, poor self-image, lack of integrity, poor self-control, no ego repression, inferiority, and feelings of insecurity. "Even with his obvious minimal education, he has a creative imagination and is resourceful. Unfortunately, he uses these skills to manipulate and control others to his advantage. This becomes an even more extreme negative situation with his propensity to aggressively express anger and frustration," the report states. The analyst remarked upon inner, unresolved conflict that colored Lindsey's interaction with women and the way in which that interaction was affected by his childhood abuse and neglect.

The analyst concluded that while most people would consider Lindsey to be "friendly, outgoing, sociable, unobtrusive, reserved, carefree and a good listener," his handwriting revealed him to be in reality "a loner, a fraud, compulsive, careless and a compulsive liar." Lindsey was seen as feeling "safe" only when distancing himself from others. He did not want to allow anyone to come to know him better, as he was afraid that they would see him for his true self. He was energetic, but quick to lose enthusiasm. The final conclusion was proved undeniably true: "He is highly capable of violent expression."

While the evidence strongly indicated Lindsey had significantly more victims than those for which he was convicted, the true extent of his killings will probably never be known, unless he should confess before he dies. The detectives most directly connected with the case, Welborn and Harrison, have repeatedly expressed a conviction based on their combined fifty years of law enforcement experience that Lindsey had undoubtedly committed many more murders.

The earliest murder for which Lindsey is serving a sentence took place in 1988 when he was fifty-three years old. In researching the records of 306 sadistic serial lust killers, the authors could locate only two who were over fifty at the time they murdered the first victim for whom they were convicted of killing. One of these men was blatantly psychotic at the time of his murders.

While it seems highly probable that William Lindsey committed far more murders than the six to which he pleaded guilty—his own estimate of "twelve to twenty" murders may even be an understatement—it is also reasonable to assume that unless by some freak circumstance he is released from prison, none of these cases will be prosecuted. Unlike TV courtroom dramas, real-life murders do not always come tied up in a neat package stamped CONVICTED.

Chapter 20

An Interrogation Ends in Drama

At their St. Johns County headquarters, Welborn and Strickrott, along with other task force members, continued the tedious and time-consuming task of checking out the information they had obtained from Lindsey. As weeks went by, they developed a detailed timeline of his movements and activities over the years. In this way they were able to determine where Lindsey was around the time of each of the six murders, what kind of vehicle he owned, whom he had been seen with, etc. As the information accumulated, it became obvious that Lindsey was, at the very least, a strongly viable suspect in six of the St. Augustine killings.

It was learned that he had frequently utilized the services of prostitutes in Ocala, Palatka, and St. Augustine. Information gathered during the investigation also revealed that Diana Richardson may have been acquainted with Lindsey prior to her disappearance. In attempting to verify some statements Lindsey made, a number of inconsistencies appeared, so it became necessary to clarify these by reinterviewing him.

Despite Lindsey's seeming cooperation during their initial interview with him, what they had since discovered suggested that he had been lying about many details and revealed a number of discrepancies in the account he had given them of his activities. Another aspect of Lindsey that raised red flags for the investigators was his troubled childhood and disturbed marriages, a pattern typical of many serial killers.

On March 24, 1997, armed with this information and photographs of the victims, the task force members returned to North Carolina, well prepared to confront Lindsey with incriminating circumstantial evidence. Rather than meeting with him in the typical sterile "interrogation room," it was decided to bring him to the large, comfortable conference room on the second floor of the Buncombe County Jail. In these surroundings they felt they would be able to make Lindsey feel he was simply being questioned as a possible witness, rather than being accused of any particular crimes. Welborn, Strickrott, and Detective Jennifer Ponce sat surrounding Lindsey at a large table.

Ponce noted that none of the law enforcement officers were armed during this meeting. This was possibly a jail requirement or may have been done in order to confront Lindsey in a nonthreatening manner. A critical part of the interviewers' strategy was to make Lindsey feel that he was being listened to and understood. As seasoned interviewers they knew it was important to allow the suspect the opportunity to justify himself and what he had done.

Detective Ponce took notes as the interview proceeded. For about fifteen hours with breaks for food and rest, the interview continued. When questioned regarding the discrepancies in his previous interview, Lindsey became increasingly nervous and defensive.

He backpedaled on a number of the details he had given them. He also continued to insist that he had no criminal record in Florida.

As the questioning became more intensely focused, Lindsey began talking about God, his religious beliefs, and the fact that as a Christian he couldn't possibly be lying.

"We were looking for a crack in Lindsey's armor," Strickrott recalled. "When he started talking about religion, I felt this might be the opportunity to apply more pressure. During a break from the interview, I had one of the jail personnel bring me a Bible."

When the interview resumed, Strickrott said to Lindsey, "I'm a religious person and you say you are a religious man. Let's, the two of us, sit down and put our hands on this Bible. If you tell me then that you are telling the truth, we'll let you alone."

Confronted with the Bible, Lindsey kept changing the subject. Now his previously calm demeanor gave way to nervousness and fidgeting. A line of sweat appeared on his forehead. When pressed for an answer, he would remove his hand from the Bible before responding. "He couldn't lie to us with his hands on the Bible," Strickrott said. "But even though he was becoming more and more nervous, there was still no admission of guilt in the St. Augustine murders."

The task force investigators took another break from the questioning to discuss their strategy. They went over Lindsey's background, including the facts of his adoption, his childhood under a stern, abusive mother, and his anger toward his wife after learning she had been a prostitute. The investigators felt that these events had instilled in Lindsey a tremendous rage toward women and the inability to perform sexually unless the act was accompanied by violence. This hypothesis was substantiated further by the brutal manner in which the St. Augustine victims had been murdered. To attack so savagely, a man would have to hate women.

The detectives reasoned that, having had these kinds of experiences and feelings about two of the key women in his life, Lindsey would have considerable anger and resentment against any woman who tried to control him. If they were able to get Lindsey to exhibit this anger against women, they felt they would be able to get a confession from him. Strickrott had noticed that during the interview Lindsey had focused frequently on Detective Jennifer Ponce, an attractive, well-endowed young woman. Strickrott suggested that before the next questioning session, she unbutton the top button of her blouse. "Then, the next time he seems to be lying or evading the question, I want you to get up and lean over and stick your fist in Lindsey's face and scold him."

At an appropriate moment in the interview, Ponce made her move. She put on an impressive performance, screaming at Lindsey like a U.S. Marine drill sergeant. "Blessed him out like he was a three-year-old she was scolding," Strickrott later recalled.

The results were dramatic and Lindsey's reaction was all that the investigators could have hoped for. He erupted violently, eyes blazing like those of an enraged animal. He grabbed Ponce's hand and shoved it aside, and it was obvious that if the two male detectives hadn't been in the room, he would have attacked her. "It still sticks in my mind—the fire in that man's eyes," Strickrott recalled. "He was like a caged animal that had been backed into a corner, an aggressor. There's no doubt in my mind that he wanted to rape her."

Ponce also described the incident in vivid terms. "When I did that—made him angry—I knew what every single girl he killed experienced. I could see that he wanted to kill me. I had talked to some of the women he attacked who survived and they all reported that he displayed a 'haze' when he got angry. That's what I saw when I confronted him in North Carolina—that haze."

The aftermath of the confrontation was equally dramatic. Just as suddenly as he had lunged toward Ponce, Lindsey stood up, went to a corner of the room, placed his head against the wall, and started sobbing. "He cried like a whipped child," Ponce said.

"At that point," Strickrott said, "I knew we had him. The game was over."

Ponce, shaken herself, walked out of the room to regain her composure.

Welborn and Strickrott showed Lindsey a chart they had prepared of the St. Augustine victims, allowing him to examine their photographs, but concealing their names, vital statistics, and details of their murders. Lindsey studied the chart for some length of time. Then he went through it, pointing with his finger, and said, "I killed this girl. I know I did not kill this girl. And I killed this one."

The two for whom he gave most positive identification were Diana Richardson and Cheryl Lucas, his most recent victims. He drew a map of the area where the body had been abandoned. The map was faxed to St. Augustine and detectives there verified it as correct in regard to the area where Cheryl Lucas's body had been found. Lindsey then offered to go to Florida and help them locate Diana Richardson's body. He wanted to know how soon they could arrange to get him down there. Strickrott replied that he wasn't sure, that he would have to return to Florida and make the arrangements.

The detectives took a break and went into the hall to inform Ponce that Lindsey had admitted to the two most recent St. Augustine murders, those of Cheryl Lucas and Diana Richardson. When Ponce returned to the room, Lindsey apologized to her. He then gave a detailed description of the circumstances under which he killed Cheryl Lucas, as recorded by Detective Ponce in the following report. For the first time detectives were hearing the details of the crime from the killer himself.

The interview took place in the Buncombe County Detention Center and began at approximately 4:00 P.M. Sergeant Welborn, Detective Ponce, and FDLE Special Agent Strickrott were in the room with Lindsey. After Lindsey had been read his Miranda Rights and signed a Waiver of Rights form, he admitted his responsibility for killing Cheryl Lucas.

Lindsey said that he had picked up Cheryl after midnight in the parking lot of the Pic 'n Save at King and Palmer Streets in West Augustine. He claimed he was driving his 1988 black Ford Ranger when she flagged him down. He described her as a black female with short hair who was small and lanky and was possibly wearing a rain jacket. He said that he had never seen Cheryl before that evening, nor did he know her name.

After Cheryl got into the passenger seat of his car, Lindsey claimed that she reached into either the ashtray or the open glove compartment and stole something. He said it couldn't remember exactly what, but thought it was money she took. After that she leaped out of the truck and ran toward the railroad tracks on the west side of Palmer Street.

Infuriated, Lindsey reached under his seat for a flat bar similar to the type of pry bars used in construction and began chasing her. He caught up with her at a grassy area near the tracks a few yards from Palmer Street where he grabbed her and hit her with the bar, knocking her to the ground. He struck her three or four times more, then went back to his truck and drove it to where Cheryl's lifeless form lay crumpled

on the ground. He heaved her body into the back of
the truck and drove off.

With his macabre load in the back, Lindsey stuck to
the less-traveled Old Dixie Highway and Old Moultrie
Road until he reached Lewis Point Road. There he
turned east through the intersection with US 1 and
onto St. Augustine South. When he reached the boat
ramp several miles farther along, he turned off his
headlights and backed the truck as close as possible
to the riverbank as if intending to launch a boat.

He seized Cheryl's body by the waistband of her
shorts and pulled her from the truck bed. He claimed
that as he did so, her shirt and shorts came off and
her underwear was pulled down. He dragged her to
the water's edge, threw her in the river, then tossed
her clothing into the water.

As to his reason for killing her, Lindsey testified that
it was because she tried to "rip him off" and that this
made him very angry.

After this confession was completed, Lindsey told of
the murder of Diana Richardson. Again he had a remarkable recall of details of the killing.

He stated that he had met Diana Richardson in September, 1995, at an apartment complex on Masters
Drive where a friend of Diana's was living. On this occasion, Diana revealed to him that she lived nearby on
Davidson Street off State Road 16. He claimed that at
a later date he went to Diana's house and gave her
thirty dollars for what he referred to as a "finder's fee."
He inferred that he paid this sum to Diana in order to
arrange a tryst with her friend, but this arrangement
apparently never took place.

In October of that same year when Lindsey was en
route from Asheville, North Carolina, to Florida, he
went to Diana Richardson's house again. Although it
was around two or three in the morning, when he
asked if she wanted to go for a ride with him, she

agreed and they set off for what was to be a paid sexual encounter. From Davidson Street, Lindsey turned his white Monte Carlo west onto State Road 16 and then onto Four Mile Road. From there he proceeded toward the Holmes Boulevard put area where he had previously abandoned Connie Terrell's body.

Lindsey told investigators that while he drove Diana was rubbing his penis and he obtained an erection. He stopped the vehicle and backed it into a small driveway area by the pond. After killing the motor, he unzipped his pants and moved to the middle of the front seat. Diana, still fully clothed, proceeded to give him a blow job as they had previously agreed upon. At some point during this process she bit his penis. Angered, he hit her on the back of her head with a blow that knocked her unconscious. She collapsed with her head resting on Lindsey's upper right thigh.

Lindsey reported that he got out of the vehicle and walked around to the passenger side where he opened the door and seized Diana's body in a fireman's carry. He hauled her to the edge of the pond, threw her in, and watched as her body floated six or eight feet from the shore. He estimated that the pond's depth at that point was about thirty feet.

Lindsey signed an affidavit attesting to these facts. He then also implicated himself in some of the other St. Augustine killings, but because they were older cases, Lindsey said he needed "time to get his facts straight." He also claimed that he "wanted to do the Lord's work" by admitting to his involvement. At this point the task force investigators decided not to press for more detail, but to give him time to think things over.

In an attempt to explain his motive for the killings, Lindsey told the investigators, "You've got to understand that there's a Good Bill and a Bad Bill. Good Bill is a decent person, does the right thing. Bad Bill is someone society needs to be afraid of."

At this point the tension and emotions were running so high that the investigators did not press for much more information. In all, during their second trip to North Carolina, they spent approximately thirty hours of intense interviewing, not counting time out for meals and sleep. It had proved a traumatic and draining process for everyone involved.

Between 3:00 and 4:00 A.M., Lindsey was led back to his cell and the investigators walked out into the chill of the mountain dawn. "We felt as if we should be jubilant at having gotten the confession, but it was odd," Detective Jennifer Ponce recalled. "Our reaction was just the opposite. We were emotionally drained, barely dragging ourselves. I think we all knew our work was just starting."

Chapter 21

Lindsey Returns to Florida

Some months after his dramatic disclosure in Asheville, Lindsey was returned to St. Johns County, this time to identify the places where he had discarded his victims' bodies. While still incarcerated in North Carolina, he had obtained representation from a local attorney, David Belser. Belser was appointed to represent Lindsey. Belser, a graduate of Harvard and University of South Carolina Law School, was a veteran criminal defense lawyer with nine years of experience as a public defender and about ten years of private practice. In that time he had represented seventy-five to one hundred people charged with first-degree murder.

Lindsey seemed to be growing increasingly anxious to return to St. Augustine. On March 27, Detective John Harrison had received a page from the detention center saying that Lindsey wanted to speak to him or Sheriff Medford. When Harrison arrived at the jail, Lindsey told him that he wanted to go to St. Augustine as soon as possible, that there was a matter he needed to clear up with one of the detectives. Sheriff Medford said they would get hold of attorney Belser and let him know what Lindsey wished to do. To this, Lindsey responded, "Well, I'm going to Florida against my attorney's wishes or not. I want to travel to Florida and I want to go as soon as possible."

Attorney Belser received a call from Buncombe County district attorney (DA) Ron Moore saying that Lindsey had confessed to at least some of the Florida murders and that if he was cooperative and helped locate the missing bodies, the district attorney's office would not seek the death penalty in North Carolina. Belser was disturbed that Lindsey had offered the confessions to the Florida detectives without his attorney present. This issue would later present a stumbling block to Florida prosecutors.

Finally the arrangements to transport Lindsey from Buncombe County Detention Center to the St. Johns County Detention Center were completed. On Tuesday, April 1, 1997, Buncombe County sheriff Bobby Medford, Sergeant John Harrison, and Sergeant Jimmy Medford escorted Lindsey from North Carolina. Lindsey had voluntarily agreed to come to St. Augustine to assist the task force by revealing where he had disposed of Diana Richardson's body, as well as that of Cheryl Lucas. He had also cautiously alluded to the possibility that he might be responsible for several more of the female victims whose homicides they were investigating.

During the trip down, traveling to the various crime sites, Lindsey was in shackles, wearing both leg and arm restraints. Conversation during the five-hundred-mile trip was casual and nonconfrontational. The investigators were hoping to continue the rapport they had previously established with Lindsey in order that he would fulfill his promise and lead them to the sites where he had committed his murders and abandoned the bodies of his victims.

One of the major concerns Lindsey expressed about returning to St. Augustine was that his mother would learn the details of his crimes. "He was scared to death she'd know," Special Agent Strickrott said.

Optimism warred with caution as the detectives began escorting Lindsey to the sites he had indicated as being where he had disposed of the women's bodies. With Lindsey in the lead car directing the North Carolina officers from one location to the next, Detectives Ponce and Welborn, Jimmy Medford, and Special Agent Strickrott followed in other vehicles. Since the North Carolina officers were unfamiliar with the area, it was felt there was no chance of any of them indicating to Lindsey where the bodies were left. This was of critical importance because if he could identify those sites accurately without any help, it would go a long way toward proving his guilt.

Detective Jennifer Ponce recorded that at approximately 9:00 A.M., the task force and the North Carolina officers met at the Task Force Office on Lewis Speedway to escort Lindsey to the sites where he had abandoned his victims' bodies. The first area they visited was the Holmes Boulevard pit area. When the arrived there, Lindsey motioned for them to stop at a narrow, unpaved road on the east side of Holmes Boulevard. From there, they parked and walked down to the pond. He directed them to a clearing on the bank of the pond and told them that this was where he had thrown Diana Richardson's body. Previously, while being interviewed in Asheville, he had drawn a map of this pit area, which became an important piece of evidence in the case. This map identified the exact location to which Lindsey led them.

Under Lindsey's direction, the officers next proceeded to the boat ramp in the St. Augustine South area, following the same route Lindsey had taken the night he transported Cheryl Lucas's body to that spot. They pulled into a boat ramp, but after checking out the area Lindsey said this was not the correct boat

ramp. They continued driving until they reached the
north St. Augustine boat ramp. This spot Lindsey
identified as the correct one where he had disposed
of Cheryl's body along the bank.

Lindsey's next revelation was in reference to the Lisa
Foley murder, which had occurred in 1983, five years
before Anita Stevens was killed. Lindsey directed the detectives to the spot where he thought he had disposed
of her body, a marshy area off the intracoastal waterway.
A dirt mound he indicated in the middle of the road
prevented the vehicles from going any farther. He mentioned having picked up the girl at the Tradewinds
Lounge, but could not recall her name. He was uncertain if this was Lisa Foley or some other girl he had
killed and disposed of at that location.

The caravan then proceeded north and crossed
the 312 Bridge. As they did so, Lindsey proceeded
to say that he "had killed someone at this location"
and that he had disposed of the body along the bank
of a pond.

After having lunch at Long John Silver's seafood
house, the homicide task force escorted Lindsey back
to their office. At 2:30 in the afternoon, they read
Lindsey his Miranda rights, he signed the waiver of
rights form, and a detailed interview was begun. He
began talking about Anita Stevens's murder, describ-
ing exactly the manner in which she had been killed
and how her body had been left. This testimony was
first taken verbally; then, when asked for a written
statement, he asked that Detective Ponce write it for
him as he dictated.

At this point optimism was running high among
members of the task force, who actually could see a
glimmer of hope that their yearslong investigations
were beginning to show results. On April 1, 1997, the
sheriff's office issued a news release revealing the results to date of their investigation of Lindsey as a

suspect in "several unsolved murder cases in St. Johns County." The release went on to state:

Further interviews with Lindsey today (Tuesday) confirmed investigators' suspicions that Lindsey has direct knowledge of at least two St. Johns County unsolved cases. These cases include an unsolved homicide of Cheryl Lucas who was found in the marsh near St. Augustine South in 1995 and the disappearance of a St. Augustine woman identified as Diana Richardson, who has been missing since November 1995. Efforts are being made now to locate her body. Detectives will continue to interview Lindsey on additional unsolved homicide cases as well.

Sheriff Perry and FDLE Special Agent-in-Charge Rick Look (who assigned Special Agent Allen Stickrott to the task force) were pleased with the progress that the Joint Task Force has made over the past 14 months. Agent Look added, "We are certainly encouraged by the information supplied and the cooperation from Sheriff Medford and his staff to assist with this complex investigation."

During the time Lindsey was being held for questioning in St. Augustine, one afternoon as Sheriff Perry was on his way home, he stopped by the task force location, where Lindsey was being questioned. The sheriff hadn't previously met Lindsey, but he was aware that Lindsey had grown up in St. Augustine. Perry also knew that Lindsey had attended Ketterlinus High School at about the same time Perry's own brother and sister were students there. "I just wanted to get some sense of what kind of person he was," Sheriff Perry reported.

Perry didn't directly question Lindsey about the crimes, but he chatted with him about people they knew in common. Lindsey was quite pleasant during this interchange, interested in hearing about mutual acquaintances and asked about several of the people he had gone to school with. For about half an hour, the two men chatted and reminisced.

But the conversation took an unexpected turn when Lindsey asked about another school acquaintance, Jackie Bennett. Perry replied, "He's not doing very well. Bill, Jackie's daughter is one of the women who was killed."

Lindsey's reaction to that information was astonishing. "At that moment his facial expression changed from an open, friendly one to a hard, secretive look," Perry said. "His eyes turned absolutely cold."

It was obvious that Lindsey had not been aware previously that one of his victims was his friend's daughter. It was also obvious that the conversation was over. But, to Perry's further surprise, Lindsey then asked that he bring the detectives back in, that he wanted to "tell them something."

Lindsey then gave a chillingly detailed account of the murder of Connie Terrell, his second known St. Augustine victim. "On or about June 10, 1989," he stated, "I came to St. Augustine to visit my mother. I left that evening about dusk and went riding in the West Augustine area." Lindsey recalled that while driving his 1985 dark blue Ford LTD in the area of King and Davis streets, he spotted a small, thin white female wearing a cotton shirt and jeans. He stopped to roll down his window and asked if she dated. She said that she did, got into the car, and directed him toward the Holmes Boulevard pit area where they parked in a clearing by the pond.

Their sexual encounter began, but Lindsey claimed that when he was unable to obtain an erection, Connie laughed at him. That, he said, provoked his attack on the small defenseless woman, during which he placed a noose around her neck and dragged her from the car as she pleaded for mercy.

He beat and kicked her, then dragged her back toward the car and seized his Marlin .22 caliber semi-automatic rifle from the back seat. This was a gun he had purchased at a garage sale in Palatka. Connie, down on all fours, begged for her life as Lindsey, yelling and cursing at her, held the gun to her head. Pointing the barrel directly at her face, he pulled the trigger.

After determining that Connie was dead, Lindsey laid down the gun, picked up her limp body, and carried her to the pond where he dumped her along the bank.

He then described hunting for the spent cartridge, using his vehicle's headlights to find it.

> Then I drove back towards my mother's house. I threw the spent cartridge out of this window toward the median of the road. I can't remember exactly what I did with the remainder of her clothes, but I probably threw them in the Sebastian Creek on my way home.

In the report taken by Detective Jennifer Ponce during this interview, she recorded:

> It should be noted that during the course of the interview W. Lindsey commented that he wanted to execute her (Connie) and there were times when he was hitting her, he commented that he just was not ready.

Ponce took this to mean that he wanted to enjoy seeing the terror in his victim and seeing her suffer before finally killing her. This is behavior typical of sadistic serial lust killers.

Detective Ponce recalled that the only time Lindsey showed great emotion when talking about the cases was when he described shooting Connie. "When he talked about that, you could just see his heart pounding," she said.

Later, after offering more information about the rest of the victims, Lindsey agreed to take the detectives to the murder sites and point out the locations where the bodies had been discarded.

Given that some time had passed—nearly nine years in the case of Anita Stevens—Lindsey was not entirely clear as to all of the locations, but he was able to identify most. It appeared he was willing to cooperate in solving these cold cases. He pointed out the locations for the bodies of Anita Stevens, Lashawna Streeter, Cheryl Lucas, and Connie Terrell.

In a confession taken on April 1, 1997 by Detective Ponce, Lindsey gave a detailed account of the events leading up to his slaying of Anita Stevens. "I was going down King Street about 6 to 7 P.M., driving my '85 LTD Ford car. A little past Riberia I saw this girl walking. I honked at her and she waved."

Lindsey stated that he asked Anita where he could get a date and she "said she would do me for forty dollars." With that matter settled, they headed down US 1 onto State Road 312 and crossed over the Matanzas River. On the east side of the bridge, Anita directed him to a turnaround near a pond on Fish Island Road. Once there, they climbed into the back seat.

Lindsey stated, "We threw our clothes on the floor board and messed around, but no intercourse." Sometime later, he claimed, they got into a fight, although he could not recall what had instigated it. He said Anita scratched him on his arm and shoulder and the violence escalated. He described it as not a "solid fight" but a struggle, interrupted by periods of chasing and fighting. But it was obvious from his words that the situation soon became a perilous one for Anita. "We were fighting outside the car and I picked up a three-foot-long piece of board, maybe about 1-by-6. I hit her several times on the upper portion of her body."

According to Lindsey's account, Anita continued yelling, screaming and cursing at him as she fought back and tried to pick up something with which to defend herself. He landed more blows with the board. She went down and he continued to pound her face and body. When she was finally still, he threw away the board. "I then took a piece of tree branch from the ground and stuck it in her vagina and her butt. After that, I carried her about fifteen feet to the pond and threw her in."

He could not remember whether or not he had inflicted the bites the coroner later found on Anita's body but he did admit to having choked her with her own necklace. He said that after disposing of Anita's body he wiped the blood off his arms and hands then returned to the car and put his clothes on. Leaving the scene, he drove to a 7-11 Store at King Street and US 1 where he washed himself in the bathroom. After that, he stated, "I went home to my Mom's at Sylvan Drive."

(At the bottom of this confession under the words "I swear/affirm the above statement is true and correct," he signed his name, *William D. Lindsey*.)

His confession to Lashawna Streeter's murder, again recorded by Detective Ponce, was equally detailed. He stated that he had driven from Palatka to St. Augustine and ended up at what he referred to as Crack Head Corner, where a lot of people were sitting around on a bench. He described the manner in which a black female approached his Ford Granada and that he had told her he wanted a white girl. She said she knew where he could find one for a fee of thirty dollars.

He then related that as they were driving in the car,

she grabbed some money that was sitting on the seat and tried to jump out:

> *She managed to get the door open, but I hit her. I stopped the car and started hitting her more. I knocked her unconscious. I shut the door, turned the car around, and headed back towards King Street.*

He said that when he got to a clearing off a deserted road, he pulled Lashawna out of the car by her head and started beating her again. After kicking her and strangling her with a chokehold, he carried her body into the woods and laid it in a low-lying area with standing water. "But I didn't feel comfortable how she was too exposed," he added, "so I covered her body with some underbrush and then left."

Lindsey was not able to explain how Lashawna's shirt was pulled up or how her jeans were pulled down, and he did not indicate that any sexual activity occurred. Almost as eerie as the killing was his final admission:

"She didn't mention her name, and I did not know her."

In four of the six cases the detectives were focusing on, they found the bodies where Lindsey indicated he had left them. However, with Donetha Snead-Haile and Diana Richardson, no bodies had been recovered. He led the investigators to alligator and snake-infested Cracker Swamp, near Hastings, where he claimed to have deposited Donetha's body. Detective Welborn marked the spot Lindsey indicated by driving a stake through a tin pie plate. Cadaver dogs and their handlers were called to the scene. The dogs focused on the area near the pie plate. At that time the sheriff's diving team was called into action in hopes they might find Donetha's body.

St. Augustine and surrounding St. Johns County are

bordered by the Atlantic Ocean and abound with rivers, marshes, lakes, ponds, and borrow pits. These areas were often used by criminals to dispose of bodies, guns, and cars containing evidence, such as blood or finger-prints or sometimes drugs. For the past twenty-five years, the St. Johns County Sheriff's Office has had its own dive team composed of law enforcement person-nel who take on this sometimes dangerous task in addition to their regular duties.

To become a member of the dive team, an officer must have Advanced Open Water Division Certifica-tion, which meant he must have acquired basic scuba-diving skills. Once on the team, he continued training in areas such as mixed-air and tri-mixed div-ing, which involved using various gases in the tanks that team members carry strapped to their backs.

The number of divers was decided by the diver in charge, depending on the job. Often the dive team must work in swift-flowing rivers, where currents were strong and visibility poor, making the work extremely dangerous. In the local waters alligators and snakes abounded; in the Atlantic Ocean divers might en-counter sharks. Officer Tim Willingham, formerly of the St. Augustine Police Department and now a mem-ber of the Jacksonville Sheriff's Office Dive Team, reported that he never had encountered an aggres-sive alligator. "They have always given me a wide berth," he said. "But on several occasions I have had a sharpshooter on the surface 'just in case.'" Willing-ham also noted that with the current threat of terrorism, the dive team might also work with the bomb squad to check regularly the pilings around bridges, piers, and other potentially vulnerable un-derwater targets for terrorists.

Most often the divers were called upon to locate and retrieve bodies in homicide and accident cases, and to retrieve wrecked and stolen autos, guns, and other objects involved in crimes and accidents. In the Lindsey murders the team would be called upon to search for both Donetha Snead-Haile's body and Diana Richardson's.

Willingham provided a description of his equipment. A Public Safety Dive Team normally wore a wet suit in a thickness suitable to the season or a dry suit in very cold weather or polluted water. A full face mask was also commonly used to protect the face from exposure to hazards. A "buoyancy compensator"(BC) was a vest that could be inflated or deflated to adjust buoyancy in the water. Public Safety Divers normally wore BCs that have a lot of extra air capacity or more "lift." They also carried a scuba regulator and a tank of the appropriate gas for the dive.

Equipment varied for the mission, but a diver normally carried a small knife or tool for cutting entangling lines. They also had at least two lights, usually a main light and a smaller backup, plus emergency strobe lights, attached to their BCs for emergency rescue. Lift bags, reels, and various hand tools might be carried. Most divers carried a small slate and pencil for notes.

Human remains were placed in a bag and lifted slowly to the surface. There would be help waiting on the surface to enable control of the remains at all times.

In Donetha's case, despite prolonged efforts by the diving team, no evidence of the dead woman was found. Because the search occurred some four years after Donetha's disappearance, it was highly probable that animals had consumed her remains. A purse and shoe were recovered from the area, but it could not be determined whether they were hers or someone else's.

However, Lindsey's account of the killing of Donetha Snead-Haile was complete enough so that the investigators felt they could charge him with this crime as well.

He described how on April 4, 1993, he was driving down King Street in St. Augustine in his white Jeep Comanche truck: (The date Lindsey gave in his confession does not coincide with her mother's report that Donetha was missing on April 21. However, details he revealed of the crime convinced the investigators that she had been the victim he was referring to.)

> As I passed the railroad tracks, about 100 feet, I noticed a black girl alone, walking along the street by herself. I did not know her name. She was a very small-framed build. I pulled over and started talking to her and she agreed on $50.00 for a long while. ("A long while" apparently meant she would spend more than the usual twenty to thirty minutes with him. This is borne out by the fact that they went to his trailer and were there for several hours.) She got in. We discussed about where to go, and decided to go to the trailer where I lived on Master's Farm.

He described their activities upon arrival at his trailer:

> We went inside and drank a few beers and talked for a while. We watched a little T.V. the six o'clock news, and then I cooked something to eat. After we ate, about 20 minutes later, we went into the bedroom. We both had our clothes off. She gave me a "blow job," and then we had sexual intercourse for about 10 minutes. I ejaculated. I was not wearing a condom. Afterwards we both laid down and took a very short nap, about 20 to 30 minutes.

He claimed that it was only later, when he was driving her back to King Street, that she revealed that she was HIV positive:

> *I did not say anything else to her. I was very, very angry. I started planning to kill her. When we got to the end of the paved road I just stopped the truck and started beating her. I hit her with my fist about six or seven times and she went out. I did not get out of the truck. She was completely unconscious.*

As in his previous killings, Lindsey then found a swampy, wooded area in which to abandon Donetha's body:

> *I went into the woods about 30 feet along the bank and threw her in the creek. I then walked back to my truck and went back home.*
>
> *I remember taking many showers, scrubbing and scrubbing. I did not even sleep in the bed, I slept on the floor that night. I burned the sheets the next morning, then a couple of weeks later I burned the bed.*

Lindsey ultimately provided enough verifiable detail about the Florida crimes to convince the task force that he had committed them. He did not appear to embellish his crimes, nor did he seem to crave the publicity and attention sought by many other serial killers, such as Ted Bundy, Richard Ramirez, aka "the Night Stalker," and Keith Hunter Jesperson, aka "the Happy Face Killer." When unsure of details, Lindsey would respond, "That's what I remember and that's all I can say."

When escorted to the site where Anita's body had been found, he immediately noted, "This whole place has changed." He was referring to the absence of the piles of debris that had been present on the site at the time of the murder and the fact that a transmission tower had since been erected nearby. He was also quite specific about the rope ligatures on Connie's neck and the .22-caliber rifle he had used to kill her.

The strategy the interviewers used in their sessions with Lindsey grew out of their years of experience questioning suspects and the excellent police and psychological training that had been provided them during their law enforcement careers. Without the information gained from these lengthy interviews with the suspect, it would have been difficult, if not impossible, to have persuaded him to plead guilty to the St. Augustine murders. Had he not pleaded guilty, they would have faced even greater difficulty in attempting to convict him of the crimes.

Sheriff Neil Perry credited the discipline and stick-to-it-iveness of his staff for the success in bringing Lindsey to justice. "They never lost sight of the fact that we needed to get this monster off the street. The willingness of all the folks in law enforcement to stay with it was critical."

However, Sheriff Perry pointed out, confessions were not enough to convict a killer. Like eyewitness accounts, they have to be viewed with extreme caution, as just a piece to the larger puzzle. Even after Lindsey confessed to all six St. Augustine murders, the detectives' work was not done. Each confession had to be backed up with solid, factual evidence.

When the interviews were completed and the confessions for all the St. Augustine victims taken in detail, Lindsey waived extradition from North Carolina and was given over to Florida's custody.

While awaiting his trial, Lindsey was incarcerated in St. Johns County Detention Center. As a murder suspect he was held in Delta Block, the prison's highest-security area. Corrections Officer Jody Beasley reported that he was unfailingly polite to prison personnel, responding with "yes, ma'am," and "yes, sir," when addressed. Beasley, a seasoned corrections officer, also said that when accompanying Lindsey from one area of the detention center to another, he was so mannerly and congenial that she was forced to remind herself that this was a man accused of murdering numerous women.

Sheriff Perry recalled that while Lindsey was rather sulky and withdrawn, he presented no particular problems during his incarceration in the detention center. "Serious offenders, such as Lindsey, are less likely to cause problems in prison because they don't have to prove to anyone that they're bad. And they usually get along well in prison because they know that this is the end of the road for them. . . . They are never going to be released."

Authorities had hoped that when he arrived in Florida, Lindsey would agree to a plea of second-degree murder in all six cases. However, on the day of his initial hearing, he formally rejected the plea, fired his North Carolina attorney, and requested a public defender. Thus began a battle in which a number of legal issues would be raised, some of which, if upheld, could have damaged or destroyed the case against William Lindsey.

Chapter 22

The Legal Issues

The legal issues that arose between December 1996, when William Lindsey was arrested, until his final sentencing on July 8, 1999, yield an interesting picture of the strategies that can appear in complex homicide cases.

In William Lindsey's case the first step was to have a public defender appointed to represent him. Even this seemingly simple step was not easy. Because Lindsey was incarcerated in North Carolina and charged with the murder of Lucy Raymer, which had taken place there, the Buncombe County Public Defender's Office was assigned his defense. On December 30, 1996, public defender Bill Almond was appointed to serve as Lindsey's defense attorney. On that same day Faye Burner, another public defender, was in the Buncombe County Jail seeing a client. She overheard Butch Oxner, of the Asheville Police Department, interviewing Lindsey about where he lived and other questions of relevance to Lindsey's past. Burner reported this to public defender Almond, who then informed Oxner that any further questioning from that point on would have to come through him.

However, it was later discovered that the public defender's office had once represented Lucy Raymer in a case in which she was a defendant and their client. This prior involvement with the murdered woman meant Almond would have a conflict of interest if he defended Lindsey. Additionally, because of the conversation she had overheard, Burner could have become a witness in the ensuing suppression case.

On January 13 and 14, 1997, detectives of the task force from Florida interviewed Lindsey in the Buncombe County Jail. Lindsey's attorney, David Belser later claimed that it wasn't until January 23 that he learned that Lindsey had talked to the detectives from Florida and those from Virginia as well. Two years afterward, in a suppression hearing in Florida, Detective John Harrison, who headed the investigation of Lucy Raymer's murder, stated that he had contacted Belser and received permission from him for the other detectives to interview Lindsey. At the same hearing Belser denied having given this permission. The issue would prove to be a major point of contention at the suppression hearing.

On January 15, 1997, a search warrant affidavit permitting detectives to search Lindsey's person, his car, and the trailer in which he lived was executed and placed in the court file.

On March 21, 1997, after Lindsey's startling confession to the Florida task force detectives, attorney Belser received a call from Ron Moore, district attorney for Buncombe County. Moore told Belser that he was aware Lindsey had confessed to the murders in St. Augustine and that, if Lindsey would cooperate with the Florida authorities in solving the crimes there, his office would not seek the death penalty in North Carolina. Belser agreed that sounded like a viable option. He discussed this with his client, and Lindsey confirmed that he had made a confession to the Florida authorities. He also said that the Florida detectives had promised he would avoid the death penalty if he helped them find the missing bodies. Belser then confirmed these agreements with Buncombe County sheriff Bobby Medford.

Conversations between the two jurisdictions continued and eventually it was worked out that, in return for his cooperation with Florida authorities, Lindsey would be allowed to plead guilty to six counts of second-degree murder and receive a sentence of thirty years for each, to run concurrent with whatever sentence he received in North Carolina. One problem that arose was that under North Carolina law the death penalty cannot be waived in a first-degree murder case. This was resolved by reducing the charge to second-degree murder. With this, North Carolina authorities and those in Florida reached an agreement that there would not be a death penalty and that whatever sentences were given for the Florida murders would run concurrently.

Sheriff Neil Perry also confirmed that such an offer had been extended to Lindsey by Florida state's attorney John Tanner. The reason given for this offer was that, in the opinion of both Perry and Tanner, the physical evidence they had in the case was not sufficient to put Lindsey in the electric chair. However, they were convinced of his guilt as a serial killer and were determined to put him behind bars for the rest of his life. (Lindsey was sixty-two at the time.) Sheriff Perry stated, "I'm convinced if he ever gets out of prison, he will kill again."

Because of consternation expressed by some of the victims' families about the fact that Lindsey was being allowed to plea-bargain out of a death sentence, the sheriff met at the McQuaig home with twenty-three of the victims' family members to explain the reason for the offer. He said it had been given because the case against Lindsey was too weak to guarantee a conviction if it went to trial. "We're never going to get

Lindsey in the electric chair," Perry stated. Understandably, many of those present felt Lindsey should
be executed, but most agreed to the plea-bargaining
offer in the face of the nature of the case against him.

At this time Lindsey had been charged with first-degree murder in the Lucy Raymer case and was still
awaiting trial in North Carolina, but he had not been
officially charged with in any crimes in St. Johns
County. The agreement was offered to Lindsey as an
inducement to him to plead guilty to six charges of
second-degree murder in the Florida cases. (A seventh case, that of Lisa Foley's murder, was dropped,
due to the lapse of time and insufficient evidence.)
It is not unusual for different options to be discussed
in this manner before charges are filed. The issue of
the exact terms of the plea bargain would go on between Lindsey's attorneys and the prosecutor's office
for nearly two years.

By October 1997 Lindsey had been remanded to the
custody of Florida authorities and was transferred to St.
Johns County Detention Center. The warrant on which
he was transferred to Florida listed him as a suspect in
the death of Donetha Snead-Haile. Her body had not
been found, although Lindsey had pointed out in
March the location where he abandoned it. A public
defender, Douglas Withee, was appointed to defend
him in the Florida cases. Assistant State's Attorney
Robin Strickler withheld formal charges until Withee
had an opportunity to study the Snead-Haile case,
which was an especially difficult one owing to the absence of any remains or significant physical evidence.
Sheriff Perry thought the circumstantial evidence they
had was sufficient to charge Lindsey with her murder,
although he knew it would be an uphill battle to prove
him guilty at trial.

On November 10, 1997, Lindsey appeared before a
grand jury hearing at which prosecutors presented

evidence charging him with murdering the six women, one by shooting and the others by bludgeoning. The panel handed down a two-page indictment on the murders extending back to Anita Stevens's killing in November 1988. The following day, circuit court judge John Alexander announced that charges would be issued against Lindsey in all six cases.

But Lindsey, for reasons that have never been explained, abruptly fired his North Carolina attorney, David Belser, and announced that he was rejecting the plea offer that had been made to him. This startling development meant that the state's attorney's office was faced with the possibility of a long, tedious trial. His current attorney, public defender Douglas Withee, had an equally startling announcement on the day Lindsey was formally charged in Judge Peggy Ready's courtroom. Withee stated that he intended for the trials of the six victims to be conducted separately. This would have meant that the legal process could easily take six years or more. Withee pointed out that, in general, murder cases in St. Johns County required a year just to get from the point where the suspect was charged with the crime until the actual trial began. While it was suspected that this was a legal maneuver to gain a better agreement for his client, it caused consternation among the prosecutors and even more concern among the victims' family members who were present at the hearing.

At an arraignment hearing before Judge Richard Weinberg in December 1997, Withee again indicated he would be making a motion that the charges in each murder be separated, which meant each case would be tried separately. His rationale was that this would enable him to prepare each case better.

At this hearing Withee also asked to have a transcript of the grand jury proceedings. (Defense attorneys are not permitted to participate in grand jury hearings, which are held solely for the purpose of allowing the prosecution to show that there is sufficient evidence to proceed to trial. This evidence is sealed and can only be released if the judge so orders.)

During this procedure Lindsey sat slumped and seemingly emotionless as the charges against him were read. This would be his demeanor throughout all of the subsequent hearings.

In November 1998 Withee, after months of preparation, filed a motion with circuit court judge Robert Mathis to suppress the confessions Lindsey had made in Florida in March 1997. He supported his motion by claiming that during that period Lindsey had not been adequately advised of his rights, i.e., given his Miranda waiver. Assistant State's Attorney R. J. Larizza questioned Sheriff Bobby Medford and the St. Johns County detectives who were present when Lindsey pointed out the sites where he had deposited the bodies. All indicated that Lindsey had been given the Miranda waiver appropriately and as frequently as was required under the Fifth Amendment.

In addition, Withee asked that three of the six murder charges against his client be dismissed. Withee argued that with regard to Donetha Snead-Haile and Diana Richardson the state could not prove they were dead or even that any crime had occurred as their bodies never had been found. He also noted that prostitutes frequently led nomadic lives, moving from one town to another and leaving no forwarding address.

Withee also attempted to have the case of Lashawna Streeter set aside. His position was that, due to the extensive decomposition of her body, the cause of death could not be established. He implied that her demise could have been the result of an accident, disease, heart attack, or some circumstance other than murder.

Larizza rebutted Withee's arguments, saying there

was sufficient circumstantial evidence to try the cases on all of the counts specified.

The final issue Withee raised was to challenge Judge Mathis's previous agreement to allow the prosecution to obtain blood from Lindsey so it could be compared to that found at the various crime scenes.

Judge Mathis made his rulings on Withee's motions later in November. He refused to suppress the confessions made in March 1997 to St. Johns County detectives. In his opinion the investigators had followed appropriate procedures and had neither coerced nor forced Lindsey to confess to the crimes.

On the issue of Donetha Snead-Haile's and Diana Richardson's cases, the prosecution suffered a defeat as Mathis ruled that there was insufficient evidence to justify trying their cases. In his opinion, other than Lindsey's confession, the state had only the fact that the two women were missing. His decision rested on the fact that to prove murder the state must first demonstrate corpus delicti, meaning material evidence that a crime had been committed.

To the families of Diana Richardson and Donetha Snead-Haile, it was a bitter irony to find that, in spite of Lindsey's confession to having killed their loved ones, he could not be brought to trial in their cases.

Mathis's third ruling was that because the county's medical examiner had described Lashawna's death to have been a homicide, there was sufficient evidence to go to trial. He allowed that charge to stand. As Lindsey had rejected the plea bargain offered him, the case was now scheduled to go to trial in February 1999.

These decisions would prove critical in the upcoming trial. They were especially important to Lindsey as the state's attorney's office had earlier filed a motion to seek the death penalty. Now, instead of the thirty-year sentence that he would have received under the plea bargain he had rejected, he faced the very real possibility of being sent to the electric chair.

In response to Judge Mathis's ruling regarding the two women whose bodies had not been found, Robin Strickler, chief prosecutor in the St. Augustine Attorney's Office, argued that the grand jury had previously indicted Lindsey on the basis of the same evidence Judge Mathis was now rejecting. For this reason Strickler indicated that the state might appeal the decision.

A few months later public defender Withee came to Judge Mathis with an unusual request. He wanted St. Johns County to pay $2,400 for Lindsey to have cataract surgery in both eyes. His rationale was that Lindsey could not see well enough to read the legal documents involved in the case and therefore was not able to participate fully in his own defense. Assistant State's Attorney Maureen Sullivan Christine rebutted the request, indicating Lindsey must first apply to the jail's doctor, the sheriff's attorney, and the county attorney. "We can't just take this guy's word that he needs surgery," she maintained.

Judge Mathis ruled that he did not have the authority to order surgery for an inmate without medical testimony and denied Withee's motion. Because Lindsey was indigent, the county would have been obligated to pay for the operation if it was approved.

On February 16, 1999, a rather contentious hearing was held in Judge Robert Mathis's courtroom. It was to address the issue of the admissibility of evidence gained as a result of confessions and evidence obtained in the interviews of Lindsey by Florida detectives on January 13 and 14, 1997. This was a crucial point upon which the entire case against Lindsey could have collapsed. At this time, although Lindsey was being represented by attorney Douglas Withee, his former attorney, David Belser, appeared as a witness for the defense.

In this hearing Maureen Sullivan Christine, of the Florida State's Attorney's Office, was the prosecuting attorney. Christine, daughter of an engineer for the National Oceanic and Atmospheric Administration, was a graduate of Duke University and Stetson Law School. Robin Strickler, division chief of the state's attorney's office in Palatka, had done the indictment hearing after which the case was handed over to Christine. Christine credited the cold case task force for the remarkable job they did in putting together the case against Lindsey.

As many of the victims' family members were becoming upset at the ongoing legal struggle, Christine met with them before the hearing of February 16, 1999. She wanted them to understand the reason for the procedure and to give them confidence in her ability to handle the issues that might arise.

Under questioning by Withee, attorney Belser stated that he had not given permission for the Florida detectives to interview his client on January 13 and 14 in Asheville, and that any evidence obtained as a result of these interviews should not be admissible in court. The same held true, he said, for any other confession Lindsey might have made at that time. In rebuttal to Belser's statements, Sergeant John Harrison testified that he had requested and received permission from Belser for the Florida detectives to do the interviews, provided they did not discuss the Lucy Raymer case, which occurred in North Carolina.

When questioned further, Belser stated that when discussing these interviews, Lindsey told him he had asked for an attorney to be present and that his request was denied. Prosecutor Maureen Christine immediately objected to this testimony and her objection was sustained. She made the point that such testimony was hearsay and that Mr. Lindsey was present in the courtroom and could clear up the matter if he would testify. The defense, however, declined to put Lindsey on the stand. Had they done so, Christine would have been able to cross-examine him, which the defense did not want to happen.

Noting the conflicting statements, Judge Mathis said that up to that point in the hearing he had assumed the detectives had obtained Belser's permission for the interviews. While he was withholding a decision on that issue for the present, he wanted clarification of the terms under which the plea agreement had been reached. "My understanding at the last hearing we had was that all the times Mr. Lindsey was interviewed between January and March, counsel (attorney Belser) had agreed to allow him to do that and that contact was not made initially by the law enforcement but by Mr. Lindsey or his attorney. Is that still the position?"

Christine responded, "That is still [the prosecution's] position."

Belser repeated his earlier declaration that he had not agreed to interviews by Florida detectives prior to March 31, 1997. "I absolutely did not give Sergeant Harrison or Bobby Medford permission to discuss anything with my client on March twenty-seventh," he stated. However, he did indicate that he understood Detective Frank Welborn was eager to solve the Florida cases. Belser also admitted that he had agreed to Lindsey coming to Florida to help in the unsolved murders and to give consolation and closure to the victims' families. "In Ron Moore's presence I called Frank Welborn and confirmed the promises that were made to Lindsey the previous week on March twenty-seventh," he said. "And from Ron Moore's office and in his presence, I called Sheriff Bobby Medford and confirmed the agreement that had been made and the promise not to seek the death penalty in Florida. Only on the basis of these assurances did I allow Mr. Lindsey to go to Florida and continue his cooperation."

Belser testified that in the negotiations between North Carolina and Florida, his goal had been to save Lindsey from the death penalty. He had not considered the possibility that Lindsey would later reject the plea bargain after having accepted it. Nor had he anticipated that Lindsey would abruptly dismiss him as his attorney and waive extradition to Florida against his advice.

In regard to Belser's statement that he had not given his client permission to be interviewed by the Florida detectives, prosecutor Christine brought up an interesting point of Florida law. She maintained that the only time the Fifth Amendment (which protects a witness from self-incrimination) can be invoked is when questioning is imminent, meaning just about to happen. "You cannot just file a 'You cannot ever talk to my client' notice. Instead, notice must be filed shortly before each interview is requested," she stated.

As the hearing neared an end, Christine presented three witnesses to rebut Belser's claim that he had not given consent for the Florida detectives to conduct the January and March 1997 interviews with Lindsey. The first witness was Special Agent Allen Strickrott, of the Florida Department of Law Enforcement, and a member of the task force. He testified that he was told by Sheriff Bobby Medford that Lindsey's attorney David Belser had been contacted, knew the detectives were there to talk to his client, and had given permission for them to speak with Lindsey. "I was told that we were not to discuss any events in the North Carolina crimes, but that so long as we were talking about events in Florida, it was okay."

Referring to the second trip to interview Lindsey in March 1997, Christine asked, who had contacted Belser for permission? "I believe it was Sergeant Harrison," Strickrott said. "I was told that just before I entered the conference room to speak to Mr. Lindsey.

I was told again by Sheriff Medford that Mr. Lindsey's attorney knew we were present and had given permission to speak with Mr. Lindsey."

Christine asked, "Did you confirm with the defendant whether or not he had spoken with his lawyer and whether his lawyer was aware you were talking with the Florida detectives?"

Strickrott replied that in January, when he first met Lindsey, his opening statement to him was, "Has your attorney come to see you?" He said that Lindsey replied he had spoken with his attorney and that his attorney knew he was being interviewed. "At that point," Strickrott testified, "I advised him of his constitutional rights and Miranda warning."

Again in March, Strickrott said, he asked Lindsey if his attorney was aware he was speaking to the detectives and again Lindsey assured him that the attorney was aware of this. After this statement Strickrott again advised Lindsey of his rights. It was at this March interview that Lindsey was shown the sheet of paper with photographs of eight possible Florida victims, from which he definitely identified Cheryl Lucas as one of his victims and confessed to her murder.

Near the end of Strickrott's testimony, Christine inquired if during that interview he had made any promises to Lindsey. His reply was, "I never made Mr. Lindsey any promises. I've never entered into any plea negotiations with Mr. Lindsey." He did say, however, that at some time in 1998 he and Belser had discussed this issue in relation to the upcoming suppression hearing. At that time Belser told Strickrott that he would have to testify that Lindsey was acting on advice of counsel when he confessed to those crimes.

This further confused the issue of whether or not Lindsey had given information to the detectives on his own initiative, or whether he felt he was acting in accordance with his attorney's instructions.

Sheriff Bobby Medford was scheduled to be prosecutor Christine's next witness, but he was unable to appear due to physical problems.

Next Sergeant John Harrison, of the Buncombe County Sheriff's Department, took the stand. He, too, was called upon to testify to the issue of whether attorney Belser had given consent for the Florida detectives to interview Lindsey. Harrison stated: "On several occasions I called Mr. Belser and told him we had Florida officers in town and he (Belser) would say, 'They can speak to him, but they can only talk about the Florida cases, not the North Carolina case.' On some occasions Sheriff Medford would arrange for the Florida detectives to call me, saying he had talked to Mr. Belser and it was all right to take them to the interview room of the detention center and that they can conduct the interview."

In reference to the March 1997 interviews, Harrison explained, "I spoke with Mr. Belser. I think Sheriff Medford also spoke with him. And he agreed to let the Florida detectives go speak with Lindsey, but only on the Florida cases."

Later in his testimony Harrison also stated that, to his knowledge, at no time in the March 1997 meetings with the Florida detectives did Lindsey ever evoke his Fifth Amendment rights or say that he did not want to talk anymore, nor did he request that his lawyer be present. Harrison went on to verify that shortly after the interviews with the Florida detectives Lindsey paged him from the jail with the message that he wanted to talk. That same weekend he and Sheriff Medford met with Lindsey, who told them that he wanted to go to Florida and "clear up a matter with one of the detectives."

To this, Harrison said, Sheriff Medford responded, "We'll get hold of Mr. Belser and let him know you want to go to Florida." Harrison said that Lindsey's response was "Well, I'm going to Florida against my attorney's wishes or not. I want to travel to Florida and I want to go as quickly as possible."

Judge Mathis then asked Harrison, "You're saying there was never, to your knowledge, an invocation of the defendant's rights anytime between January first and April first?"

Harrison answered, "No, sir. Each and every time Lindsey was spoken to by an outside agency, his attorneys were always notified. They were aware he was going to Florida, and they were aware of the subject we were going to talk about, which at that point would have been the Florida cases." He pointed out to Belser that Lindsey would be talking not to him (Harrison), but to the Florida investigators.

Detective Frank Welborn, of the St. Johns County Sheriff's Office, was Christine's third and final witness for the prosecution. In response to a question about whether or not he had been informed prior to the March interviews that attorney Belser had given consent for his client to speak with him, he replied, "I was told by either Sheriff Medford or John Harrison that they had contacted his attorney and that it was okay for us to talk with him." Welborn also stated that he had never told Belser that he had the authority to negotiate a plea bargain on behalf of the state of Florida. According to Welborn's testimony, the first mention of a plea bargain he was aware of came the first week of April 1997.

The timing of the onset of plea bargain discussions was a critical issue. If it was proven that the information Lindsey gave the Florida task force detectives was collected during plea bargain negotiations, it would have been inadmissible in court.

Robin Strickler, of the state's attorney's office, had been involved in the plea bargain negotiations between Florida and North Carolina. In response to

Christine's question as to when the plea bargain was agreed upon, he said he thought it was April 3, 1997. "At that point I told him we would be willing to waive the death penalty, run the sentences concurrent with North Carolina, but that, of course, whatever we charged Mr. Lindsey with, he'd have to plead to," Strickler said.

"Do you recall off the top of your head what that plea agreement was?" Christine asked.

Strickler replied, "He was to plead to six counts of second-degree murder and receive thirty years in the Department of Corrections to run concurrent with North Carolina. The sentences were concurrent, not coterminous, meaning that if there was a larger sentence imposed in Florida, it would not end when his North Carolina sentence ran out."

Strickler went on to explain that a date had been set for the plea to be entered before the court. "Mr. Lindsey apparently rejected it," Strickler said. "I spoke with Mr. Belser, who told me that Lindsey was no longer talking to him and that the plea could never go through. Later Mr. Withee sent me a letter saying the plea was rejected."

Attorney Belser was called to the stand by Withee to rebut Special Agent Allen Strickrott's testimony that the task force had received his permission to interview Lindsey. "I never spoke with him directly or gave him permission to interrogate my client prior to March 27, 1997. I don't know what Sheriff Medford or Harrison may have told him, so I do not know whether that's correct or not." As to Strickrott's statement that Lindsey had told him on March 27 that his attorney was aware he was being questioned, Belser said, "I do not know whether that occurred or not, since I wasn't there. But in fact I did not know they were there and there would have been no way for me to know it unless I just sensed it out of the blue. I ab-

solutely did not give anybody, whether it's Sheriff
Medford or John Harrison, permission to interrogate
my client about capital homicides in Florida without
any plea agreement and without my being present."

Later Belser stated, "He (Strickrott) said that we
had discussions later about the case in which Strickrott stated that I said I would have to testify that Mr.
Lindsey was acting on advice of counsel when he
confessed. I probably did tell that to him, but I'm
talking about things that he said *after* March thirty-
first, when his confessions were made with my
permission specific to agreements that we had. Not
regarding anything prior to March 31, 1997."

Belser also denied having given Detective John
Harrison permission for the Florida detectives to
interrogate his client, and that if detectives from
other jurisdictions wished to interview his client, he
wanted to be notified. "I absolutely did not give either Sergeant Harrison or Sheriff Bobby Medford
any permission to discuss anything with my client
on March twenty-seventh."

After hearing more contradictory testimony of this
nature, Judge Mathis finally declared, "I don't think
perjury is probably a crime in the United States anymore, but somebody is lying in this case. I think we
need to have a special prosecutor appointed from
North Carolina to find out who. And I would certainly
like to hear from Ron Moore (the North Carolina
prosecutor in charge of the case there) about this entire thing."

Christine responded, "With every single state's witness, Mr. Belser has materially and diametrically
opposed everybody's testimony. I would like an explanation for that, and I'm sure the court would, too."

Judge Mathis replied, "Ms. Christine, I've already
figured that out. It's very clear that in this case somebody is lying."

Following this hearing, on behalf of his client, Attorney Douglas Withee filed another motion to suppress. This motion argued that the confessions Lindsey had made in North Carolina were in violation of his Fifth Amendment rights against self-incrimination.

A hearing on this motion was scheduled for March 20, 1999, in Judge Robert Mathis's courtroom. Again the victims' families were in court, fearful once more that by some legal ploy Lindsey was about to escape punishment.

But a surprise awaited the families, as well as both defense and prosecutors, on that day. Rather than attempting to escape his fate through more legal maneuvering, on that day Lindsey abruptly pleaded guilty to the murders of four of the St. Augustine women—Anita Stevens, Cheryl Lucas, Connie Terrell, and Lashawna Streeter.

By virtue of this plea, Lindsey avoided the possibility of a death sentence, had he gone to trial. It is possible the impetus for his about-face was publicity at that time about an execution carried out in Florida's infamous "Old Sparky" electric chair. In that recent execution, when the electricity was turned on, flames had shot out from behind the convicted murderer's face mask, leading to a gruesome spectacle for onlookers. It was reported that Lindsey dreaded the possibility he might meet a similar fate.

Following Lindsey's surprise capitulation, prosecutor Maureen Sullivan Christine commented, "We really didn't think he was going to plea to this. If we had had the confession suppressed, I didn't have a case."

Withee explained that the plea had been discussed with his client for months prior to the hearing and that he felt it was in Lindsey's best interest.

Following acceptance of Lindsey's guilty plea, Judge Mathis met with the victims' families and explained his rationale for acceptance: "He (Lindsey) is not in good health and he has thirty years to serve. The reality is that even if he were sentenced to die, he would not live to see the death penalty." Judge Mathis was referring to the long process of appeals involved in death penalty cases and the fact that some inmates spend decades on death row.

Meanwhile, the Fifth District Court of Appeals in Daytona, Florida, had reversed Judge Mathis's ruling involving the suppression motion in the cases of Diana Richardson and Donetha Snead-Haile. In tribute to the detective work of the St. Johns County Sheriff's Office, the appeals court noted that their decision in this type of case was rare, but that enough facts had been established even without the bodies to demonstrate that a crime had been committed. Acknowledging the close bonds between the victims and their families, the court also noted: "The facts in the St. Augustine victims' disappearance indicate that such absences without contacting family or friends are out of character."

In July 1999, four months after his original plea, Lindsey again appeared in court to plead guilty to the two remaining cases, that of Diana Richardson and Donetha Snead-Haile. In signing his plea agreement, Lindsey gave up the right to appeal these cases. The terms of his sentence were stated in the agreement as follows:

> *The defendant be incarcerated in the Florida Department of Corrections for a term of 30 years. The sentence to run concurrent, not coterminous, with any sentence the defendant receives in the State of North Carolina.*

Ironically, this agreement was the same that had been worked out two years previously.

At a sentencing hearing a month later, Judge Mathis required Lindsey to give two blood samples for genetic testing, a measure designed to insure that if other murders surfaced with a possible connection to Lindsey, DNA samples would be available. The judge also recommended in his sentencing that Lindsey be put in the general prison population and not receive any special privileges.

A number of the victims' family members spoke at this hearing, expressing the depths of their sorrow and their hatred of what Lindsey had done to their loved ones. Malvera Lucas, mother of Cheryl Lucas, brought a photo of her daughter and showed it to Judge Mathis. She suggested to the judge that Lindsey be forced to have photographs of his victims, on the walls in his cell. The judge, aware that most serial lust killers like to keep pictures of their victims, which they regard as trophies, declined the request, saying, "Unfortunately, based on what I have seen, I don't think that would be punishment."

Chapter 23

The Role of
Law Enforcement

*Your skills and abilities brought to a swift conclusion
a case which might well never have been solved otherwise.*
—Sheriff Bobby L. Medford, in a letter to
Detective Sergeant John Harrison

Too frequently, police efforts to apprehend serial
killers were thwarted by interstate and interdistrict ri-
valry, jealousy, and desire for publicity. These can turn
joint endeavors into a series of battles that include
withholding information, refusal to cooperate, and efforts at one-upmanship. Such reactions add to the
difficulty of identifying and capturing serial killers.
The end result was that the perpetrator often escaped
detection for years while he continued to prey on
other victims.

Such was not the case with the Lindsey murders.
Here, two diverse police departments cooperated
fully from the very beginning. After eight years of ex-
haustive police work following the discovery of Anita
Stevens's body in 1988, the combined efforts of the St.
Johns County, Florida, Sheriff's Office and that of
Buncombe County, North Carolina, had finally re-

sulted in the arrest of a dangerous serial lust killer, William Darrell Lindsey.

It should be noted as well that the Jacksonville Sheriff's Office, whose jurisdiction was adjacent Duval County, also rendered assistance to its counterpart agency in St. Johns County. For instance, when detectives focused on Dallas Porter as a potential suspect, Lou Eliopolis, an investigator with the Duval County Medical Examiner's Office, reexamined similar cases that had occurred in Duval.

Many law enforcement officers were involved in the remarkable investigative effort. Four individuals deserve special recognition for their major contributions to his capture.

When St. Johns County sheriff Neil Perry learned that a man from St. Augustine had just confessed to a murder in North Carolina that had chilling similarities to those committed in Florida, he wasted no time assigning some of his detectives to checking out the case. It was Sheriff Perry's alertness to the information and his immediate follow-up that was key to the killer's eventual capture and confession.

This kind of attention to detail and quick, incisive action has characterized Perry's career as a law enforcement officer and former colonel in the National Guard. A descendant of the Minorcans who originally settled St. Augustine, and member of a family with generations of involvement in police work, Perry began his law enforcement career as a sheriff's deputy working road patrol at a salary of $10,000 per year. His quick insights, his ability to deal with people from all walks of life, and his success in solving a number of crimes soon got him promoted to detective. He was elected sheriff in 1984. That he has continued in that elective office for over twenty years speaks to his professionalism and dedication to duty.

A quiet, scholarly man, Sheriff Perry has pursued extensive police training throughout his career. He received his bachelor's degree from Nova University and was a graduate of several nationally recognized law enforcement programs, such as the FBI Academy, the Chief Executive Course of the Florida Criminal Justice Institute, as well as that of the U.S. Army's Command and General Staff College. His career in both the National Guard and law enforcement have resulted in numerous awards, honors, and important assignments. In 2001 Governor Jeb Bush of Florida appointed Sheriff Perry as cochair of the Northeast Florida Regional Domestic Task Force.

In addition to following up on the initial clue in the Lindsey case, Sheriff Perry supervised the entire investigation of the St. Augustine murders and also directly interrogated Lindsey, with whom he was able to establish a good rapport. His most important contribution was to assure the full and open cooperation between his department and that of his North Carolina counterpart, Sheriff Bobby Medford. This teamwork between two departments, some six hundred miles apart, speaks to the professionalism of both sheriffs.

Sheriff Bobby Medford has had thirty-two years of experience covering many facets of law enforcement. Prior to his current position as head of law enforcement in Buncombe County, North Carolina, Medford served as chief of police in Rutledge, Georgia, and has held other positions as a detective, lieutenant, and captain. His special training included areas such as arson investigation, credit card fraud, sexual offenders, and the handling of rape cases.

Sheriff Medford had initiated programs in Buncombe County schools dealing with gang-resistance education and a Safe Kids Operation, which included fingerprinting and photographing children for identification purposes. These and other youth programs have brought him national recognition.

Sheriff Medford was important in the Lindsey case for several reasons. One was his capacity to relate effectively with Lindsey in a way that contributed to Lindsey's willingness to talk to detectives from both North Carolina and Florida. His full cooperation with St. Johns County law enforcement agents was a major factor in getting Lindsey to confess to the six murders in Florida.

On a personal basis Medford always has been a quiet, modest man with a deep, genuine commitment to law enforcement and the prevention of crime.

Detective Frank Welborn, of St. Johns County Sheriff's Office, headed the investigation team assigned to the six murders Lindsey committed in St. Augustine. Welborn has recently risen to the rank of lieutenant.

Despite the notoriety of the Lindsey case and the kudos it had earned for him, Welborn's greatest satisfaction in police work came from cases in which he was able to locate lost children. The Welborns have two children of their own.

In the Lindsey case, based on what Detective Welborn knew about serial killers and the brutality of the murders, he fully expected the killer to be a younger man. Lindsey was sixty-one years old when initially apprehended. This has led Detective Welborn to feel certain Lindsey killed many more victims than those to which he confessed. In fact, he and Detective Harrison felt so strongly about this that in September 2003, almost four years after Lindsey confessed, the two men drove to the Marion County Correctional Institute, where Lindsey was incarcerated, to attempt to interview him further. But by this time Lindsey had been advised by attorneys not to offer any additional information and refused to discuss any matters related to other possible murders.

Lindsey was the second high-profile killer Lieutenant Welborn has helped apprehend and convict. The other was Darnell Apple, a huge mountain of muscle and anger who was sentenced to life in prison ten years ago for a murder. (He remains a suspect in other homicides.) At the time of his sentencing, he threatened to kill Welborn when he got out of prison. Such threats were among the many dangers a career officer such as Welborn has to face.

In addition to his profession as a police officer, Frank Welborn was an expert craftsman who restored old tractors and Bronco automobiles. He is currently building with his own hands a home on the beautiful St. Johns River. He and his wife, who works in the state's attorney's office, plan to retire there when their careers are over.

Two other officers from the task force, Special Agent Allen Strickrott and Detective Jennifer Ponce, were key investigators in the Lindsey case. They, too, played significant roles in gathering the data that led to Lindsey's arrest and sentencing. Strickrott was the lead investigator in the task force, and several of the confessions about specific victims were obtained by Detective Ponce.

Like Frank Welborn, John Harrison, of the Buncombe County Sheriff's Department, had a long, distinguished record in law enforcement to which his many awards bore testimony. His career spanned over four decades. Harrison's courage was reflected by his single-handed capture of serial killer William Lindsey, who, at the time he was arrested, owned a .22-caliber pistol. Harrison's skills as an interrogator were demonstrated by his obtaining a confession to the Raymer murder within hours of Lindsey's arrest.

He, too, felt strongly that Lindsey undoubtedly killed many more victims than those to which he had confessed. Both Harrison and Welborn expressed the conviction that Lindsey's frequent moves from town to town were designed to escape detection and usually took place after he had committed another murder.

Harrison's interviews with prostitutes, drug dealers, and pimps in the Asheville area also validated other information regarding the sadistic treatment Lindsey wreaked upon prostitutes, even those he did not kill.

Along with his vast experience and training in law enforcement, John Harrison was also well known in his home area as an athlete, first playing varsity high-school football and basketball, and later officiating for many years at high-school sports events throughout North Carolina. He also enjoyed deep-sea fishing and was an avid fan of ACC basketball.

Harrison's previous experience with serial killers came with the Lesley Eugene Warren case. Warren, who, like Lindsey, had a violent temper, killed five or six young women before being apprehended and convicted.

What appealed most to Harrison about police work was catching offenders and seeing justice done. What he found most distasteful was the time it took to get final closure on a case.

Police work was often hard on a marriage, owing to the stresses of the job, such as irregular hours, the night work, and exposure to the temptations of the seamy side of life, with which officers must deal.

When asked about this, Detective Harrison explained that for him it had not been a problem, in part because his wife was the widow of a sheriff and knew what was involved in being married to a law enforcement officer.

As a result of his outstanding work on the Lindsey case, Harrison received a glowing commendation from Buncombe County Sheriff Bobby Medford. In his letter, Medford stated that Harrison's skills and abilities had brought a swift conclusion to a case that might otherwise never have been solved. He also mentioned other unlawful death cases, which Harrison had brought to successful conclusions. "If we have been successful in providing efficient, quality law enforcement and public service to the citizens of Buncombe County, such success has been greatly enhanced by your efficiency, experience, knowledge, and dedication to duty," he said.

Medford also commented on the close friendship and he and Harrison had enjoyed during their years of public service.

Sadistic serial lust killers, such as William Darrell Lindsey, are among the most difficult of all felony offenders to capture and convict. Were it not for the outstanding work of these law enforcement officers, Lindsey would be a free man today, prowling the streets of Asheville, St. Augustine, or some other town, seeking defenseless women to rape, torture, and murder.

Maureen Sullivan Christine was the prosecutor in the Lindsey case. A graduate of Duke University, where she played varsity basketball, Christine received her law degree from Stetson University Law School in Tampa, Florida.

A veteran of several high-profile court battles in Florida, she entered the Lindsey case late, but, despite this handicap, she was able to bring it to a successful conclusion. A crucial step in this victory was when she won on appeal in the Richardson and Snead-Haile murder cases after an initial ruling that there was insufficient evidence to bring them to trial. This not only led to Lindsey pleading guilty to their murders, but also meant that Lindsey would serve a minimum of 85 percent of his sentence. The law requiring this amount of time to be served was passed before Lindsey's last Florida murder, that of Diana Richardson.

Maureen Christine is married and the mother of a nine-year-old daughter.

Chapter 24

The Making of a Serial Lust Killer

There is something the matter with me. I just couldn't contain it. . . . It got too strong. I tried to suppress it. All the time I could feel the force building in me.
—Ted Bundy, in E. Kendall's *The Phantom Prince: My Life with Ted Bundy*

What made William Lindsey—in many respects, an average man—commit acts that brought incredible pain and gruesome deaths to his victims, and intense grief to those who loved them? What has driven Lindsey and hundreds of other serial lust killers to murder not once, but time and again—despite the high risk of such behavior to themselves and the strong probability that their killings will ultimately result in arrest, incarceration, and a possible death sentence?

Those questions are ones that psychologists, psychiatrists, and criminologists find almost as difficult to answer as those of us who read about these killer's bloody deeds in the daily newspaper. Repulsed by the act itself, we as a society are at the same time intrigued and mystified that a fellow human has behaved in such an inhumane fashion. To understand more fully the forces that impelled William Lindsey to kill, it is necessary to examine not only his life, but the lives of others who have committed similar crimes.

William Lindsey personified a particular type of murderer known as a sadistic serial lust killer. These are men who get sexual pleasure from raping, torturing, and gaining total control over women in the process of killing them. In its more extreme forms, this behavior may involve mutilation, dismemberment, cannibalism, and necrophilia. Some lust killers are sexually impotent unless they see the women with whom they are having intercourse screaming in pain, terrified, and begging for their lives. A number of them achieve orgasms simply through the torture, independent of actual intercourse or oral sex.

In almost every case the seeds that grow into sadistic serial lust killing begin in childhood with fantasies involving the torture, killing, and sometimes the dissection of animals and/or people. This raises a fundamental question about serial killers: What causes them to associate the expression of their sexuality with such extreme sadistic behaviors? Why are they fixated on sadistic fantasies as opposed to the relatively normal sexual fantasies of most boys and men? This is not to say that the fantasy life of average people does not become extreme at times, but the vast majority do not act out those fantasies.

The best explanation comes from an understanding of how most human learning occurs. A baby learns to cry when hungry because that will usually result in his being fed. Having a full tummy feels good. Hence the rationale is discovered: if I cry, I will get fed and then I will experience pleasant feelings. Conversely, people learn to avoid touching a hot stove burner because when they do it hurts. A rat in a cage quickly learns that when he presses the red lever, food appears, but if he touches the green one, he will get an electric shock. These simplistic examples illustrate one of the basic principles of learning known as conditioning.

The author's interviews with a number of Lindsey's schoolmates, former neighbors, and acquaintances revealed that his adoptive mother was a harsh disciplinarian. Consistently, they reported that as a child he was beaten with belts, chains, a frying pan, and other objects and that he became the family scapegoat for most mishaps in the home. After Lindsey's capture, this was confirmed in interviews he and his first wife, Willa Jean, gave to detectives.

In *The Killers Among Us*, S. A. Egger discusses how a child who is consistently mistreated in this fashion develops hostile fantasies about his abuser, fantasies in which he "gets even" by inflicting similar kinds of punishment, or worse, on his abuser. Because these fantasies are pleasurable and provide some outlet for the child's anger, he repeats them over and over. Eventually they become indelibly entrenched in the neural wiring and synaptic connections in his brain.

In his younger years, Lindsey would have been powerless to act out such hostile fantasies with adult women. Many such abused children, when denied an outlet for their hostility, turn to torturing animals. A neighbor of the Lindsey family reported that in at least one instance Lindsey deliberately killed a cat. Later in life, as a hunter and fisherman, he may have found pleasure in the cruelty and killing involved in these sports.

During puberty, a time when sexual preferences are still in the formative stage, abused children often mentally play out fantasies of torture and killing women while masturbating. With each orgasm—a pleasurable and rewarding experience—the association between sadism and sexual pleasure becomes reinforced. This at a critical stage of development; sex becomes associated with cruelty. This association of sex and sadism—involves the concept known as "critical stage learning."

The rationale underlying this concept is complex. Its basic theoretical framework is that in early childhood the brain is more receptive to learning than at any other time in life. For example, young children, especially those between the ages of two and four, attain relative fluency in their native languages at an amazingly fast rate with no formal instruction. On the other hand, most adults in their forties never attain fluency in a new language. Regardless of how hard they try, they will forever speak it with an accent and limited vocabulary and syntax.

In human sexuality, puberty is one of the critical stages for developing sexual preferences. If young Bill Lindsey followed the pattern of most abused children, it is highly likely that during this time he was associating his fantasies of aggression against his mother with the orgasms resulting from masturbation and that they were becoming fixated in his mind. Only when he grew older would he have the opportunities to act them out. Some scientists have posited that fetishes are acquired through such early imprinting. In this sense, serial lust killing is a fetish.

Another possible reinforcer of William Lindsey's need to torture, murder, and rape his victims is hypersexuality. The role of hypersexuality in the development of a serial killer is analogous to what happens in laboratory studies of rats. A rat that is always hungry will be more active in his cage. The more active he is, the greater the likelihood he will push the lever that releases food, whereas a more passive rat lacks a strong appetite and is less likely to push the lever. The hungry rat is rewarded by a full stomach and quickly associates pushing the lever with obtaining food. In short, the stronger the drive—be it hunger, sex, or thirst—the quicker and more strongly the behavior will be learned.

The same principle applies with a hypersexual male. An example of this is Albert DeSalvo, known as "the Boston Strangler." He desired sexual relations five to seven times a day. When a woman was not available, he would masturbate that often. Like Lindsey, DeSalvo's brutal home life had reinforced his hostility and sadistic feelings toward women that led him to rape and torture them. A man with less intense sexual drive might entertain those same fantasies, but would be less compelled to act them out. That doesn't mean that such an individual could not become a serial killer, but it would be less likely to occur. Nor are all serial killers hypersexual.

Evidence in Lindsey's records does suggest hypersexuality. According to information collected by the Asheville Sheriff's Office, even at age sixty-one he was obtaining prostitutes from a pimp four or five times a week in addition to soliciting women on his own.

Many other serial lust killers exhibit the same hypersexual tendencies. Mike DeBardeleben, an amazingly successful and versatile criminal, was reported by the FBI to have an insatiable sexual appetite. He escaped capture for eighteen years, during which time he tortured and killed up to twenty women. A highly intelligent man, he meticulously recorded his crimes. At his trial prosecutors presented to the court the following vivid description DeBardeleben wrote about the pleasurable reinforcement he derived from sadism:

> *The wish to inflict pain on others is not the essence of sadism. The central impulse is to have complete mastery of another person, to make him/her a helpless object of our will, to become the absolute ruler over her, to become her god, to do with her as one pleases, to humiliate her,*

to enslave her. . . . The most radical aim is to make her
suffer. . . . There is no greater power over another per-
son than that of inflicting pain on her. To force her to
undergo suffering without her being able to defend her-
self. The pleasure in the complete domination of another
person is the very essence of the sadistic drive.

Carroll Edward Cole, a sexual sadist with a genius
level IQ (152) who tortured and killed between twelve
and fifty women, was also hypersexual. He mastur-
bated at least four times daily. Harvey Glatman,
another bright, sadistic lust killer, was hypersexual,
with a passion for violent pornography. By the time he
was twelve, he was already practicing autoerotic as-
phyxia, a condition in which men achieve orgasm
through near-strangulation. These cases and many
others provide ample evidence of the role hypersexuality plays in serial sadistic crime. Unfortunately in
terms of research studies of serial lust killers, data has
rarely been obtained regarding their degree of hypersexuality.

Another primary factor that influenced Lindsey's
becoming a serial lust killer was his explosive temper.
Even as a young boy, Lindsey could not accept "no"
for an answer, especially if it came from a woman. As
he grew older, such a refusal could arouse in him uncontrollable rage, especially if the "no" meant a denial
of sex.

The possibility also exists that Lindsey was subject
to petit mal seizures. Several people who knew him
well have noted that he had "strange staring spells"
during which he seemed "out of it." His first wife,
Willa Jean, noted that Lindsey had bottles of phenobarbital in his closet. At the time she made this
discovery, this medicine was the major prescription
drug used to treat epilepsy. In certain epileptic patients petit mal is associated with aggression and

explosive behavior. The aggression results from an electrical discharge in the brain, which, by definition, is what constitutes a seizure. The discharge causes the neural connections in the brain to malfunction, impairing the brain's capacity to inhibit aggression. This is similar to the manner in which an electrical surge might cause a computer to lose its connection with the program it was working on.

In petit mal epilepsy, the individual may just appear dazed, stare off into space, or have a mild tremor of the hands. When the episode passes, the individual is left confused and still unable to inhibit his aggression effectively. At this stage, if angry, the person may act out his rage in an attack upon another person or possibly commit murder. After the anger has been expressed through violence and the episode is over, the individual may express regret. On occasion the condition may progress to a grand mal seizure and the person eventually passes out and has no recollection of what he has done. However, the actual physical attack occurs prior to the grand mal seizure because the movements during a grand mal seizure are random and not directed to fighting or killing.

Several incidents suggest that this may explain some of Lindsey's explosive episodes. He exhibited this type of behavior with Sandra Sullivan upon her refusal to go into his bedroom with him. After a brief staring spell, he attacked her without warning. Then, moments later, he apologized. A similar incident occurred with Rosalie Dawes who tried to steal some money from him as they were riding in his car. After a similar spell Lindsey flew into a rage and attacked her with a baseball bat, then stopped the car and apologized. His former sister-in-law, who lived with him and his second wife in Asheville for several years, reported that he would average about three rage episodes a week. These occurred after he had suffered a head injury in a serious car accident. Such injuries often precipitate epilepsy and epilepticlike episodes.

The background of several other serial lust killers also points to epilepsy as a motivating factor in rage outbursts like those Lindsey had exhibited. One such individual was Ken Bianchi, whose seizures started when he was a child. Along with his cousin and partner, Angelo Buono, Bianchi formed a team known as "the Hillside Stranglers." These two men tortured, raped, and strangled ten women.

Another epileptic killer is John Reginald Halliday Christie, who in addition to raping and strangling to death seven female victims, also engaged in necrophilia with their corpses. He shared Lindsey's problem of sometimes being unable to have an erection, earning him the nickname "Can't-get-it-up Christie." Unable to have intercourse until after two years of marriage, he was able to achieve orgasm only when raping and torturing his wife and the prostitutes he used. After his death in 1953, the bodies of his victims were found buried in and around his house. His story formed the basis for the film *10 Rillington Place.*

In *The Encyclopedia of Serial Killers* by B. Lane and W. Gregg and in *Dead of Night* by D. Lassiter, it is noted that Dayton Leroy Rogers, also an epileptic, committed some of the more bizarre sadistic lust killings. He would hogtie women, then torture and rape them. With three of his eight victims, he cut off their feet because he liked to see them bleed.

While it is unlikely that epilepsy is often the direct cause of sadistic serial lust killing, in some cases it appears to be a contributing factor to the degree of uncontrollable rage expressed in some of the killings and to the killer's lack of ability to control his aggression. With the increasing sophistication of medical imaging techniques, such as MRIs and PET scans, it is almost certain that some of the more subtle forms of seizure disorder will become diagnosable. When that occurs, the role epilepsy plays in determining aggressive behavior in general—and sadistic killing in particular—will be better understood. It should be noted that seizures can be triggered by forms of excitement other than rage, one example being sexual arousal. It is also important to emphasize that many individuals with seizure disorders are no more violent than the average person.

In addition to epilepsy, other forms of brain damage, including traumas and neurological diseases, are a significant cause of explosive anger, a condition present in William Lindsey. Frequently a relatively trivial incident triggered his outbursts. He would be momentarily swept away by anger, then feel remorse and embarrassment after it passed. Of the 180,000 people who suffer serious brain damage in automobile accidents each year, 70 percent have some degree of constant irritability or explosive aggression, and some are left with epilepsy. While brain damage rarely causes the sexual component of serial lust killing, it can be a significant factor in the aggressive aspect of some of these murders. When combined with sadistic tendencies, certain forms of brain damage heighten the risk of an individual's becoming a serial lust killer because they impair the brain's capacity to inhibit aggression and are associated with impulse-control problems.

Brain damage as a factor in explosive episodes leading to murder often goes unrecognized by the court system. This is especially true of indigent defendants, who lack the money required to have neurological experts testify in their cases. While it is definitely not the *cause* of most serial lust murders, a link between the two appears likely in some cases. An example is serial killer Robert Joseph Long, aka Bobby Joe Long, who killed ten or more women, whom he raped, strangled, and slashed. In E. W. Hickey's book, *Murderers and Their Victims,* Long is described as having numerous traumas to his brain, and had medical evidence of damage to his temporal lobe.

In common with many other serial killers, William Lindsey had a psychiatric history. Around the time of their divorce, he wrote Willa Jean a seven-page letter stating that he was going to kill himself. He then took his children for a drive and wrecked the car, severely injuring several of the children and inflicting a serious head injury on himself. Willa Jean was convinced this was a suicide attempt. Shortly thereafter, he voluntarily saw a psychiatrist in Gainesville for six months of outpatient therapy. No data were available on the findings from this therapy other than that he was given counseling with regard to his inability to satisfy Willa Jean sexually.

Mental problems are common among serial lust killers. Full-blown psychosis is present in some. Those with psychotic-level disorders often commit the more heinous lust murders. In *The Encyclopedia of Serial Killers* by M. Newton, Lawrence Bittaker is described as "one of the cruelest of all serial killers." He used pliers, vise clamps, and ice picks as torture instruments. The book offers a chilling account of how Bittaker stuck an ice pick through eighteen-year-old Andrea Hall's ear to her brain and recorded her screams on audiotape. He used pliers to rip off women's nipples and to mutilate their genitals.

Bittaker, who had a superior level IQ of 130+, spent most of his life in prisons and mental hospitals. With his colleague in crime, Ray Norris, he is believed to have tortured, raped, and killed thirty to forty women. At one time he was confined in Atascadero, a state mental hospital in California specializing in the treatment of sex offenders. After working with him for six years, the hospital released him as "no danger to others." That assessment was devastatingly inaccurate—Bittaker went on to torture and rape more victims.

Gary Addison, also a serial killer, spent eleven years in various mental hospitals. During his teens he began assaulting women with a hammer and later sniping at them with a rifle. Some of these incidents occurred when he was on furlough from the mental hospital to which he had been committed, even though patients judged by hospital psychologists and psychiatrists to be dangerous were not supposed to receive furloughs. Addison was diagnosed later by these same mental-health professionals to be a "safe bet" for release. Fourteen months later he had killed between four and twenty women.

These two cases are examples of mentally ill people who were sadistic lust killers. Although exact figures are not available, this type of individual represents a significant percent of all serial lust killers. These cases also illustrate the fact that social workers, psychiatrists, psychologists, and other mental-health professionals do a rather poor job of identifying and predicting the behavior of serial lust killers.

The case of Edmund Kemper, as described in the *Encyclopedia of Serial Killers* by M. Newton, also exemplifies the failure of mental-health professionals to recognize the dangers posed by such killers. At age fifteen, he killed his grandparents, after which he was consigned to a prison mental hospital for six years. When released after having received little or no treatment for his illness, his real killing spree began. A necrophiliac, he killed six young women and girls, dissecting and/or decapitating their corpses, then having sex with them. At times he cooked and ate parts of their flesh.

During the period of these murders, he was examined by a panel of psychiatrists appointed by the tate as follow-up to his previous psychiatric incarceration. The psychiatrists judged him to be "no threat to society," and they recommended that "his juvenile record of homicides be sealed for his protection." He drove away from this interview with the severed head of one of his victims, a fifteen-year-old girl, in the trunk of his car.

Later, perceiving his mother as an obstacle to his crimes, Kemper murdered her as she slept, crushing her skull with a mallet and decapitating her. Afterward, he invited a friend of his mother's to tea, then strangled and decapitated her before having sex with her dead body. He then went to a phone booth, called police, and turned himself in.

These cases in which mental-health professionals made tragic errors are not cited merely to criticize their failure but to point out the difficulty professionals have in predicting violence in general and serial killing specifically. In reaction to these kinds of errors, legislators have passed new laws, such as the Jimmy Ryce Act. This legislation mandates that sexual predators who are judged to be a threat to commit further sexual offenses can be retained in prison and provided therapy even after they have completed their sentences. Should such offenders be released, Megan's Law requires them to notify local police when they move into an area and to provide their address.

The recent public and professional interest in serial killers and serial lust killers is providing more insight into the nature of these pathologies and should lead to better prediction of their behavior. For example, the FBI has now engaged a psychologist, Dr. Kristen Beyer, to conduct an in-depth study of these offenders.

It should be emphasized that most serial lust killers are not psychotic, meaning that they do not have a major mental disorder characterized by loss of con-

tact with reality and often involving delusions and hallucinations. Schizophrenia is an example of a
psychosis. In fact, serial killers are usually sane med-
ically and legally. However, Lindsey and others like
him have what is called in psychiatric terminology,
personality disorders. These are not classified as mental illnesses, but as mental disorders. They are, in
brief, conditions that primarily involve persistent behaviors that deviate from what is expected by the
society in which the diagnosed live. The personality
disorder most often seen in serial lust killers involves
failure to behave in a lawful manner, deceitfulness
(lying, use of aliases, and conning people), rash, and
impulsive acts, and aggressive behavior, including
physical attacks.

Lindsey exemplified most of these behaviors: his
stealing on the job, his apparent scamming of the
insurance company in Annie Laurie's death, his
pathological lying, and in the impulsive manner
of some of his killings.

Another characteristic seen in Lindsey and common
in most serial killers is that they leave a "signature" as
part of the crime scene. Lindsey's signature was to leave
his victim's partially nude corpses in borrow pits,
streams, or other bodies of water. This signature is part
of his sexual fantasy. It provides an important clue to
law enforcement investigators who distinguish between
it and the killer's modus operandi, or method of operation (MO), that describes how the criminal has carried
out his crime.

Perhaps the clearest example of utilizing a signature
is Charles Albright, a former professor, professional musician, college football player, writer, and con man.
Albright acquired a fascination with eyeballs through
his boyhood hobby of taxidermy. As an adult serial lust
killer, he removed the eyeballs of his victims with a sur-
geon's skill and knowledge of anatomy.

While those interviewed for this book offered vary-ing perspectives on William Lindsey, they all agreed on one point: he was an inveterate liar. He claimed to his friends in North Carolina that his occupation was airline pilot, yet he did not even know how to fly a plane. While living in a small travel trailer on rented space in an RV/mobile home park, he regaled others with tales of the fancy houses he owned in various locations around the country. Those who liked him enjoyed listening to his tales, but with no expectation that there was any truth in them. Some saw his lies as revealing low self-confidence or as obvious efforts to cover up his conspicuous lack of achievement.

The underachievement and feelings of inferiority present in Lindsey are also characteristics found in many serial killers. In his case much of his negative self-image no doubt resulted from his mother constantly putting him down and scapegoating him.

The background of Keith Hunter Jesperson, "the Happy Face Killer" of eight women, mirrors Lindsey's in many ways. Perceived by his parents as the slowest of five siblings, Jesperson became the family scapegoat, demeaned and beaten by his father, much as Lindsey was mistreated by his mother. As was the case with Lindsey and his mother, Jesperson had a love/hate relationship with a parent, although in his case the parent was his father. Jesperson's father also set a model that his son followed as an adult in that "he treated women like they took up too much space."

Like Lindsey, many serial killers choose prostitutes as their victims. In the authors' study of 299 lust killers, they obtained data on the type of victim the murderers chose in 264 of the cases. Approximately one-fourth chose prostitutes. The reasons for this are fairly obvious—these women are available, they are easy to lure into isolated settings, and their disappearances normally do not attract much attention. This is particularly true if their bodies are not found.

While most serial killers limit their victims to persons of their own ethnicity, Lindsey did not. Three of the six victims to whose deaths he pleaded guilty were Caucasian and three were African American. A number of the prostitutes he dated in the St. Augustine area were also African Americans. This seems somewhat ironic, since those who knew Lindsey saw him as a racist, one who often referred to African Americans as "niggers."

As mentioned elsewhere, one way in which Lindsey is very different from the overwhelming majority of serial lust murderers is the age at which his killings allegedly started. At the time he killed Anita Stevens, the first murder for which he was charged, he was fifty-three years old, an almost unheard-of age for a sadistic serial lust killer to begin his murders. It is highly possible, of course, that the actual killings began much earlier in his life. (This view is strongly held by Detectives Harrison and Welborn and the authors.)

A number of serial lust killers further desecrate their victims' bodies by placing foreign objects in their anuses or vaginas. Whether or not this was done can usually be determined only if the body is discovered prior to decomposition. In the case of Lindsey's victims, it has been clearly established that he did this to Anita Stevens. This extreme act of hostility and lack of respect is usually performed only by the most brutal killers and/or those who are severely mentally deranged.

An extreme example of such a killer was Jeff Adams. According to *The Mammoth Book of True Crime* by C. Wilson, Adams started out by writing threatening letters to beautiful women married to rich men. One recipient of his letters, Sally Wimbush, was attacked by Adams in her swimming pool. He bound her hands and feet to a bench, raped her, then stuck foreign objects into every orifice of her body. These included chopsticks in her ears, dog feces in her mouth, a bottle in her vagina, and a pen in her anus. Adams killed and mutilated a total of three women in this fashion before being captured and sentenced to life in prison.

In Jack Olsen's book, *Charmer*, the author describes how George Russell, another sadistic killer, strangled, bludgeoned, knifed, and raped his victims, then forced foreign objects into their anuses and vaginas. Son of a well-to-do African American family—his father was a physician and his mother held a Ph.D.—he located his prey among college girls who frequented the club scene. In 1991 he was captured and sentenced to two consecutive life terms plus twenty-eight years.

According to *The Want Ad Killer* by Ann Rule, Harvey Carignan tortured, raped, and killed seven women, then placed foreign objects in their anuses and vaginas. His nickname was derived from the fact that he obtained his victims through newspaper ads saying he wanted a young lady to fill a clerical position.

William Lindsey's criminal record is minor compared to that of many serial killers. In the authors' review of the case histories of 299 sadistic lust killers, eighty-eight had records of felonies and imprisonment. This is a conservative estimate, as many of the case histories were not comprehensive enough to include this information. Although Lindsey had no felony convictions on his record when captured, he had been arrested for robbing a gas station and for aggravated assault. However, neither case was prosecuted. He had also been charged with writing worthless checks and had two misdemeanor charges pending in North Carolina, one for fishing without a license. He had been fired from numerous jobs for stealing, but his employers did not take these cases to court.

In summary, several important factors regarding the

causes of serial lust killing can be gleaned from the study of William Lindsey's history and that of other serial lust killers. One is an early history that generates tremendous hostility. It may be a parent who beats or is otherwise severely punitive toward the child. In some cases the child's vulnerabilities and social ineptness leads to vicious teasing and abuse from his peers. Often it is early placement in poor foster homes that are punitive or in juvenile correctional facilities in which weaker, more passive boys are subjected to constant bullying and, frequently, sexual abuse. A history of confinement in a juvenile correction facility in particular is prevalent in the histories of serial lust killers. The common thread in all of these situations is early traumatic abuse of the child or adolescent, which generates in him intense hostility and initial feelings of helplessness to do anything about it.

This hostility manifests in fantasies in which the child revenges himself on his tormentor through torture, debasement, and murder. Often these fantasies are first carried out on animals. Such acts give the young person pleasure and some feeling of being superior and in control. They may also have a calming effect when he is upset. As the child approaches the teenage years, he finds that these fantasies stimulate masturbatory behavior. At this point sex becomes the main reinforcer, with orgasm as the ultimate impetus for the behavior. Now the fantasies involve both sex and torture of the person upon whom the youth focuses his feelings of anger and revenge. In the case of the serial killer, this behavior generalizes and ultimately results in his carrying out his lust for sadism and murder against innocent women. As would be expected, in the case of pedophiles, the torture and murders are directed against children, and with homosexuals, against men.

Because sexual orgasms are the primary reinforcers of the fantasies that are fixated in the serial killer's mind, the more often they occur, the stronger the drive becomes to fulfill the fantasy and repeat the pleasure it brings. In this respect hypersexuality can be seen as a primary causal factor in the making of many serial killers.

While these are the motivating factors involved in most serial lust killing, the need for power and control are also key factors as the quote from DeBardeleben earlier in this chapter vividly demonstrates. Other elements that may provide impetus for serial killing are pornography, early sexual abuse, impotence, and substance abuse. Certain psychoses, endocrine disorders, chromosomally caused conditions, and other genetic factors may also play a role.

While it is not possible to identify in every serial lust killer the exact combination of these and other etiologic factors that have determined his destiny, it is clear that early conditioning, imprinting, critical stages, sexual abuse, and hypersexuality often set the psychological foundation for this sadistic behavior. With William Lindsey, these elements clearly contributed to his criminal actions.

Lindsey's rage episodes were important for another reason. On some occasions when the victims survived, they noted that he underwent strange staring spells prior to attacking them. At those times he would seem dazed and stare off into space as if disoriented. These were possibly petit mal epilepsy attacks as previously mentioned. In his forensic work, McCay Vernon has been involved with two cases in which the killings were preceded by petit mal epileptic episodes followed by explosive rage attacks: one was a serial killer. The other man stabbed to death his girlfriend and her mother, inflicting seventy distinct stab wounds.

The theory in these kinds of cases is that the random firing of the neurons in the brain that constitutes a petit mal epileptic seizure and/or an interictal period interferes with the synaptic connections involved in inhibiting aggression. This kind of seizurelike behavior is analogous to many short circuits occurring simultaneously in a large electric fuse box. As a result the current flows randomly and cannot be controlled by the switches that normally regulate the amount of power that flows to each outlet. In the human brain it involves impairment of synapses that would normally inhibit aggression. The result is that the individual loses the power to inhibit the physical expression of his anger, releasing an orgy of violence. In some cases, during or after the release of the rage, the individuals will have a grand mal seizure and be unable to recall the violence that took place.

Chapter 25

Crack Cocaine: The Real Killer

There is no medical condition [other than alcohol and drug addiction] for which the American public would tolerate only $11.9 billion in treatment expenditures while enduring over $294 billion in social costs.
—S. Martin, "Most Substance Abusers Aren't Getting Treatment," *Monitor on Psychology,* June 2001

William Lindsey's victims died from bludgeoning, beatings, strangulation, and bullets. But, in a larger sense, their lives were sacrificed to a much more insidious killer. It was the unceasing, ever-gnawing hunger for crack cocaine that caused these women to go on the streets, to steal, lie, and prostitute themselves. To the casual observer, it might seem that this was a moral choice that they themselves made, that no one was forcing them to continue their drug habit, that they could have escaped at any time, had they chosen to do so. But the truth is far more complex than that: the grip cocaine has on addicts is so powerful and its attraction so great that all other aspects of their lives—family, children, careers, education—become secondary to the desperate quest for the next high. Anita Stevens's desperate and ultimately futile attempts to retain custody of her children is an excellent example of how even the strong bond of motherhood snaps under the lure of crack cocaine.

Anita was also of the generation most affected when, in the late 1980s, rock cocaine hit the drug scene with devastating effects. Cocaine itself had been around for hundreds of years. An alkaloid found in the leaves of the South American shrub *Erythroxylon coca,* its use was once reserved for royalty. Through the centuries such notables as Arthur Conan Doyle, Sigmund Freud, and Robert Louis Stevenson claimed it benefited creativity, enhanced self-confidence, and generally promoted good feelings. Freud, a physician, became addicted, cured himself, and was thereafter strongly opposed to cocaine use.

Cocaine was sold over the counter until 1916, even in such exclusive venues as Harrods department store in London. The drug was widely used in a variety of medicines, tonics, and beverages—until 1903 the formula for Coca-Cola contained about sixty milligrams per serving. During that era the powder form of cocaine became the preferred drug of certain musicians, performers, and a segment of the rich. Today this form is still widely used as a recreational drug, but its cost makes it unavailable to those of modest means.

In the 1970s powdered cocaine use entered the mainstream; well-to-do yuppies snorted lines in clubs and homes across the nation. At Studio 54 in New York City, celebrities from such diverse segments of society as high government officials, name clothing designers, artists, lawyers, and transvestites discoed together beneath a ceiling hung with a giant cocaine spoon. For a while New York police looked the other way, allowing such clubs to permit open public consumption of the drug. (Eventually the party at Studio 54 ended when its owners were imprisoned for tax evasion. A brief re-opening under new ownership failed and in 1986 the club's doors closed permanently.)

It wasn't until the late 1980s that crack—a form of cocaine processed with baking soda to produce smokable rocks—appeared on the streets. Techni-cally, this is cocaine hydrochloride combined with ammonia, ether, and baking soda to create cocaine base/crack. Crack is also known by a wide variety of street names, including "real tops," "raw," "Roca (Spanish)," "Rooster," "Roxanne," "Rox," "Roz," and "Rocky III." A good hit of crack is referred to as a "ringer." When smoked, crack's stimulus reaches the brain much faster than by other methods, in-cluding snorting. The intense high it produces lasts about five minutes.

Crack is far cheaper than the pure cocaine powder. Consequently it became the drug of choice for the less affluent. The cream-colored rocks, typically about the size of rock salt, sold in the '80s and '90s in St. Au-gustine for $10 to $20 for a vial that contained three or four small rocks. This put crack within the price range of working-class people, teenagers, and young adults. In the April 1987 issue of *Medical Times*, Mar-cus S. Gold, M.D., reported: "Widespread crack use has sent the age of the user spiraling downward to the point that many adolescents now begin their drug use with crack." Because crack was inexpensive, inner-city African Americans could afford to buy it. Soon they became the major street dealers, despite the severe penalties and long sentences imposed for its use and sale. By contrast, the forms of cocaine used by the af-fluent involved far lesser penalties. Leaders in the African American community felt justified in de-nouncing this as blatant racism.

From the late '80s to the present, rock cocaine has

dominated the lower-economic drug scene. In the process it has become a major currency of Crack Head Corner's economy. On a daily basis the distribution of crack and the quest to obtain it constitute the central hub around which the lives of the prostitutes, dealers, and pimps revolve. Many of the johns are also users and will have the prostitute procure the rock for them as well as providing them sex. Prostitutes, in turn, quickly learn to inflate the cost of the crack, thereby earning money for both the sex and the drugs. The financial transactions revolving around the sale and purchase of crack offer numerous opportunities for chicanery. In addition, the money to acquire the drug provides the impetus for much of the petty crime that occurs in St. Augustine and other towns and cities across the United States.

Law enforcement attempts to halt the illicit traffic in crack cocaine have proven largely unsuccessful. Occasionally a sting operation nets police a few of the dealers and users, but within days they—or others like them—are back on the streets. For instance, on Sunday, January 12, 2003, the *St. Augustine Record* reported that ten to fifteen officers from the city and county police departments set up a sting operation in the Lincolnville area of town to "slow drug traffickers downtown and arrest addicts who circle the streets searching for them." They served seventeen warrants. As evidence of the desperation to which crack reduces its addicts, although the raid was conducted during a torrential downpour, one addict, who was later arrested, attempted to trade the raincoat off his back for a rock of crack cocaine.

Police admit that their efforts to stem the tide of crack are ultimately futile. As the *Record* article noted, "Unfortunately, the numbers [of drug dealers] haven't dropped significantly over the years." Or, as Lieutenant Dale Bryant, commander of the Organized Crime Unit, which conducted the raid, admitted, "It's the same thing, different faces."

Again, on May 2, 2003, the *St. Augustine Record* reported that a sweep—"Operation End of the Line"—by the Tri-County Narcotics Task Force had rounded up twenty dealers, eleven pounds of cocaine, and $386,274 in cash.

While some have tried to picture the neighborhood drug dealers as simply entrepreneurs taking advantage of an opportunity to earn a living, there is a far more sinister side to the drug traffic. In the *Record*'s article, written by reporter Bryan Noonan, the regional director of the Florida Department of Law Enforcement, Kenneth Tucker, stated, "Unfortunately, kids in the neighborhoods look up to the dealers because of the flashy cars they drive and the fear they instill in the community." Dealers regularly threaten and intimidate the residents to the point that they are afraid to report the drug trafficking or to testify in court against the dealers.

Sheriff Neil Perry of St. Johns County confirms that this fear can make investigations more difficult. "Drug dealers often take over neighborhoods," he said.

Crack-addicted prostitutes are especially susceptible to control. One dealer in particular was noted for photographing the women nude in a variety of sexual poses with multiple companions and with animals.

As the lowest level in the distribution chain, street dealers obtain their crack from midlevel sources with larger bankrolls and connections to major suppliers. At the top level of the drug chain, the cocaine importers have networks of carriers and are capable of transporting huge caches of drugs throughout the country. A June 7, 2003, account by reporter Bryan Noonan detailed a police operation labeled "Upper Deck." That particular sting netted eleven midlevel crack dealers in the West Augustine and Lincolnville area. "[They] are

the ones selling drugs for around $100 and often deal
with the street dealers," Noonan wrote. "They don'
fool with a $20 crack rock buy or sell."

In the same article, Sergeant David Fiveash, of the
St. Johns County Sheriff's Office Organized Crime
Unit, reported that those arrested "were a network
but not organized with a leader. They just watch each
other's backs. A lot of these guys that we were target
ing, their criminal histories are so bad they face
fifteen to thirty to life." He also said that while the
dealers sell drugs mostly to people they know, "greed
for money will take precedent and they will sell to
most anybody."

Sergeant Fiveash noted that police often rely on the
street dealers as informants: "[Street dealers] tal
when they are pressured by police. They roll over on
each other because if their competition is removed
from the street, sales open up for them."

Fiveash echoed Lieutenant Bryant's lack of opti
mism about the possibility of stopping or ever
stemming the drug trade in St. Augustine. "It is no
possible to completely disassemble the drug trade a
long as there is a demand. We're just chipping away a
their enterprise. As they rebuild, we're going to con
tinue to tear down." This is the nature of the drug wa
nationally, as well as in St. Augustine.

For users such as Lindsey's victims, the major dan
ger of crack—although not the only risk—is that it i
so highly addictive, the most addictive of all stree
drugs. A crack high creates an almost superhuman
sense of total well-being. The pleasure is so intense
that a single dose is all it takes for some people to be
come addicted.

Malvera Lucas, mother of one of the killer's victims
described addicts' behavior thusly: "When people ar

on crack, they can't be still. They got to 'dance and
nntz,' especially when they need a fix."

The craving that develops from crack cocaine use is
not too dissimilar to a starving person's craving for
food. The same midbrain area that controls hunger
urges also contains the "reward center," responsible
for generating the intense desire for cocaine. In tests
with laboratory monkeys, it was observed that the animals will self-administer the drug in preference to
choosing food or sex and will continue doing so until
death results. Human beings are no different from
their Darwinian cousins in this regard.

As indicated earlier, another reason users become
so easily addicted is that rocks are relatively cheap
compared to the powdered form, which is usually
snorted. A kilo of cocaine costs about $24,000. After
it is cut and cooked into crack, it will net the dealer
$50,000 to $100,000 or more when sold at $20 and up
for a vial containing three or four small rocks.

Once a crack high is over, it is followed by an un-
pleasant crash lasting thirty to sixty minutes.
Hallucinations are one possible consequence—a
user may experience "coke bugs," a sensation of in-
sects crawling on his/her skin. During this down
time, the user tends to experience agitation and irritability, feelings that create an intense craving for
more cocaine. At this point prostitutes such as those
who became the killer's victims, were especially in-
clined to take on high-risk johns as clients. The
ultimate danger of crack cocaine use is that it an
endless, self-perpetuating cycle. The higher the addict gets and the more rock that is absorbed, the
worse the crash from euphoria to misery. The
deeper the crash, the more desperate the need for
more crack.

This high/low cycle has particular significance
for women. Detective Ponce has noted that men can

sometimes get off crack, but women addicts can't
She attributed this partly to the sense of helpless
ness and worthlessness that sets in once they ar
addicted. Her perceptions are borne out by recen
studies that have shown females to be more sus
ceptible to crack addiction than males, partly owing
to their smaller body mass and differences in me
tabolism. Once addicted, the women become highly
vulnerable to rape and violence. Studies have also
shown that certain personality types, such as those
with conduct disorders, sociopaths, risk takers, and
persons with attention deficit disorder, are predis
posed to drug addiction. Depressed individual
frequently self-medicate using cocaine as well a
other drugs.

The addict's craving for the drug, and the means to
which he/she must resort to obtain it, contribute to
the physical toll it exerts on the body. Long and short
term effects of cocaine use include heart problems
strokes, seizures, suicidal tendencies, paranoid be
havior, weight loss, mood swings, birth defects, and
death from overdose. In the toxicology report follow
ing Connie Terrell's death, National Medical Services
reported cocaine was present in the blood sample
they had examined. The report included a chilling
analysis of the potential effects of cocaine usage:

> Seizures and agonal cardiovascular events (heart at-
> tacks, in lay terms) have occurred in subjects with
> blood cocaine levels ranging from 0.9 to 21.
> Seizures induced by direct cortical stimulation due
> to cocaine overdosage in otherwise healthy, non-hyper-
> sensitive adults occur at blood cocaine levels averaging
> over 5 micrograms per milligram.
> Cardiac irregularities of sufficient severity to result
> in circulatory collapse and seizure due to the resulting

brain hypoxia occur at blood levels which range from
less than 1 microgram per milligram upwards.

Connie's blood level was at 1.6 micrograms per milligram at the time of her death. In addition, the forensic chemist who analyzed her samples reported that they also contained 7.8 micrograms per milligram of Benzoylecgonina, a product that is formed by chemical breakdown of cocaine after blood is removed from the body.

While Connie's death was a murder, it was obvious that she was constantly in danger of death from an overdose. She was equally at risk for death from AIDS and was, in fact, HIV positive at the time of her death. For the women who prostitute themselves to obtain the drug, HIV and AIDS are very real threats as are other sexually transmitted diseases. At least one other victim—Donetha Snead-Haile—also had AIDS.

The social consequences of heavy crack use are equally negative. As users become increasingly isolated and suspicious, they alienate their friends and families and turn away those who would help them. Interestingly, a strong association has been proved between cocaine and sex. The user's "cocaine trigger" (craving for the drug) may be stimulated by X-rated movies, phone sex, or any sexual situation.

By the time crack users reach the addict stage, they use crack not to feel good, but in order not to be depressed. Without it the user feels it is impossible to go on living. At this stage the addict will stop at nothing to get a fix.

The life of a crack cocaine addict becomes incredibly difficult. The necessity to conceal the addiction from friends, family, children, spouses and employers leads to endless lies and deceptions. In order to feed her habit she is forced to beg and steal, often from those closest to her. Her attempts to persuade the dealer to sell her crack cocaine on credit are met with humiliating laughter.

Each of the women whose lives and deaths are recorded in this book struggled to escape from crack cocaine addiction. Families begged government agencies for help for their addicted member. Those who could afford it paid for private facilities that they hoped would effect a cure. Each woman entered at least one rehabilitation program, some entered repeatedly. None succeeded in breaking free of her addiction.

As Mary Alice Colson, victims' advocate for St. Johns County Sheriff's Office, noted: "I can see no solution to the problem. You can't put these people in lockdown to keep them away from the drugs."

The statistics for those seeking to escape addiction are not good—those who do make it through rehabilitation manage to do so on the average only after three to five relapses. Nor is our society willing to commit the funds necessary to provide adequate treatment despite the enormous social consequences of drug abuse. (It was estimated that the total economic cost of drug abuse for the year 2001 was approximately $97 billion.)

During their impressionable teen years, many of the victims faced pressure from their peers—especially boyfriends—to engage in drug use. They knew this would lead to loss of inhibition regarding sexual activity. A survey by the Henry J. Kaiser Family Foundation found that nearly nine out of ten teens said that their peers used alcohol or drugs before having sex at least some of the time, and many young people reported that condoms were often not used when people were drinking or using drugs. Thus it is understandable that several of the women Lindsey murdered became pregnant in their early teens before completing their educations.

While we may refer to the murdered women as

the killer's "victims," it is equally true that they were
destroyed by crack cocaine. Once addicted, their
futures were severely truncated, and their lives took
on a depressing similarity: prostitution . . . criminal
behavior . . . society's scorn . . . abandonment of eth-
ical values . . . and, ultimately, death.

Even sadder, the elusive killer is still at large. Crack
cocaine is still cheap, still easily obtainable, still de-
vouring its victims.

Afterword

Yet we have gone on living,
Living and partly living.
—T.S. Eliot, *Murder in the Cathedral*

At the time of this writing, more than seventeen years have passed since Anita Stevens's murder. Even Lucy Raymer's death is now nearly a decade in the past. Today, gravestones mark the final resting places of most of William Darrell Lindsey's victims. The perpetrator himself is in prison.

Seemingly, this brings closure to a grievous period in St. Augustine history. But in a sense, there can be no finality in such situations. The families of the victims still live with the memory of the cruel death their loved ones endured.

In dealing with the segment of society that Lindsey and his victims inhabited, the authors were forced to present a picture of West Augustine as an ill-kempt, crime-ridden area. It should be noted that the majority of West Augustine's inhabitants are not part of this underworld of crime and prostitution. Those outside that dark circle care deeply about their community and support efforts to improve it. The churches of West Augustine play a significant role, serving as a focus for community efforts to push for affordable housing, improved community services, and reduced crime.

Within the wider community there are also attempts

to bring together St. Augustine's racially diverse elements. Following a recent incident in which a black man died while being taken into police custody, Mayor George Gardner visited churches in West Augustine to listen to the black community's comments and complaints about the tragedy.

At Crack Head Corner, a fence has been erected around the vacant purple building that once housed a car wash. The convenience store has been newly decorated with coats of bright red and yellow paint. Z's Fried Chicken is featured. A sign erected nearby advertises that THE AFRICAN AMERICAN ARCHIVES AND MUSEUM is a work in progress. Some homes along West King Street have also been given a fresh coat of paint.

But progress in the area comes with painful slowness. As recently as January 2003, the *St. Augustine Record* found it newsworthy that trash cans had been installed on West King Street, even though the rest of downtown Augustine already has over 190 such receptacles. A suggestion from a bicycle-patrol police officer brought about the improvement.

Victims' advocate Mary Alice Colson, now retired, feels that great strides have been made in Lincolnville toward eliminating criminal activity in that neighborhood. Formerly an area where much of the drug activity took place, it has undergone drastic change in recent years. Buyers seeking in-town locations have bought up many of the old Victorian houses in the area and remodeled them, causing real estate prices in the area to rise significantly. Intense efforts by residents to take the area back from the drug dealers and prostitutes are slowly but surely paying off.

The Pic 'n Save, mentioned frequently in this story as a rendezvous for drug pushers and prostitutes, has been turned into what is advertised as "St. Augustine's Only 100% Climate-Controlled Self-Storage Facility." A real estate office occupies part of the building.

Fabian Stiles, one of the men investigated for Cheryl Lucas's murder, is back in jail, charged with distribution of drugs. He was turned in by a prostitute to whom he had sold crack. Dallas Porter, a prime suspect in Cheryl's murder, left St. Augustine. Several years later he died in a house fire of unknown origin.

Several of the suspects, witnesses, and informants interviewed by detectives during the course of the investigation have died of AIDS or drug overdoses. A few have drifted off to other communities, while others are still on the streets.

For Detectives Frank Welborn and John Harrison, their collaboration did not end with Lindsey's imprisonment. Despite living six hundred miles apart, they have found and shared many interests in common. They and their families have become close friends and visit one another whenever possible. As a result of his excellent police work in the Lindsey case, Frank Welborn has been promoted to the rank of lieutenant.

Bill Haggerty, the profiler who assisted in the case, is now retired from the FBI and has his own profiling business.

In April 2004 Sheriff Neil Perry announced his retirement from the elective position he has held for over two decades, saying he wants to travel and spend more time with his family. While not closing any doors to a future in politics, Perry insists that for the time being he is content to look back on a forty-year career in law enforcement and enjoy his home and family.

When asked if modern law-enforcement techniques could have brought Lindsey to justice sooner, Sheriff Neil Perry responded, "Even with today's technology, more sophisticated law-enforcement techniques, and our increased personnel resources, we could not have done better in locating the killer. Bill left us with so little in the form of evidence. And nothing he had done previously would have provided a DNA match. Even the twenty-two handgun he used in killing Connie is almost impossible to identify through matching the bullet."

Detective Jennifer Ponce, whose actions were critical in helping to break down Lindsey's defenses, is no longer in police work. She is now employed by a local insurance agency. As a single mother with two young daughters, she felt she owed it to them to take a job less demanding of her time and energy.

She admits that after the thrill of helping to track down a serial killer, it has been hard to find that kind of passion for other work, especially since, during her years in law enforcement, not only her working life but her social life as well centered on her work and her police colleagues. She credits her experience in law enforcement with having introduced her to a world she would never otherwise have known. "I've been through experiences ordinary people will never see or think about," she says. "When you're in law enforcement," she says, "it's like being in a cubicle. That is your whole world."

Now that she's out of the "cubicle," she finds it difficult to choose the direction in which she wishes to go. "I always wanted to be a boat captain like my grandfather," she says. "Do you think it's too late for that?"

On February 21, 2003, Kay Blaisdell Mora, the psychic known as Kaimora, died in Gainesville, Florida, at age seventy-four.

Retired victims' advocate Mary Alice Colson stays in touch with the victims' families, even though she has now officially stepped down from her law enforcement duties. When she learns of a family's need, she uses her influence with various civic organizations to arrange financial aid for such items as purchase of school materials and Christmas gifts for children. At his retirement Sheriff Perry credited her with true compassion and a commitment to her job of helping others. Colson has also been instrumental in the establishment of a shelter for battered women in St. Augustine. The Betty Griffin House, where women and their children find shelter and help, is named for Mary Alice's grandmother. She has also remained highly active in fund-raising and programs for victims' rights and victims' advocacy.

For Malvera Lucas, the death of her daughter was only one of the frustrations she faced. At age fifty-three she was left with the responsibility for raising six children, some of them facing physical and emotional difficulties related to their mother's lifestyle and her drug use during pregnancy. "I've had to be a fighter," she says. "I didn't care who or what I have to fight to get help for those children. I'll fight the school board; I'll fight those teachers; I'll fight social services—whatever it takes. I ain't the kind to lay down and let them roll over me."

In dealing with her grief and anxieties, Malvera Lucas went on a forty-two-day fast, eating only one meal per day. During this time she attended regular prayer meetings at her church, praying for the strength and guidance to raise the children and that the man who killed Cheryl would be found and punished. After one particular prayer meeting at six o'clock on a Saturday morning, she and a friend went to breakfast. While they were eating, the minister entered and told Malvera that instead of praying for the man to be punished, she should pray that God would save the murderer's soul.

"I did that," she declares. "I started praying that, whoever he was, God would save his soul. It took forty-two days of my life. It took getting down on my knees. But that December, God put it in operation. God took care of it."

In spite of their grandmother's devotion to them,

the children Cheryl left behind have suffered greatly from the loss of their mother. Their mother's drug addiction has affected their ability to learn and several have had numerous problems in school. "Often times the children go down there to the cemetery and talk to their mother," Malvera says. The three oldest—Chanelle, Aaron, and Lamar Rene—are now living in New York, while the three younger ones—Mark, William, and Richard—remain in St. Augustine with their grandmother.

The pain of losing a beloved daughter was at times nearly unbearable for Mildred McQuaig, especially during the years when she did not know who had committed the horrible deed. At one point, she states, the investigators focused entirely on a young man who had been caught stealing surfboards and were not considering other possible suspects.

Searching for answers during that time, Mrs. McQuaig consulted a psychic known as Rose. Rose said she saw "the shadows of two men" who in time would be brought to trial. "Everybody is afraid to talk," Rose said. "The men are still in the area." She mentioned a "John" or a "Kevin" as being involved and claimed that Anita's children knew the person who had killed their mother. None of these data or predictions proved to be true. The closest she came to a correct guess as to the killer was when she said, "One goes far away and then comes back."

While it is easy to ridicule such prognostications, it is entirely understandable that when a child has been murdered in a horrible fashion and police can supply no answers to the killer's identity, a parent would turn to anyone who offers even the slimmest hope of an answer.

As the years passed, the McQuaigs never gave up hope that Anita's killer would be found and kept in close touch with the sheriff's office. While it is understandable that the task force was keeping the evidence against Lindsey a close-held secret until their investigation was complete, it is disturbing that the families who had been waiting so long for news of the perpetrator's capture were not informed directly. Instead, it was a TV reporter who informed the McQuaigs of Lindsey's arrest and that he had been identified as a suspect in their daughter's murder.

The McQuaigs endured further anxiety after Lindsey's arrest as the various trial motions were filed and as Lindsey's plea bargain was rejected. In an interview on November 2, 1997, with reporter Mike Grogan, of the *St. Augustine Record,* Mildred McQuaig stated, "Knowing that Mr. Lindsey is in jail hasn't eased the burden much. We still don't have closure, and aren't sure we ever will."

For the McQuaigs, and for the other parents, the years of waiting between trials were another time of confusion and distress. After Lindsey's confession led to a plea agreement, some were appalled that the sentence had seemed so light in view of the enormity of his crimes.

As Nancy Bennett, Connie Terrell's mother, told *Florida Times-Union* staff writer Dana Treen, on April 21, 1999, "It was not what a lot of us wanted. We didn't feel like justice was done, but we got a little justice."

Lashawna Streeter's mother, Nadine Jakes, was too distraught to speak after the sentencing. Through a victims' advocate, she told the court, "He (Lindsey) will burn in a lake of fire. Satan has got his soul."

When Lindsey later pleaded guilty to the murder of the two women whose remains were never discovered, Stacey Snead, Donetha Snead-Haile's sister, told reporter Peter Guinta of the *St. Augustine Record,* "There's never any closure for a mother when a child is gone. She (our mother) doesn't know where Donetha's at." Then she added, "The court wasn't able to give Lindsey the death penalty. We'll have to leave it in God's hands." On Saturday, April 12, 1997, four years after Donetha's disappearance, a memorial service was held for her at the Church of God in Christ on King Street in St. Augustine.

The children that the victims left behind are struggling toward adulthood without the help and guidance of their mothers. Some are succeeding in school and in their careers. Others have succumbed to crime and drug abuse. Diana Richardson's son, Dale, has struggled with cocaine addiction and has accumulated a criminal record that includes numerous arrests for burglary, theft, and driving under the influence. For Connie Terrell's daughter there was an even sadder legacy—Kimberly died at age twelve. Despite her best efforts to raise them properly, Mrs. Lucas reports that several of Cheryl's children have struggled without their mother's presence. Anita Stevens's son, Dustan, is employed in construction St. Augustine. Her other son, Parke, is enrolled at Northern Missouri College in Maryville, Missouri, where he is an outstanding student and a member of the U.S. Marine Corps ROTC.

William Lindsey's family members have had to cope with the pain and embarrassment of knowing a family member has committed an inexplicably vile crime. Willa Jean, Lindsey's first wife, now lives quietly in Palatka with her daughter Beverly. Her sisters, Joan Forsyth, Minnie Smith, and Shirley Hammond, live nearby. They remain a close family.

Annie Laurie Lindsey's sister Agnes Marjenhoff and her family have also remained in Palatka. They continue to feel hurt and deeply bitter about Lindsey's treatment of their sister.

Lindsey's adoptive mother, Olean Lindsey, continued to live in the same St. Augustine home where she raised Lindsey and her other children until her death at the age of ninety-two.

Downtown St. Augustine continues to thrive as a tourist mecca and historical treasure. If this book seems to have exposed the seamier side of what is otherwise a uniquely charming and gracious town, this dichotomy is by no means exclusive to St. Augustine. The scourge of drugs and prostitution is no respecter of geographical boundaries or economic status. Villages, towns, and cities across the United States share the burden of this illicit traffic.

Publicity about the Crack Head Corner murders has failed to deter other young women from adapting the same lifestyles that led to such a violent end for Anita, Connie, Lashawna, Donetha, Cheryl, and Diana. An article by Nadia Ramoutar in the July 1, 2003, issue of *Folio*, a St. Augustine weekly paper, lends weight to the argument that since the Lindsey murders very little has changed for the women who sink into crack cocaine dependency. The opening of Ramoutar's story "Tricks of the Trade" conveys that fact most pungently:

> *Sally doesn't look like a hooker. She looks like someone's daughter or sister—like the girl next door. Sally's block of West King Street is a pocket of despair in an otherwise sunny tourist town. It's a place where men looking for sex can find it anytime. A lot of times, they come looking for Sally.*

Malvera Lucas confirms that prostitution is still a serious problem in her neighborhood. "When I see one of them girls walking down the street, I stop my van and try to tell them what they're doing to themselves. I tell them about Cheryl."

Lashawna Streeter's mother, Mrs. Jakes, sat through William Lindsey's trial, heartbroken and in tears. Six months later she died of a stroke.

Some of the victims' family members express the wish that Lindsey had been executed for his crimes.

Malvera Lucas does not feel that way. "That would just be taking another life," she has said.

The bodies of Diana Richardson and Donetha Snead-Haile have never been found. The rest of the victims' families have buried their loved ones. They have suffered the public exposure of a family member's lifestyle. They have endured the trauma of Lindsey's trial in which they were confronted once again with the violence he inflicted on their child, their sister, their mother. After all the bereavement, heartbreak, and grief, how does a family mend itself? The family of Connie Terrell still struggles with that question.

Here in this house that young Connie Terrell once called home, life goes on. Nancy and Jackie Bennett, Connie's parents, have just returned from a camping trip in their new trailer. Jackie is on the roof, checking for the source of a leak. One of Connie's sisters drops by with a request that her mother hem a dress she plans to wear for a special occasion. The lawn gets mowed; meals are prepared; friends visit; holidays are celebrated. One senses that the very ordinariness of these events softens the core of pain and anger that will always exist within the hearts of those left behind.

Nancy Bennett recalls an incident from Connie's short, tragic life. "I decided to make a quilt for each of my girls," Nancy says. "I would do one for the oldest first, then on down the line. I finished the first one, and for some reason, I felt I should give it to Connie even though she wasn't the oldest. I'm glad now that she had something with her that I had made for her."

A comparison of the fresh-faced Billy Lindsey, from his high-school yearbooks, with the wretched prison-garbed figure, who appeared in court, offers visible evidence of a life tragically wasted. Like many serial killers, he was a man whose abilities could, under nor-

mal circumstances, have brought him a comfortable, rewarding life. The very cleverness that allowed him to
elude the law for long periods of time could, if applied
constructively, have resulted in positive contributions to
society. But the phantoms that haunted him precluded
a realization of his potential. Forever pursued by his
personal demons and the wrath of society, he destroyed
his own life along with those of his victims.

Lindsey's capture and conviction resolves the question of who killed six women in St. Augustine and one
in Asheville, North Carolina. The question remains:
how many other victims were there? That will forever
be unanswered unless, and until, the killer himself is
willing to divulge his secrets.

Allen Strickrott, who participated in the interviews
during which Lindsey confessed, feels that while Lindsey wrestles with guilt, he has no genuine remorse for
his deeds. "When he left his residence to solicit prostitutes, it was with the intention of killing them.
Sometimes Good Bill would be their rescuer, their sav-
ior. But he could fight his desires for only so long
before giving in to them. He seeks to avoid remorse
by assigning the crimes to Bad Bill, which helps him
to justify in his mind what he did. This way he can live
with himself, even though Good Bill knows a part of
him is a human monster. He never feels guilt or remorse in the true sense of the word, and he could
never be rehabilitated."

At the time of this writing, William Darrell Lindsey is
Inmate #V08350 in the Marion Correctional Institute
in Lowell, Florida, where he has been incarcerated
since May 26, 1999. His current release date is October
2, 2026. If he survives until then, he will be ninety-one
years old.

References

Allison, M. (1993). "Exploring the link between violence and brain injury." *Headlines, 4* #2, pp. 12–15.

Coleman, D. (August 7, 1980). "When rage explodes, brain damage may be the cause." *New York Times,* pp. C1 & C2.

Devinsley, O. & D. Bear. (1984). "Varieties of aggressive behavior in temporal lobe epilepsy." *American Journal of Psychiatry, 141,* 5, pp. 651–654.

Douglas, J. & M. Olshaker. (1999). *The Anatomy of Motive.* New York: Pocket Books.

Gold, Mark S., M.D. (April 1987). "Crack Abuse, Its Implications and Outcomes." *Medical Times.*

Hazelwood, R. C. & S. G. Michaud. (2001). *Dark Dreams: Sexual Violence, Homicide, and the Criminal Mind.* New York: St. Martin's Press.

Hickey, E. W. (1997). *Serial Murderers and Their Victims (Second Edition).* New York City: Wadsworth Publishing Company

Holmes, R. M. & S. T. Holmes. (1998). *Serial Murder (Second Edition).* Thousand Oaks, California: SAGE Publications.

Jeffers, H. P. (1992). *Bloody Business.* New York: Pharos Books.

Keppel, R. D. & W. J. Birnes. (1997). *Signature Killers.* New York: Pocket Books.

Lane, B. & W. Gregg. (1995). *The Encyclopedia of Serial Killers.* New York: Berkeley Books.

Lester, D. (1995). *Serial Killers: The Insatiable Passion.* Philadelphia: The Charles Press.

Matthews, J. & C. Wicker. (1997). *The Eyeball Killer.* New York: Pinnacle Books.

Michaud, S. G. & R. C. Hazelwood. (1998). *The Evil That Men Do.* New York: St. Martin's Press.

Newton, M. (2000). *The Encyclopedia of Serial Killers.* New York: Checkmark Books.

Newton, M. (2000) and C. Wilson. (1998). *The Mammoth Book of True Crime.* New York: Carroll & Graf Publishers, Inc.

Olsen, J. (1994). *Charmer.* New York: Avon Books.

Idem. (2002). *The Creation of a Serial Killer.* New York: St. Martin's Press.

Rule, A. (1988). *The Want-Ad Killer.* New York: Penguin Books.

Smith, D. (2001). "Move over, Agent Scully." *Monitor on Psychology, 32,* #2, pp. 31–32.

Vernon, M. & E. Lafalce. (1990). "Epilepsy and deafness: The issue of violence." *Journal of American Deafness and Rehabilitation Association, 23,* #3, pp. 64–67.

ABOUT THE AUTHORS

McCay Vernon, Ph.D., is a psychologist whose career has concentrated on the fields of deafness and forensics. He is the author of seven books, over 300 articles, award-winning documentary films, and television productions in those fields. Although his path never crossed that of William Darrell Lindsey, Dr. Vernon attended the same high school, delivered the local paper to Lindseys' family, and shared many acquaintances with the killer.

Marie Vernon is a freelance journalist whose columns, feature articles, and book reviews have appeared in such major newspapers as the *Baltimore Sun, Cleveland Plain Dealer, Atlanta Journal-Constitution, Christian Science Monitor*, and *Florida-Times-Union*. She is the author of *Speaking of Our Past: A Narrative History of Owings Mills, Maryland*.

The Vernons live near St. Augustine, Florida.

BOOK YOUR PLACE ON OUR WEBSITE AND MAKE THE READING CONNECTION!

We've created a customized website just for our very special readers, where you can get the inside scoop on everything that's going on with Zebra, Pinnacle and Kensington books.

When you come online, you'll have the exciting opportunity to:

- View covers of upcoming books
- Read sample chapters
- Learn about our future publishing schedule (listed by publication month *and author*)
- Find out when your favorite authors will be visiting a city near you
- Search for and order backlist books from our online catalog
- Check out author bios and background information
- Send e-mail to your favorite authors
- Meet the Kensington staff online
- Join us in weekly chats with authors, readers and other guests
- Get writing guidelines
- AND MUCH MORE!

Visit our website at
http://www.kensingtonbooks.com